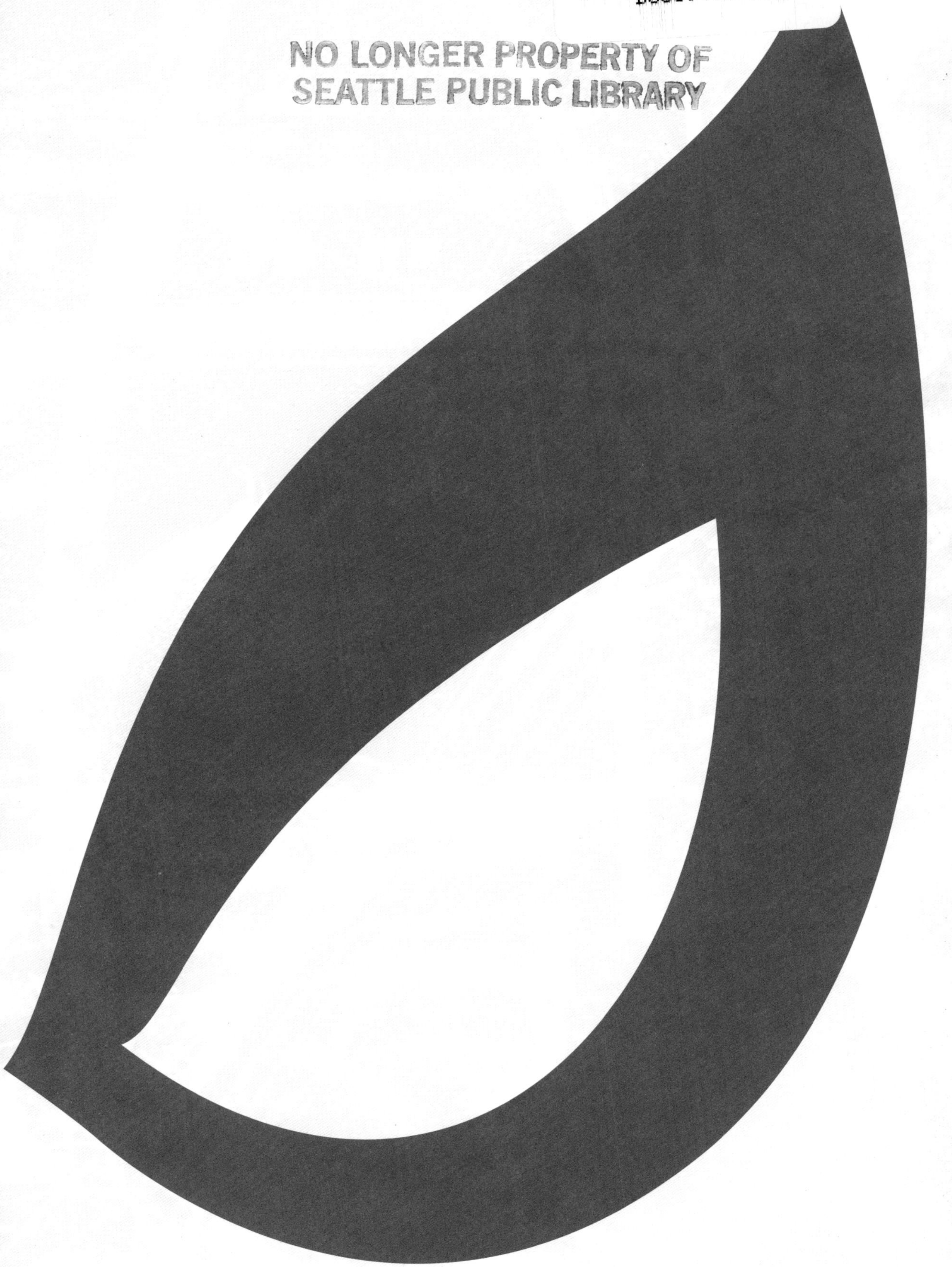

AMAZING SPIDER-MAN: FAMILY BUSINESS

First printing 2014
ISBN# 978-0-7851-8440-9

Published by MARVEL WORLDWIDE, INC.,
a subsidiary of MARVEL ENTERTAINMENT, LLC.

OFFICE OF PUBLICATION:
135 West 50th Street, New York, NY 10020.
Copyright © 2014 Marvel Characters, Inc.
All rights reserved.
All characters featured in this issue and the distinctive
names and likenesses thereof, and all related indicia are
trademarks of Marvel Characters, Inc. No similarity
between any of the names, characters, persons, and/or
institutions in this magazine with those of any living or
dead person or institution is intended, and any such
similarity which may exist is purely coincidental.

Printed in the U.S.A.

ALAN FINE, EVP
Office of the President, Marvel Worldwide, Inc.
and EVP and CMO Marvel Characters B.V.
DAN BUCKLEY
Publisher and President -
Print, Animation and Digital Divisions
JOE QUESADA
Chief Creative Officer
TOM BREVOORT
SVP of Publishing
DAVID BOGART
SVP of Operations and Procurement, Publishing
C.B. CEBULSKI
SVP of Creator and Content Development
DAVID GABRIEL
SVP Print, Sales and Marketing
JIM O'KEEFE
VP of Operations and Logistics
DAN CARR
Executive Director of Publishing Technology
SUSAN CRESPI
Editorial Operations Manager
ALEX MORALES
Publishing Operations Manager
STAN LEE
Chairman Emeritus

For information regarding advertising in Marvel Comics or
on Marvel.com, please contact NIZA DISLA Director of
Marvel Partnerships at ndisla@marvel.com.

For Marvel subscription inquiries, please call
800-217-9158.

Manufactured between 1/6/2013 and 2/17/2014
by R.R. DONNELLEY, INC., SALEM, VA, USA.

10 9 8 7 6 5 4 3 2 1

MARK WAID and JAMES ROBINSON
Writers

GABRIELE DELL'OTTO
Painted Art

WERTHER DELL'EDERA
Pencils

Vc's Joe Caramagna
Letters

Ellie Pyle and Tom Brennan
Associate Editors

Stephen Wacker
Editor

Jennifer Grünwald
Collection Editor

Alex Starbuck
Associate Managing Editor

Mark D. Beazley
Editor, Special Projects

Jeff Youngquist
Senior Editor, Special Projects

David Gabriel
SVP Print, Sales and Marketing

Rian Hughes
Book Designer

Axel Alonso
Editor In Chief

Joe Quesada
Chief Creative Officer

Dan Buckley
Publisher

Alan Fine
Executive Producer

Special thanks to
Christopher Yost

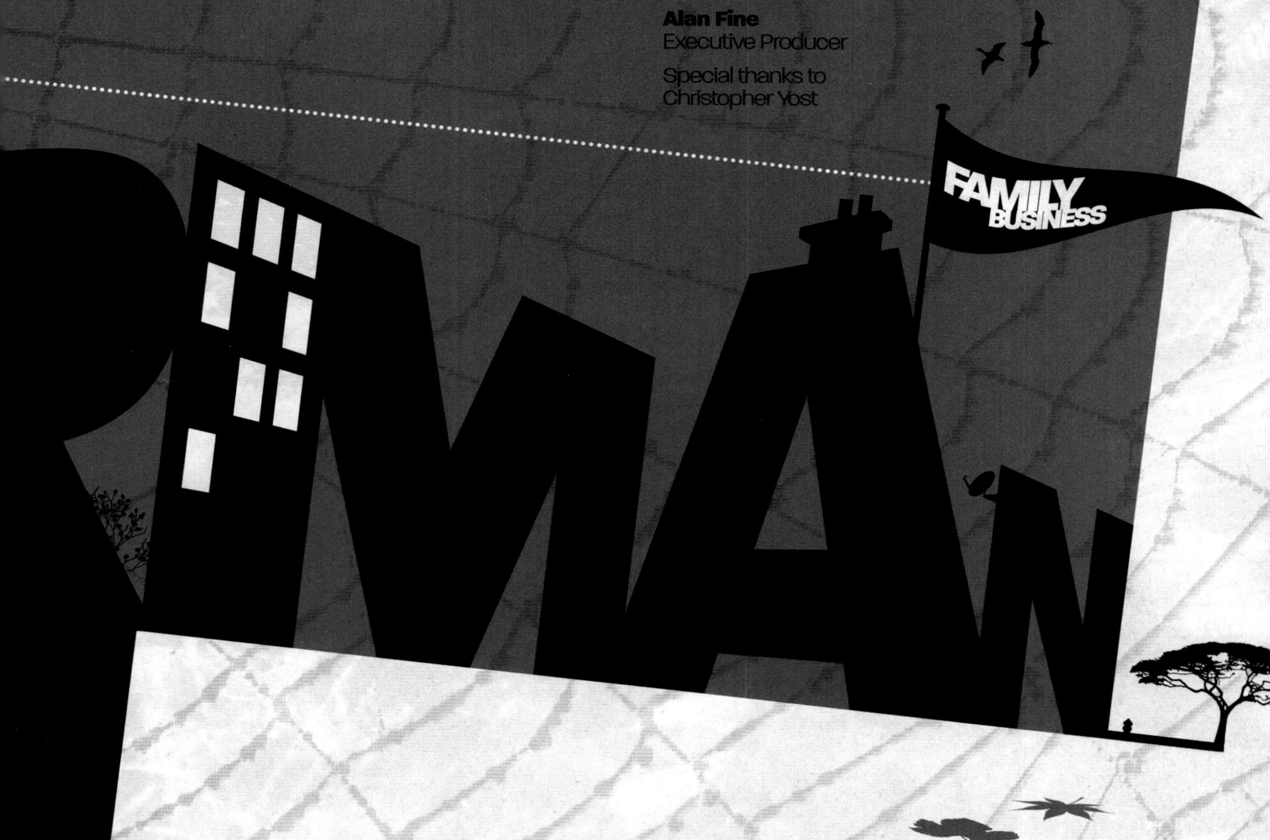
FAMILY
BUSINESS

Tell me a **Spider-Man** story. And make it a good one.

We all know **Spidey.**

He's been part of our culture for more than half a century. He's in comic books, movies, and cartoons. Action figures, lunchboxes, and pajamas. And we all know his story...

COFFEE SHOP
FREE COMIC BOOK DAY

Peter Parker—bitten by a radioactive spider—gains Great Power but learns it comes with a price: Great Responsibility.

That lesson is at the character's core and has been the fuel for every great **Spidey** story for fifty years.

So how do you keep that up and keep it fresh? How can you find a new responsibility for Pete? What will have us anxiously flipping to the next page? What's that twist no **Spidey** scribe's thought of before?

And that's where **Mark Waid** and **James Robinson** deliver. They drive this story right up to you in a super-charged sports car, fling open the door, and yell, "Jump in"—and you're off! They're taking you and **Spidey** to places he's never been... with a mysterious new character who changes everything.

Family Business gives you all the Spidey action, twists, and turns you could want—all gorgeously brought to life by **Gabriele Dell'Otto** and **Werther Dell'Edera.** This is more than a comic you'll read—it's one you'll re-read. Not just a good **Spidey** story, but a ***great*** one!

Dan Slott
December 2013

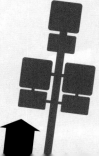

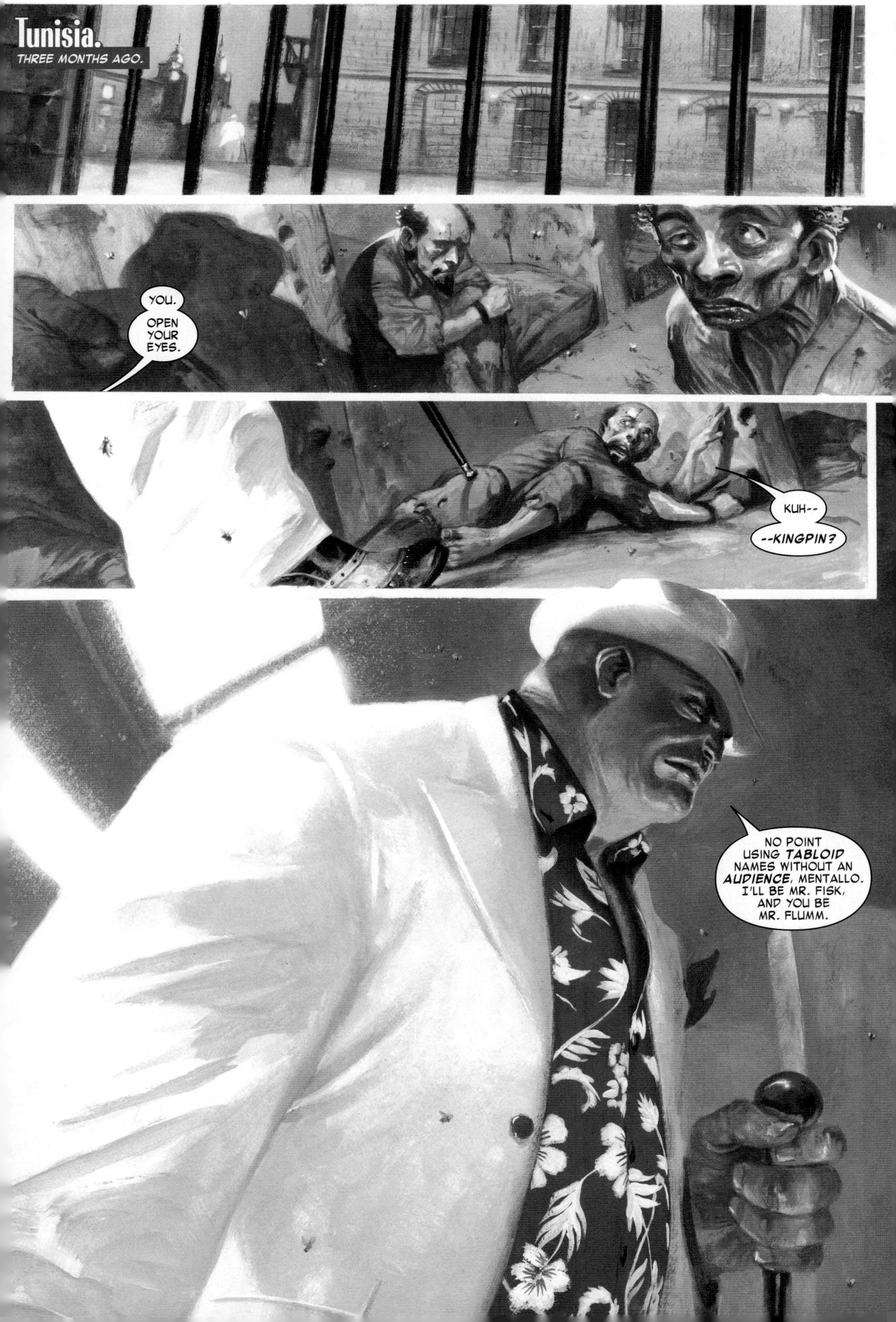

Tunisia.
THREE MONTHS AGO.
YOU. OPEN YOUR EYES.
KUH--
--KINGPIN?
NO POINT USING TABLOID NAMES WITHOUT AN AUDIENCE, MENTALLO. I'LL BE MR. FISK, AND YOU BE MR. FLUMM.

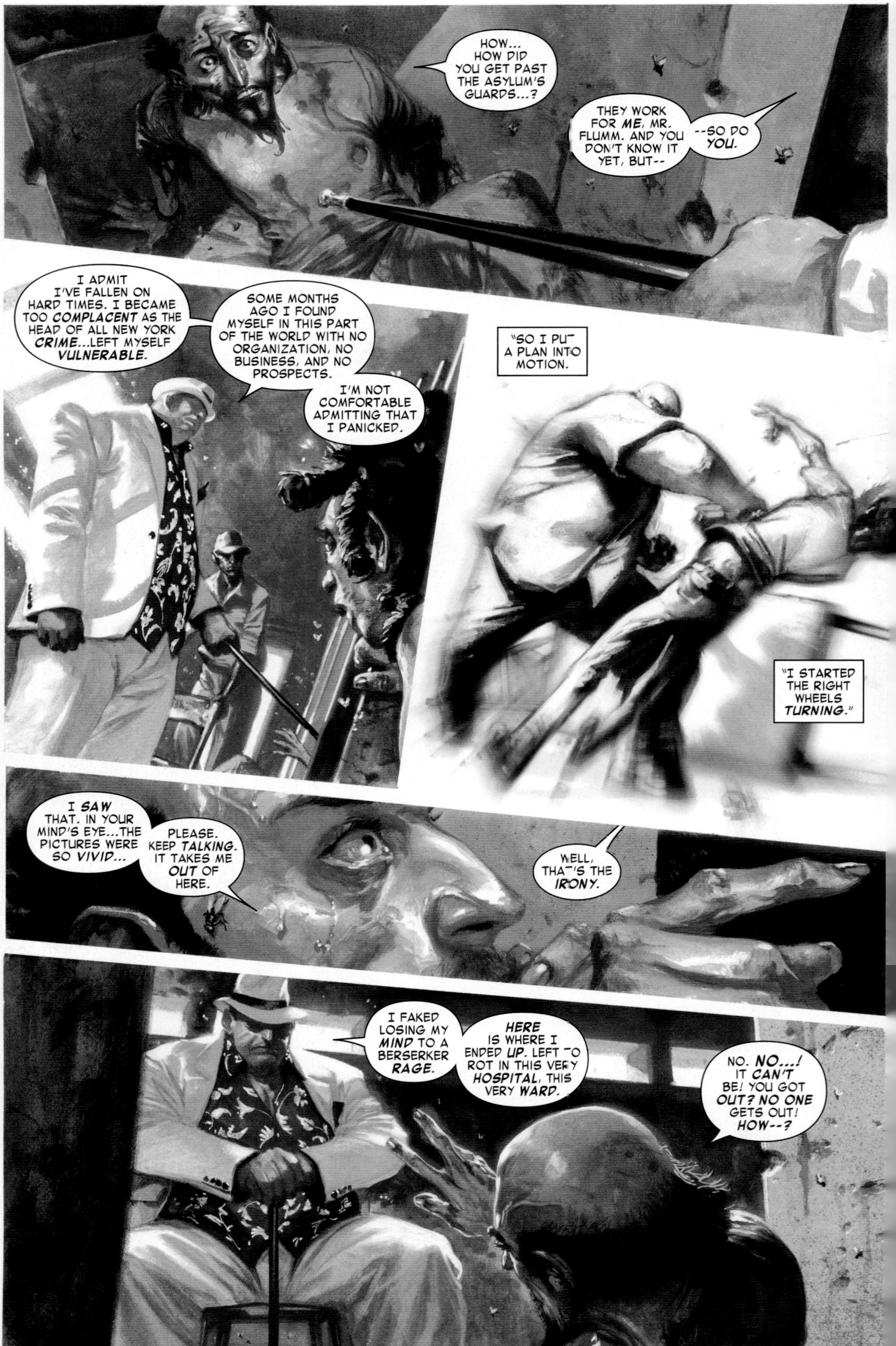

HOW... HOW DID YOU GET PAST THE ASYLUM'S GUARDS...?
THEY WORK FOR ME, MR. FLUMM. AND YOU DON'T KNOW IT YET, BUT--
--SO DO YOU.
I ADMIT I'VE FALLEN ON HARD TIMES. I BECAME TOO COMPLACENT AS THE HEAD OF ALL NEW YORK CRIME...LEFT MYSELF VULNERABLE.
SOME MONTHS AGO I FOUND MYSELF IN THIS PART OF THE WORLD WITH NO ORGANIZATION, NO BUSINESS, AND NO PROSPECTS.
I'M NOT COMFORTABLE ADMITTING THAT I PANICKED.
"SO I PUT A PLAN INTO MOTION.
"I STARTED THE RIGHT WHEELS TURNING."
I SAW THAT. IN YOUR MIND'S EYE...THE PICTURES WERE SO VIVID...
PLEASE. KEEP TALKING. IT TAKES ME OUT OF HERE.
WELL, THAT'S THE IRONY.
I FAKED LOSING MY MIND TO A BERSERKER RAGE.
HERE IS WHERE I ENDED UP. LEFT TO ROT IN THIS VERY HOSPITAL, THIS VERY WARD.
NO. NO...! IT CAN'T BE! YOU GOT OUT? NO ONE GETS OUT! HOW--?

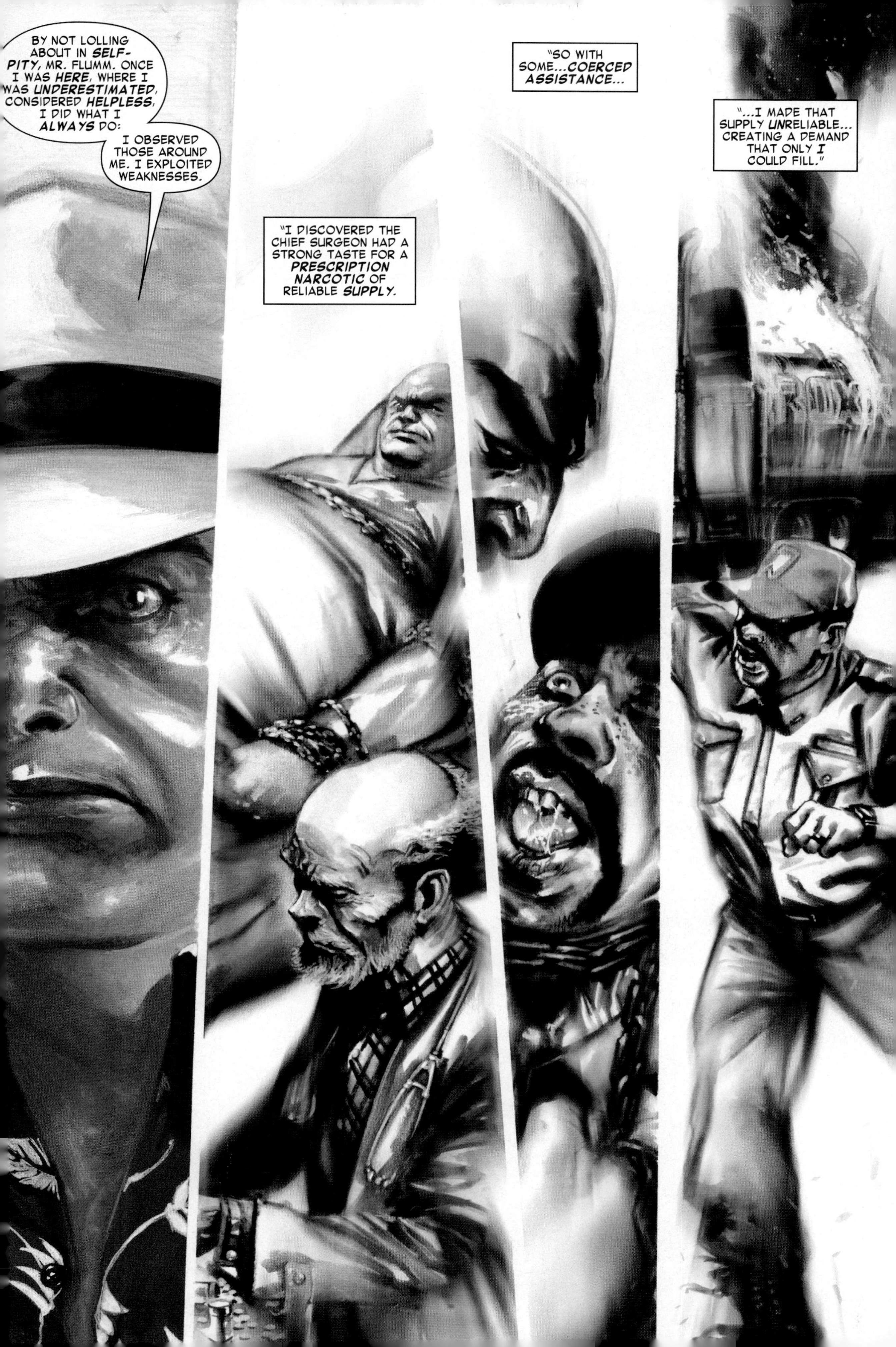
BY NOT LOLLING ABOUT IN SELF-PITY, MR. FLUMM. ONCE I WAS HERE, WHERE I WAS UNDERESTIMATED, CONSIDERED HELPLESS, I DID WHAT I ALWAYS DO:
I OBSERVED THOSE AROUND ME. I EXPLOITED WEAKNESSES.
"I DISCOVERED THE CHIEF SURGEON HAD A STRONG TASTE FOR A PRESCRIPTION NARCOTIC OF RELIABLE SUPPLY.
"SO WITH SOME...COERCED ASSISTANCE...
"...I MADE THAT SUPPLY UNRELIABLE... CREATING A DEMAND THAT ONLY I COULD FILL."

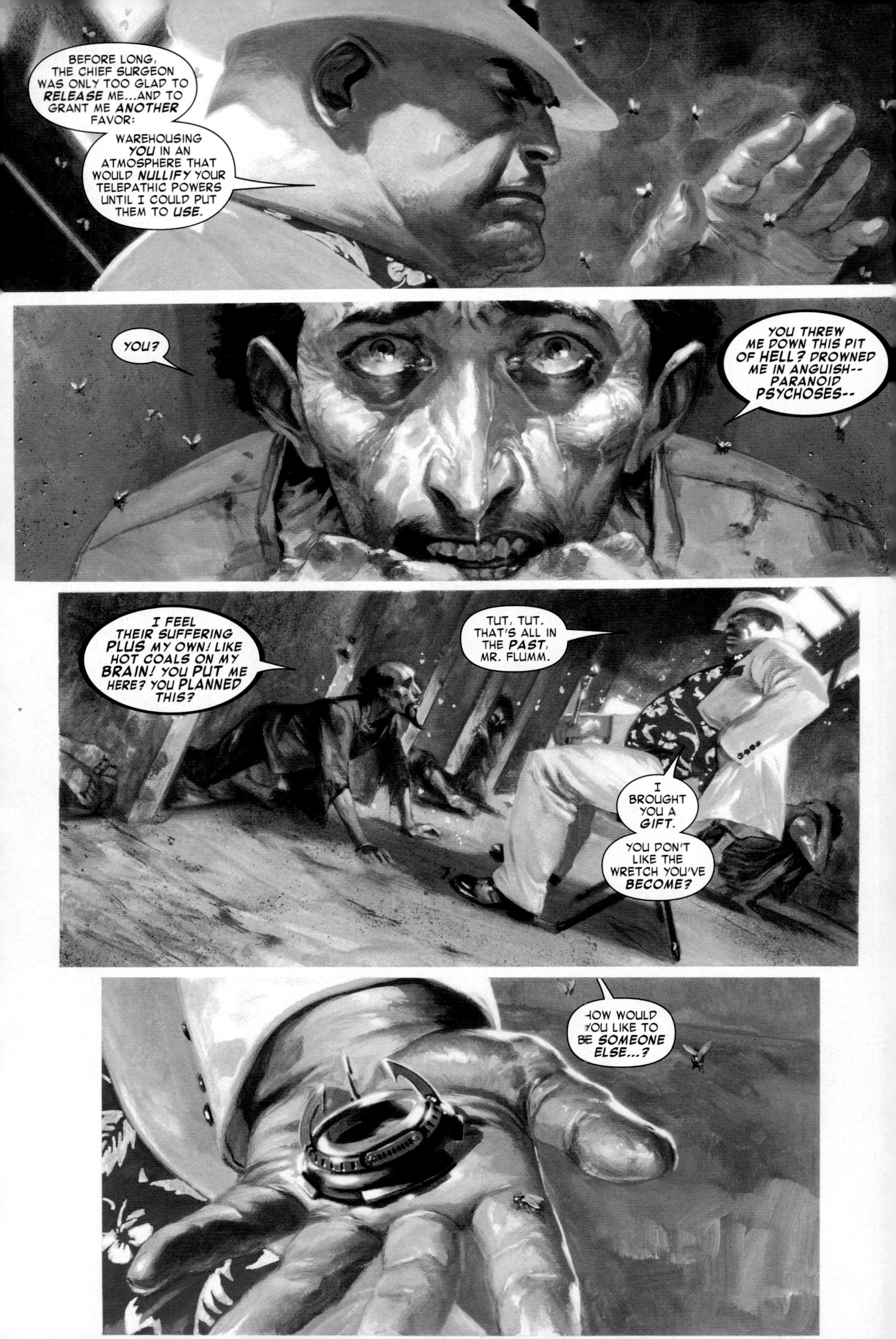
BEFORE LONG, THE CHIEF SURGEON WAS ONLY TOO GLAD TO RELEASE ME...AND TO GRANT ME ANOTHER FAVOR:
WAREHOUSING YOU IN AN ATMOSPHERE THAT WOULD NULLIFY YOUR TELEPATHIC POWERS UNTIL I COULD PUT THEM TO USE.
YOU?
YOU THREW ME DOWN THIS PIT OF HELL? DROWNED ME IN ANGUISH-- PARANOID PSYCHOSES--
I FEEL THEIR SUFFERING PLUS MY OWN! LIKE HOT COALS ON MY BRAIN! YOU PUT ME HERE? YOU PLANNED THIS?
TUT, TUT. THAT'S ALL IN THE PAST, MR. FLUMM.
I BROUGHT YOU A GIFT.
YOU DON'T LIKE THE WRETCH YOU'VE BECOME?
HOW WOULD YOU LIKE TO BE SOMEONE ELSE...?

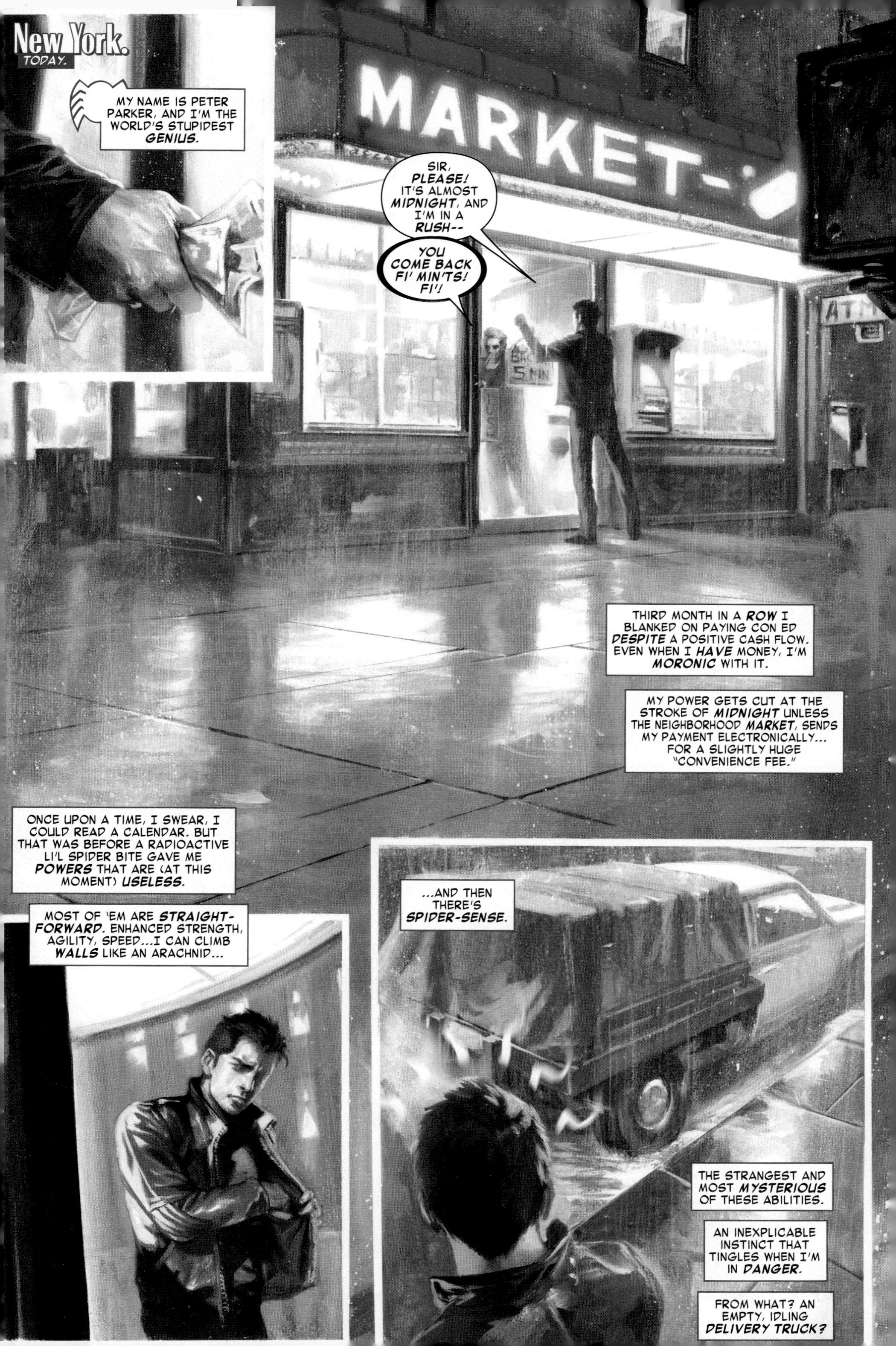
New York.
TODAY.
MY NAME IS PETER PARKER, AND I'M THE WORLD'S STUPIDEST GENIUS.
MARKET
SIR, PLEASE! IT'S ALMOST MIDNIGHT, AND I'M IN A RUSH--
YOU COME BACK FI' MIN'TS! FI'!
5 MIN
ATM
THIRD MONTH IN A ROW I BLANKED ON PAYING CON ED DESPITE A POSITIVE CASH FLOW. EVEN WHEN I HAVE MONEY, I'M MORONIC WITH IT.
MY POWER GETS CUT AT THE STROKE OF MIDNIGHT UNLESS THE NEIGHBORHOOD MARKET, SENDS MY PAYMENT ELECTRONICALLY... FOR A SLIGHTLY HUGE "CONVENIENCE FEE."
ONCE UPON A TIME, I SWEAR, I COULD READ A CALENDAR. BUT THAT WAS BEFORE A RADIOACTIVE LI'L SPIDER BITE GAVE ME POWERS THAT ARE (AT THIS MOMENT) USELESS.
MOST OF 'EM ARE STRAIGHT-FORWARD. ENHANCED STRENGTH, AGILITY, SPEED...I CAN CLIMB WALLS LIKE AN ARACHNID...
...AND THEN THERE'S SPIDER-SENSE.
THE STRANGEST AND MOST MYSTERIOUS OF THESE ABILITIES.
AN INEXPLICABLE INSTINCT THAT TINGLES WHEN I'M IN DANGER.
FROM WHAT? AN EMPTY, IDLING DELIVERY TRUCK?

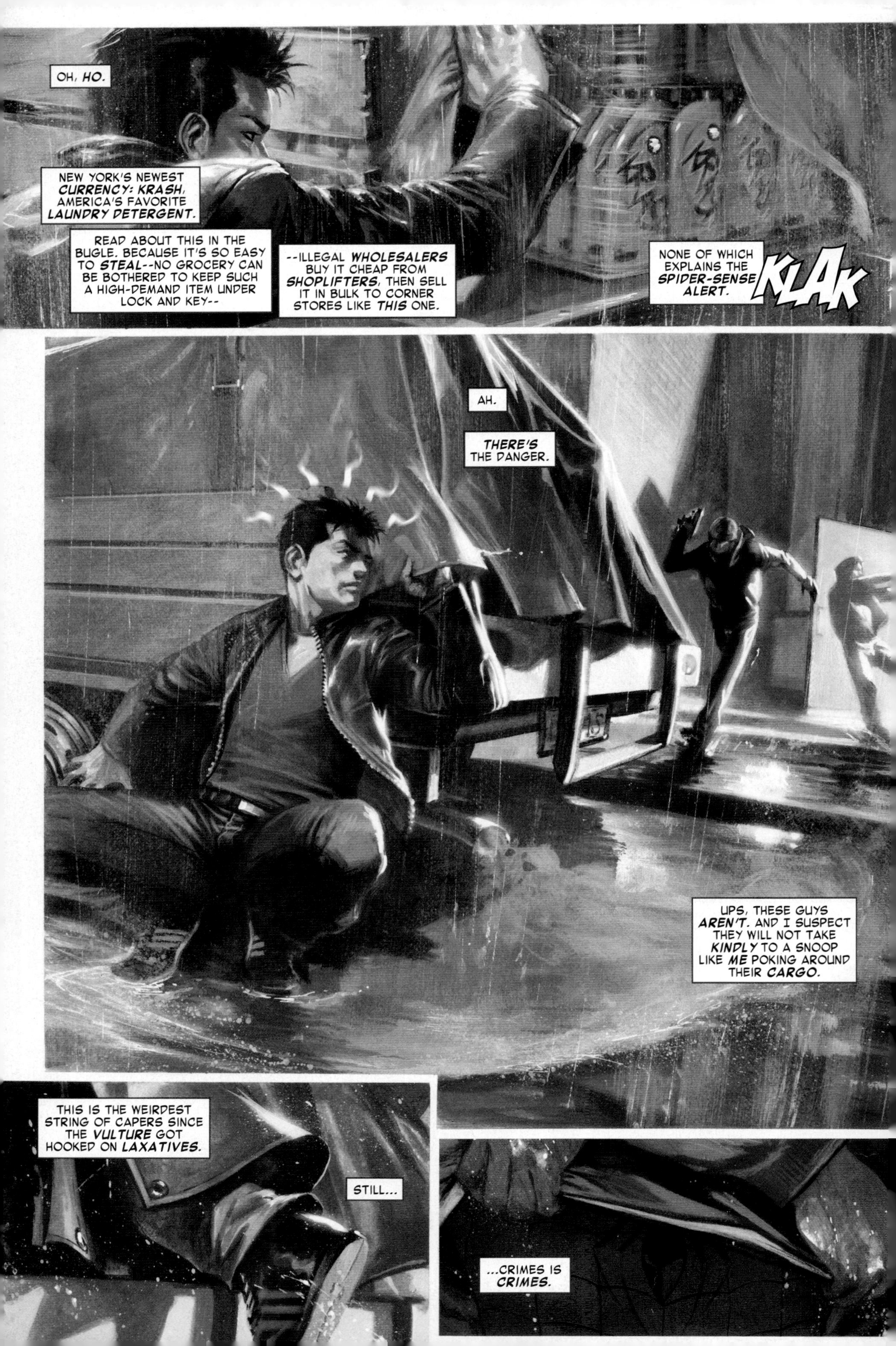
OH, HO.
NEW YORK'S NEWEST CURRENCY: KRASH, AMERICA'S FAVORITE LAUNDRY DETERGENT.
READ ABOUT THIS IN THE BUGLE. BECAUSE IT'S SO EASY TO STEAL--NO GROCERY CAN BE BOTHERED TO KEEP SUCH A HIGH-DEMAND ITEM UNDER LOCK AND KEY--
--ILLEGAL WHOLESALERS BUY IT CHEAP FROM SHOPLIFTERS, THEN SELL IT IN BULK TO CORNER STORES LIKE THIS ONE.
NONE OF WHICH EXPLAINS THE SPIDER-SENSE ALERT.
KLAK
AH.
THERE'S THE DANGER.
UPS, THESE GUYS AREN'T. AND I SUSPECT THEY WILL NOT TAKE KINDLY TO A SNOOP LIKE ME POKING AROUND THEIR CARGO.
THIS IS THE WEIRDEST STRING OF CAPERS SINCE THE VULTURE GOT HOOKED ON LAXATIVES.
STILL...
...CRIMES IS CRIMES.

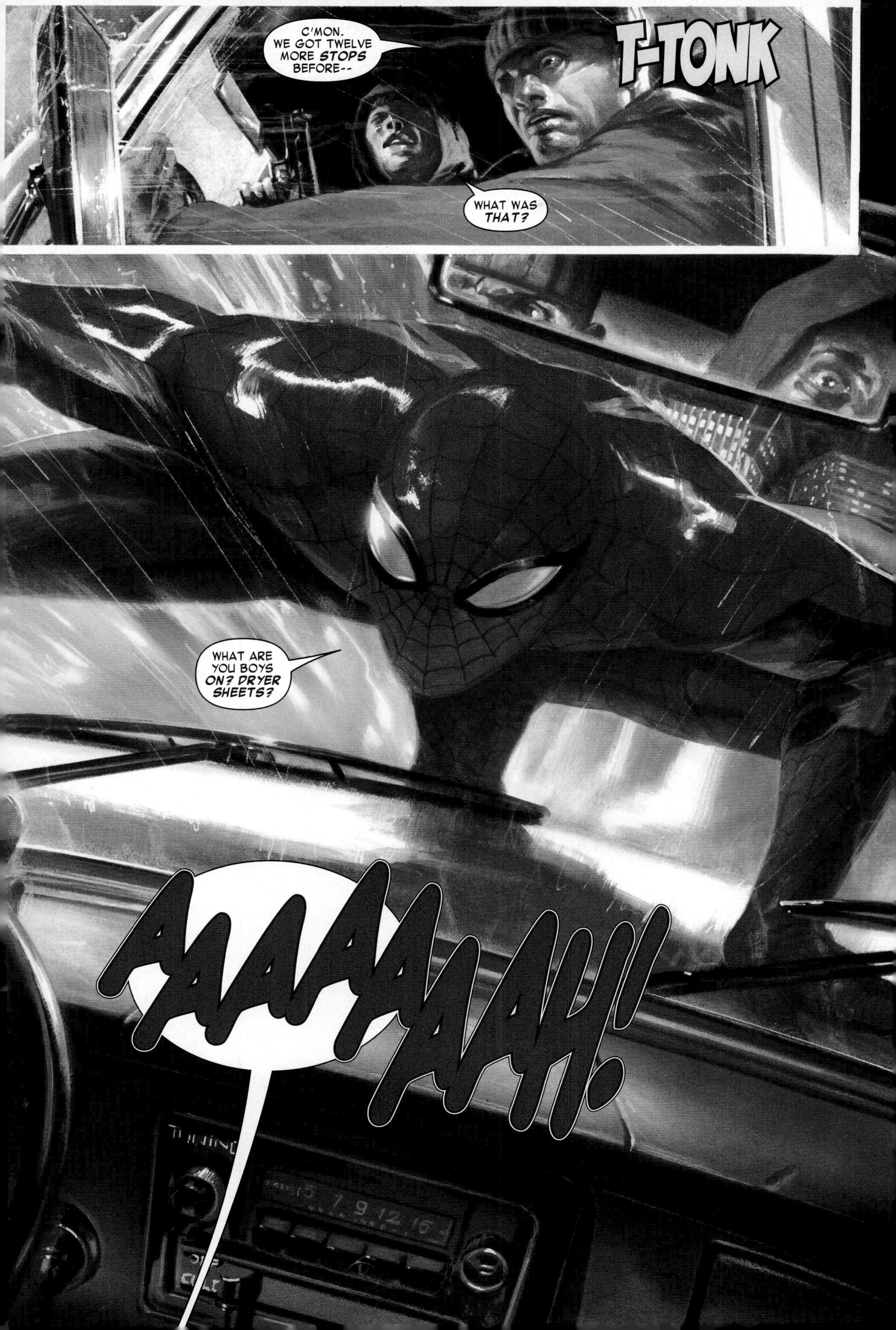
C'MON. WE GOT TWELVE MORE STOPS BEFORE--
T-TONK
WHAT WAS THAT?
WHAT ARE YOU BOYS ON? DRYER SHEETS?
AAAAAAH!!

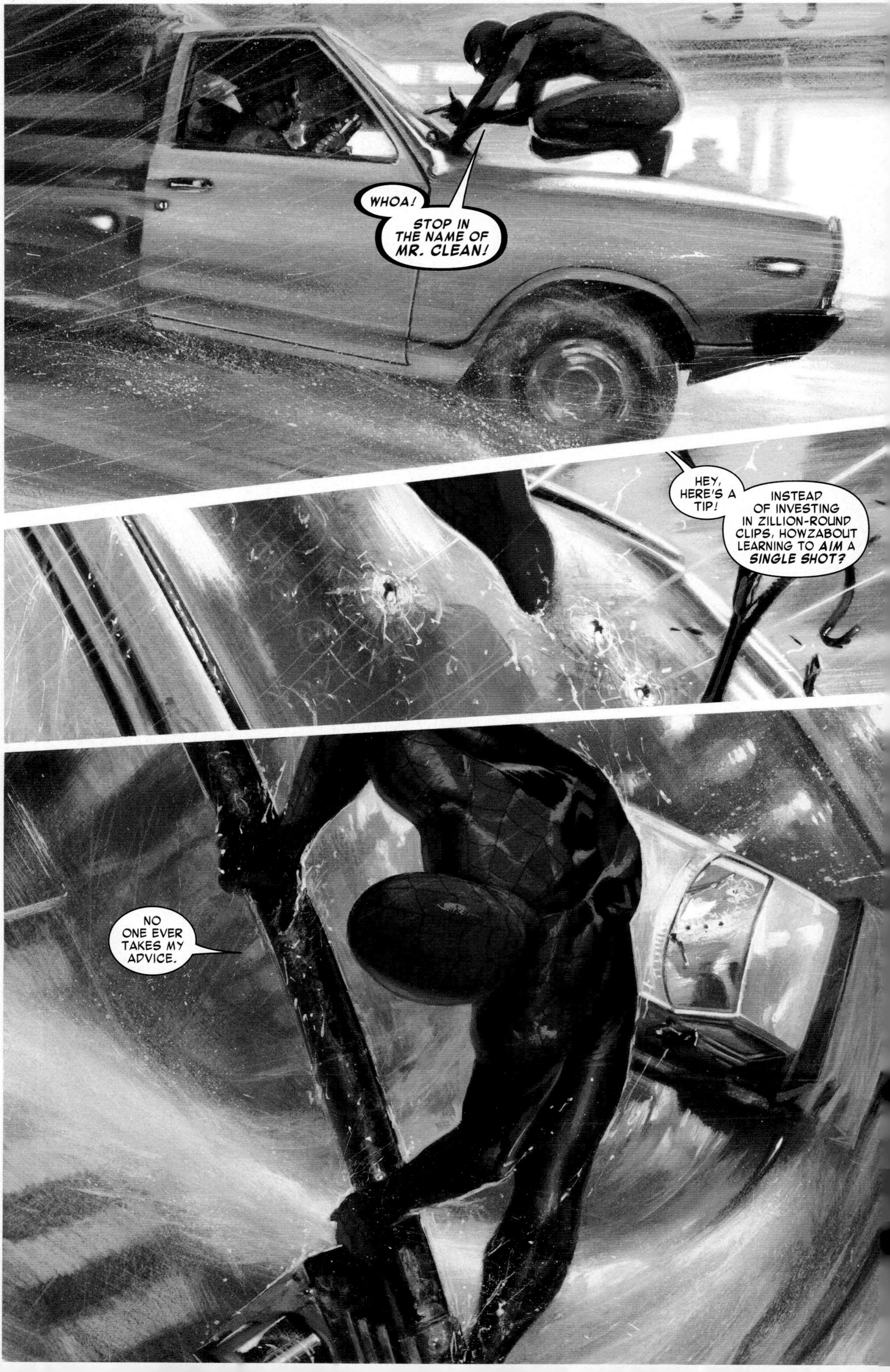
WHOA!
STOP IN THE NAME OF MR. CLEAN!
HEY, HERE'S A TIP!
INSTEAD OF INVESTING IN ZILLION-ROUND CLIPS, HOWZABOUT LEARNING TO AIM A SINGLE SHOT?
NO ONE EVER TAKES MY ADVICE.

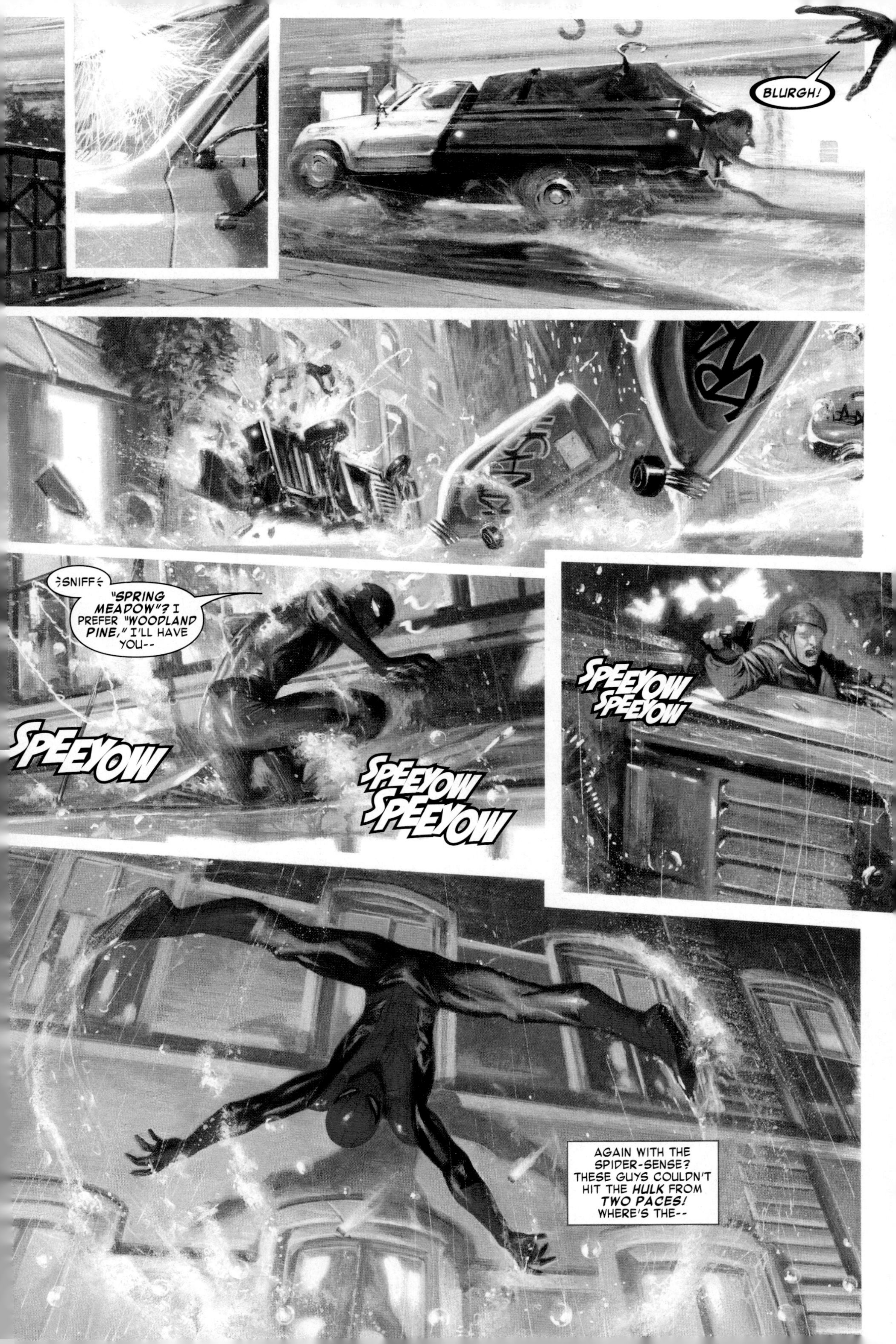
BLURGH!
SNIFF
"SPRING MEADOW"? I PREFER "WOODLAND PINE," I'LL HAVE YOU--
SPEEYOW
SPEEYOW SPEEYOW
SPEEYOW SPEEYOW
AGAIN WITH THE SPIDER-SENSE? THESE GUYS COULDN'T HIT THE HULK FROM TWO PACES! WHERE'S THE--

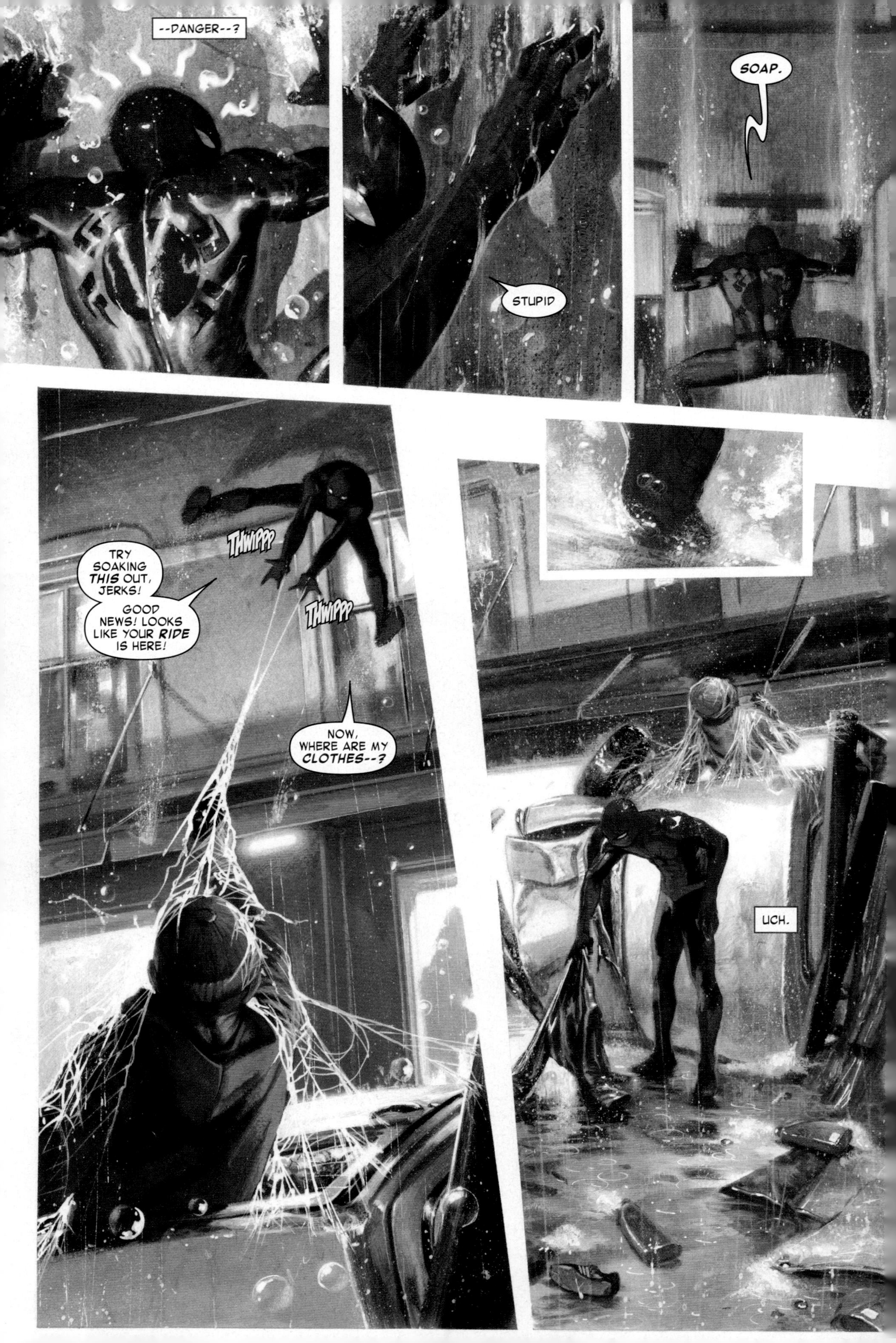
--DANGER--?
STUPID
SOAP.
THWIPPP
TRY SOAKING THIS OUT, JERKS!
GOOD NEWS! LOOKS LIKE YOUR RIDE IS HERE!
THWIPPP
NOW, WHERE ARE MY CLOTHES--?
UCH.

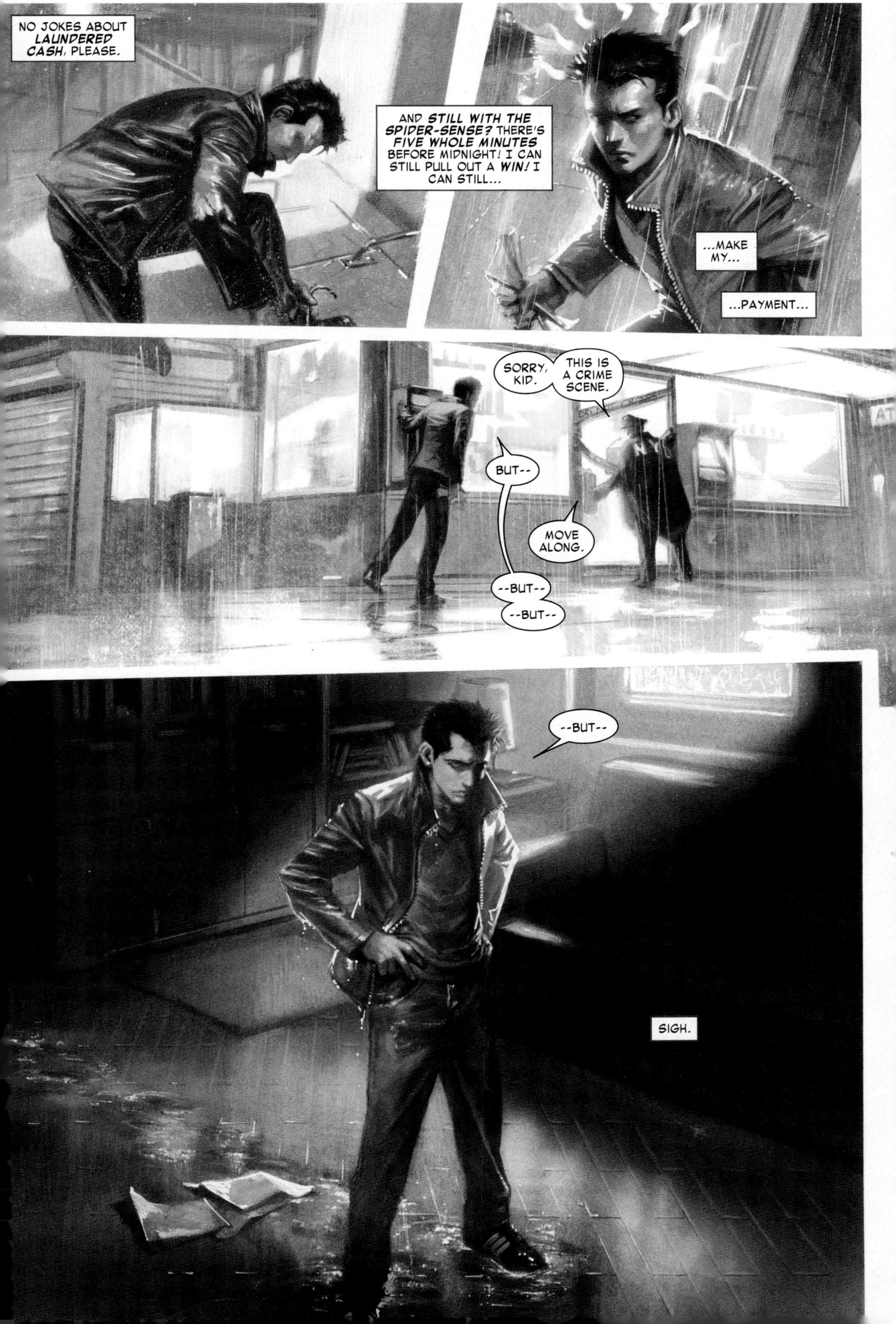
NO JOKES ABOUT LAUNDERED CASH, PLEASE.
AND STILL WITH THE SPIDER-SENSE? THERE'S FIVE WHOLE MINUTES BEFORE MIDNIGHT! I CAN STILL PULL OUT A WIN! I CAN STILL...
...MAKE MY...
...PAYMENT...
SORRY, KID.
THIS IS A CRIME SCENE.
BUT--
MOVE ALONG.
--BUT--
--BUT--
--BUT--
SIGH.

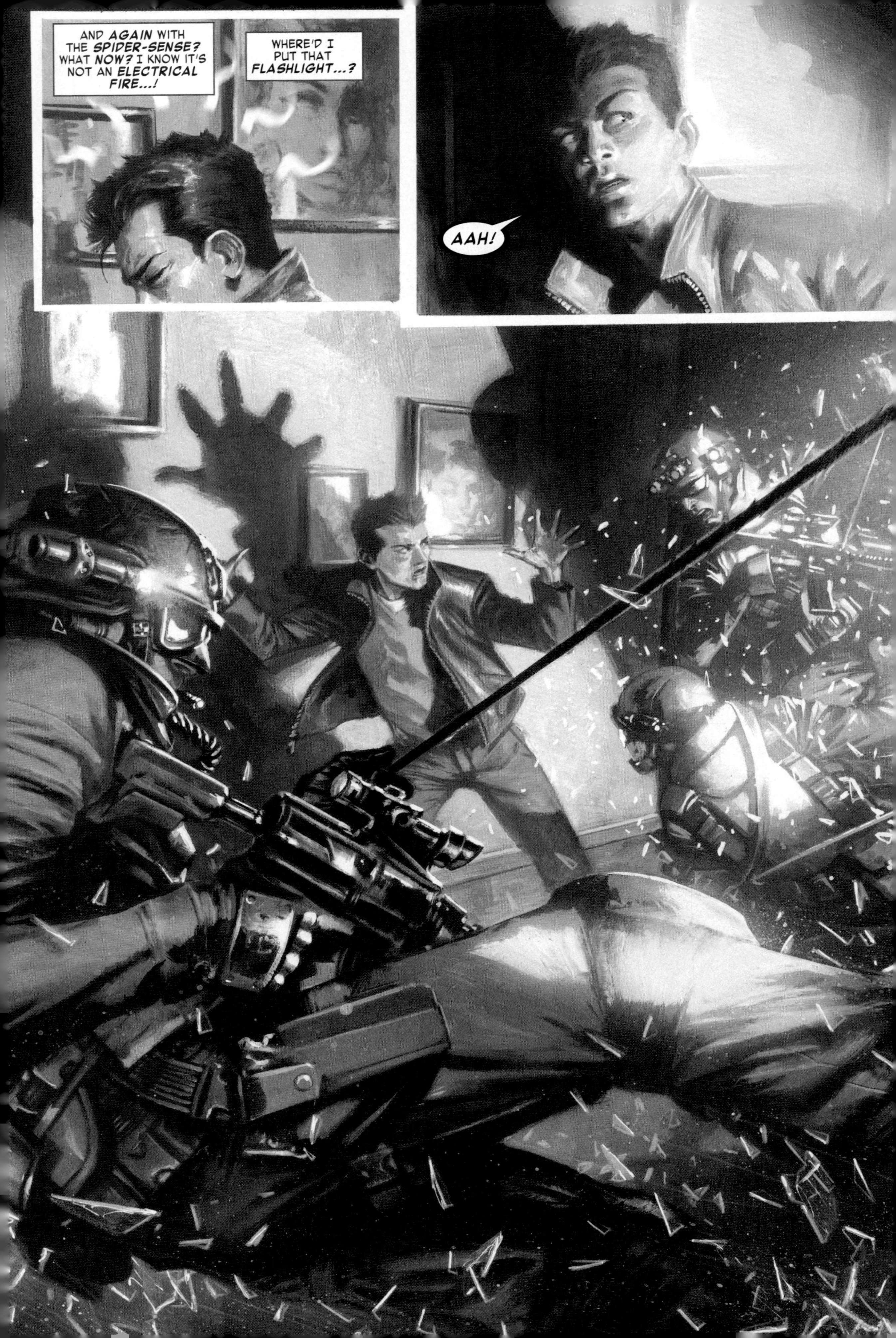
AND AGAIN WITH THE SPIDER-SENSE? WHAT NOW? I KNOW IT'S NOT AN ELECTRICAL FIRE...!
WHERE'D I PUT THAT FLASHLIGHT...?
AAH!

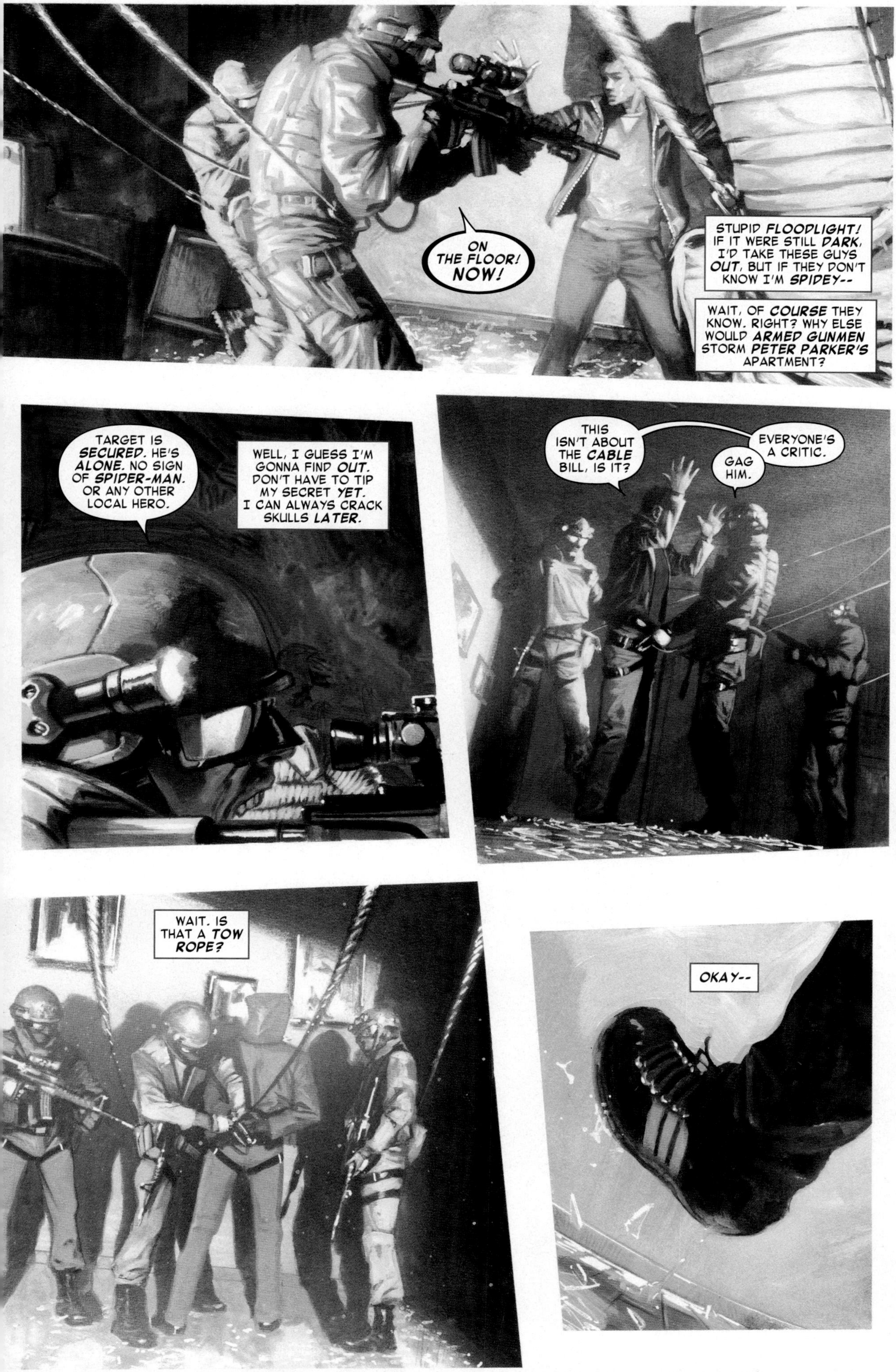
ON THE FLOOR! NOW!
STUPID FLOODLIGHT! IF IT WERE STILL DARK, I'D TAKE THESE GUYS OUT, BUT IF THEY DON'T KNOW I'M SPIDEY--
WAIT, OF COURSE THEY KNOW. RIGHT? WHY ELSE WOULD ARMED GUNMEN STORM PETER PARKER'S APARTMENT?
TARGET IS SECURED. HE'S ALONE. NO SIGN OF SPIDER-MAN. OR ANY OTHER LOCAL HERO.
WELL, I GUESS I'M GONNA FIND OUT. DON'T HAVE TO TIP MY SECRET YET. I CAN ALWAYS CRACK SKULLS LATER.
THIS ISN'T ABOUT THE CABLE BILL, IS IT?
GAG HIM.
EVERYONE'S A CRITIC.
WAIT. IS THAT A TOW ROPE?
OKAY--

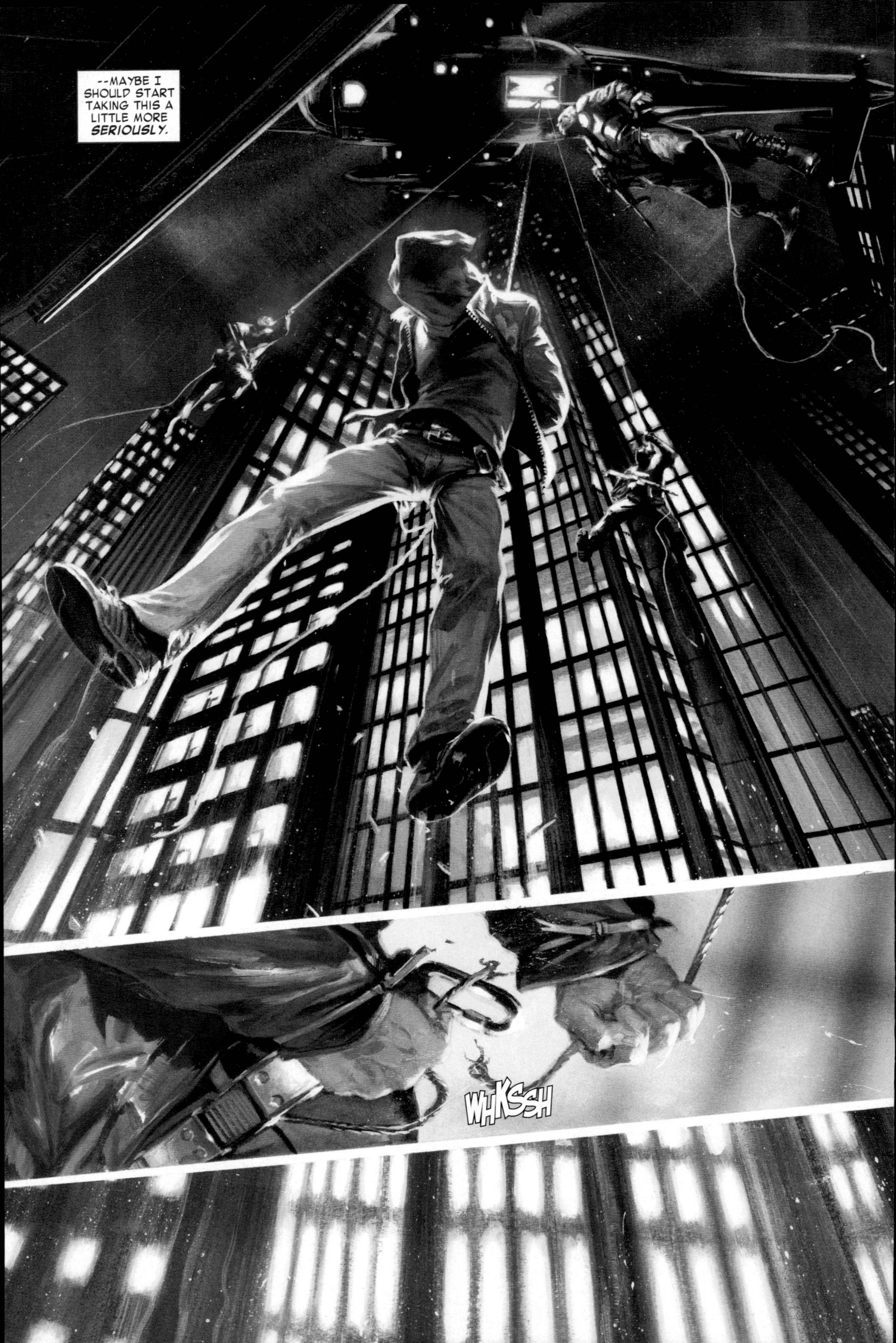
--MAYBE I SHOULD START TAKING THIS A LITTLE MORE SERIOUSLY.
WHKSSH

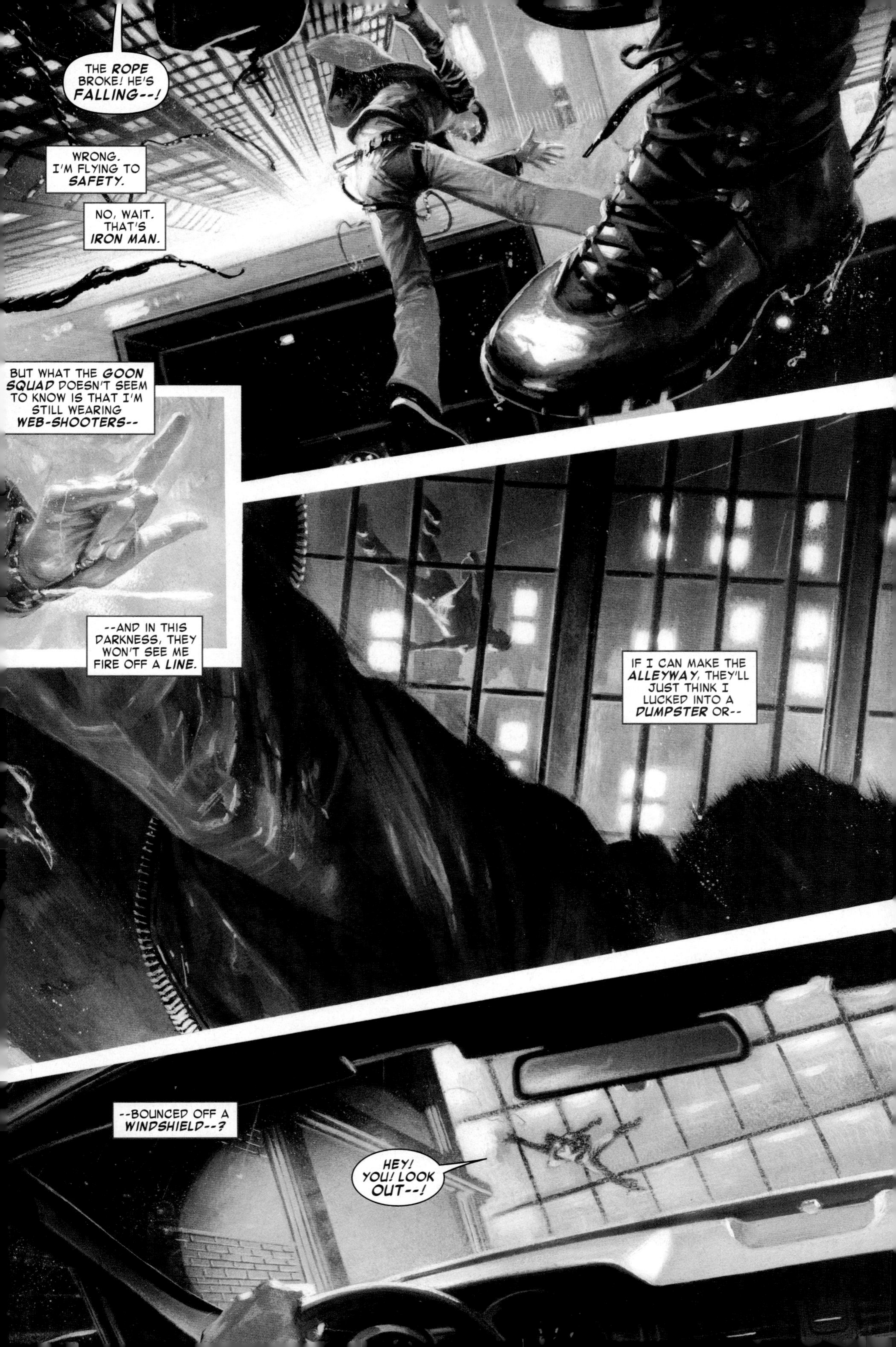
THE ROPE BROKE! HE'S FALLING--!
WRONG. I'M FLYING TO SAFETY.
NO, WAIT. THAT'S IRON MAN.
BUT WHAT THE GOON SQUAD DOESN'T SEEM TO KNOW IS THAT I'M STILL WEARING WEB-SHOOTERS--
--AND IN THIS DARKNESS, THEY WON'T SEE ME FIRE OFF A LINE.
IF I CAN MAKE THE ALLEYWAY, THEY'LL JUST THINK I LUCKED INTO A DUMPSTER OR--
--BOUNCED OFF A WINDSHIELD--?
HEY! YOU! LOOK OUT--!

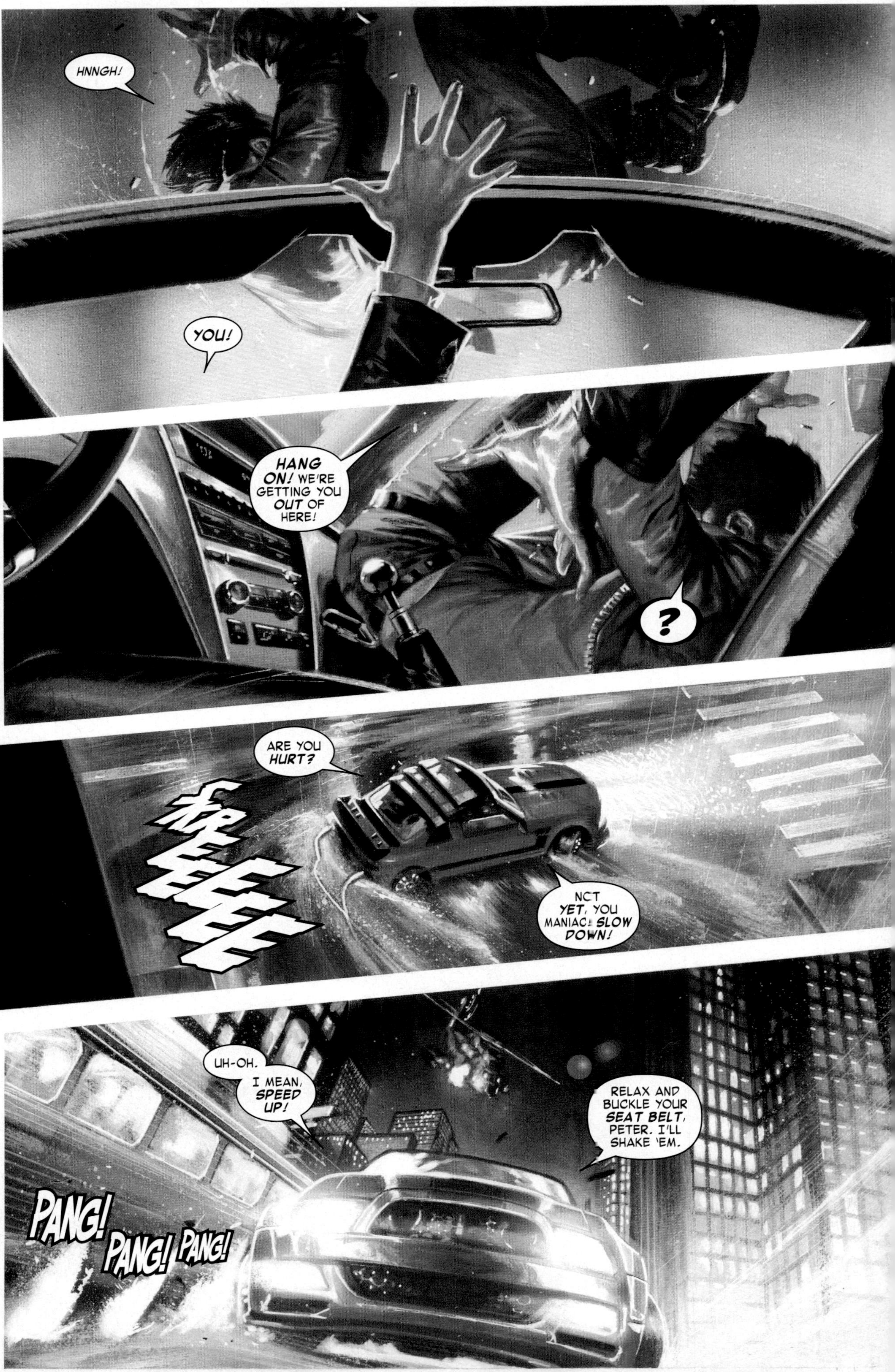
HNNGH!
YOU!
HANG ON! WE'RE GETTING YOU OUT OF HERE!
?
ARE YOU HURT?
KREEEEE
NOT YET, YOU MANIAC! SLOW DOWN!
UH-OH.
I MEAN, SPEED UP!
RELAX AND BUCKLE YOUR SEAT BELT, PETER. I'LL SHAKE 'EM.
PANG! PANG! PANG!

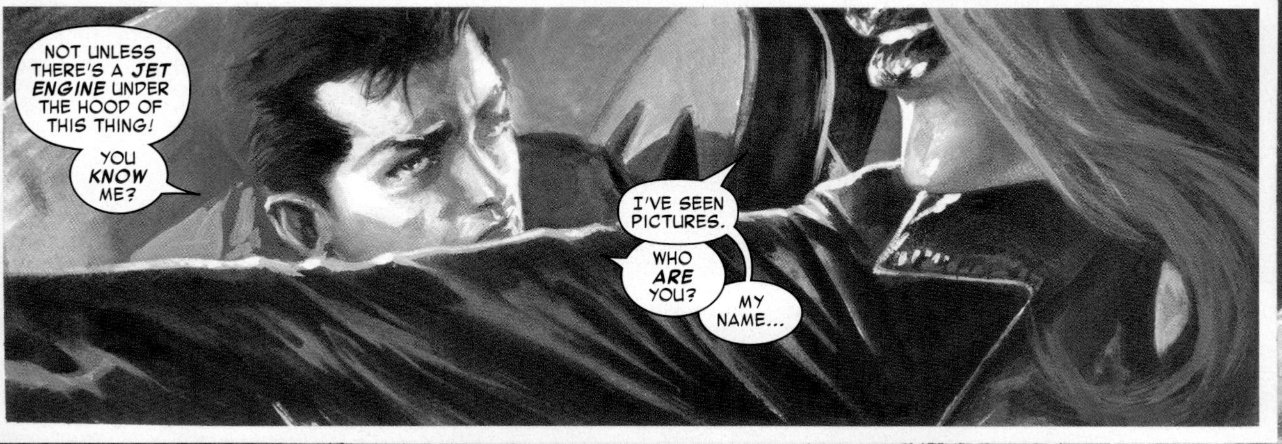
NOT UNLESS THERE'S A **JET ENGINE** UNDER THE HOOD OF THIS THING!
YOU **KNOW** ME?
I'VE SEEN PICTURES.
WHO **ARE** YOU?
MY NAME...

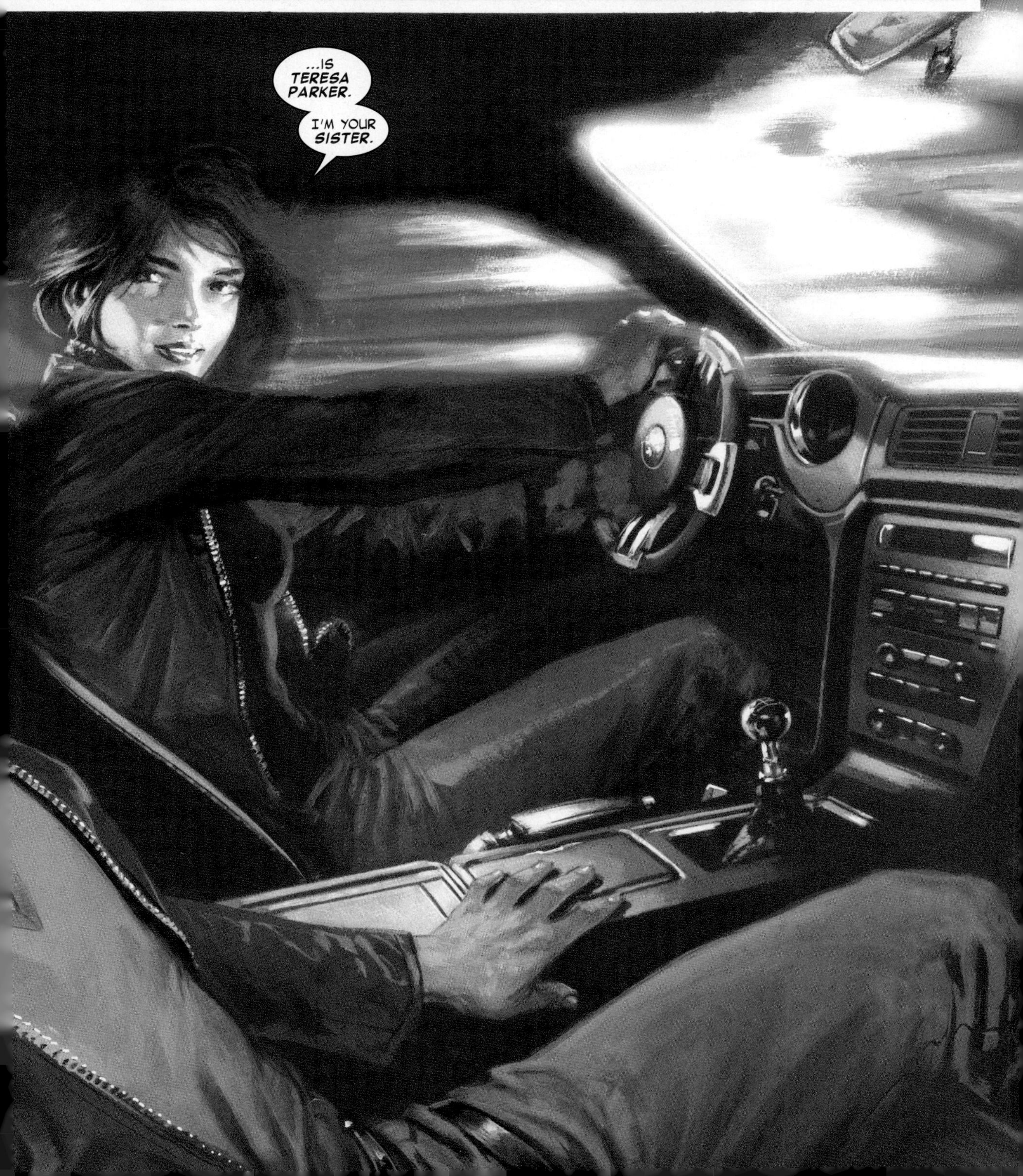
...IS **TERESA PARKER**.
I'M YOUR **SISTER**.

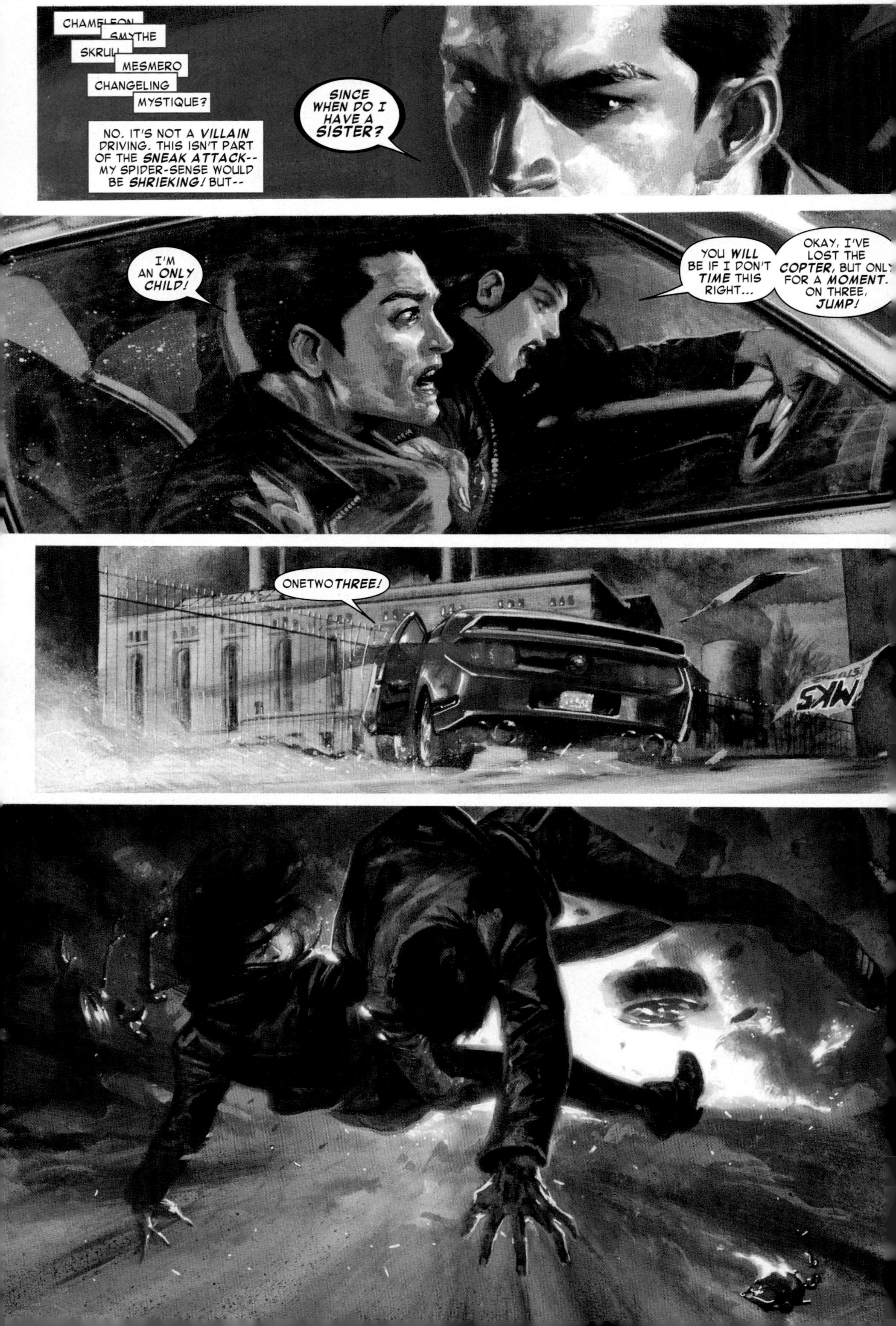
CHAMELEON
SMYTHE
SKRULL
MESMERO
CHANGELING
MYSTIQUE?
NO. IT'S NOT A VILLAIN DRIVING. THIS ISN'T PART OF THE SNEAK ATTACK-- MY SPIDER-SENSE WOULD BE SHRIEKING! BUT--
SINCE WHEN DO I HAVE A SISTER?
I'M AN ONLY CHILD!
OKAY, I'VE LOST THE COPTER, BUT ONLY FOR A MOMENT. ON THREE, JUMP!
YOU WILL BE IF I DON'T TIME THIS RIGHT...
ONETWOTHREE!

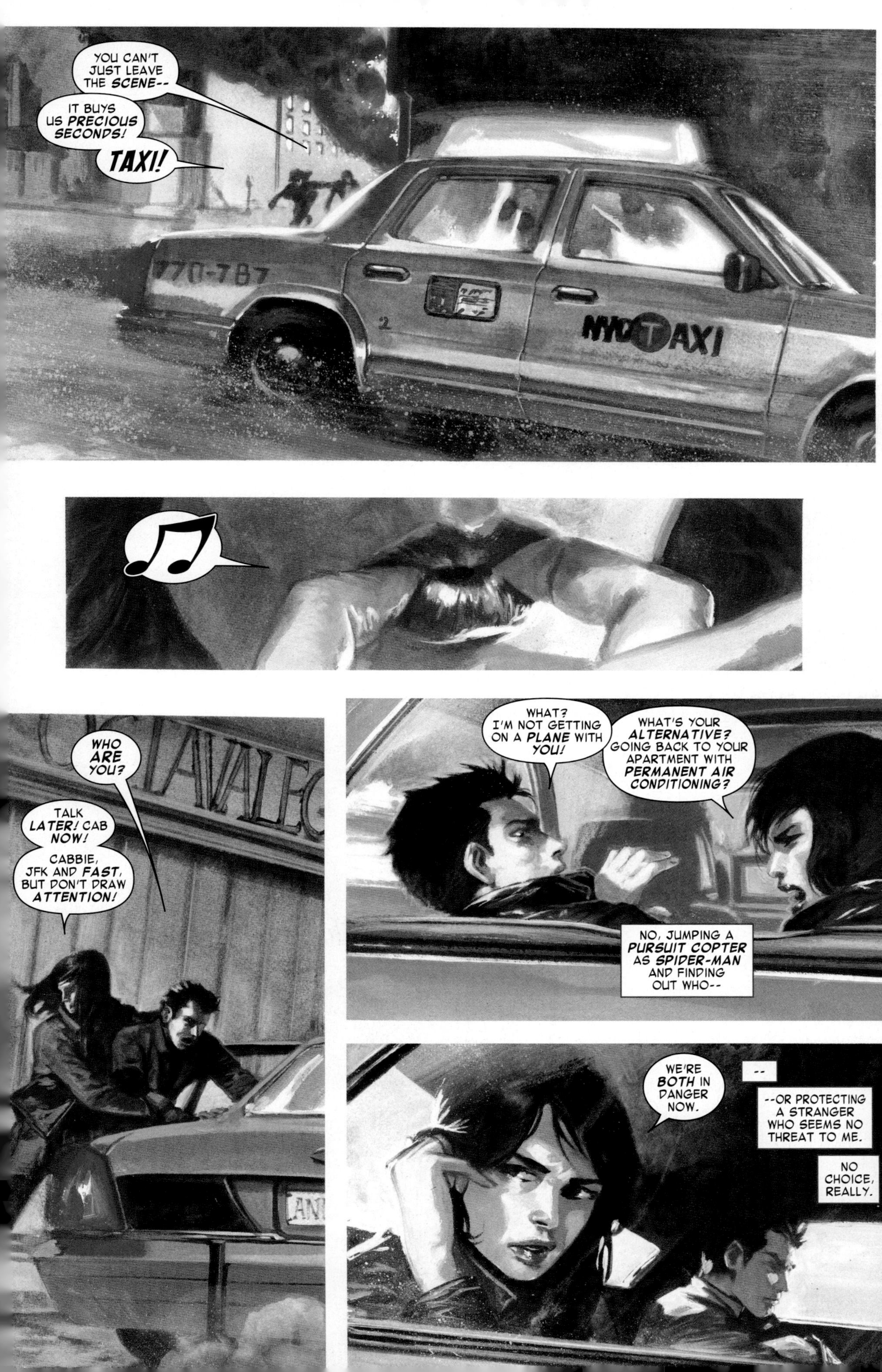
YOU CAN'T JUST LEAVE THE SCENE--
IT BUYS US PRECIOUS SECONDS!
TAXI!
770-787
NYC TAXI
WHO ARE YOU?
TALK LATER! CAB NOW!
CABBIE, JFK AND FAST, BUT DON'T DRAW ATTENTION!
WHAT? I'M NOT GETTING ON A PLANE WITH YOU!
WHAT'S YOUR ALTERNATIVE? GOING BACK TO YOUR APARTMENT WITH PERMANENT AIR CONDITIONING?
NO, JUMPING A PURSUIT COPTER AS SPIDER-MAN AND FINDING OUT WHO--
WE'RE BOTH IN DANGER NOW.
--
--OR PROTECTING A STRANGER WHO SEEMS NO THREAT TO ME.
NO CHOICE, REALLY.

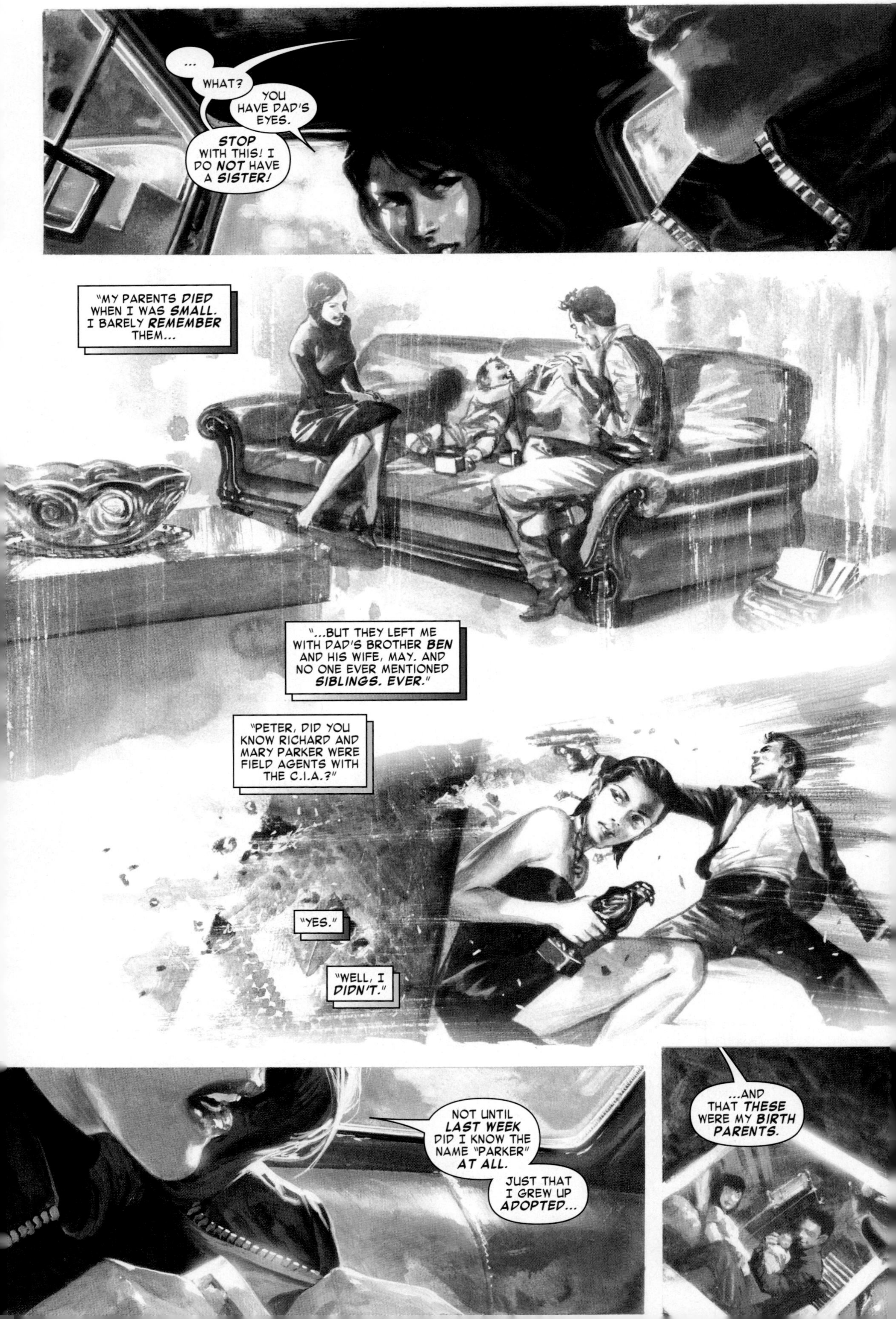
...
WHAT?
YOU HAVE DAD'S EYES.
STOP WITH THIS! I DO NOT HAVE A SISTER!
"MY PARENTS DIED WHEN I WAS SMALL. I BARELY REMEMBER THEM...
"...BUT THEY LEFT ME WITH DAD'S BROTHER BEN AND HIS WIFE, MAY. AND NO ONE EVER MENTIONED SIBLINGS. EVER."
"PETER, DID YOU KNOW RICHARD AND MARY PARKER WERE FIELD AGENTS WITH THE C.I.A.?"
"YES."
"WELL, I DIDN'T."
NOT UNTIL LAST WEEK DID I KNOW THE NAME "PARKER" AT ALL.
JUST THAT I GREW UP ADOPTED...
...AND THAT THESE WERE MY BIRTH PARENTS.

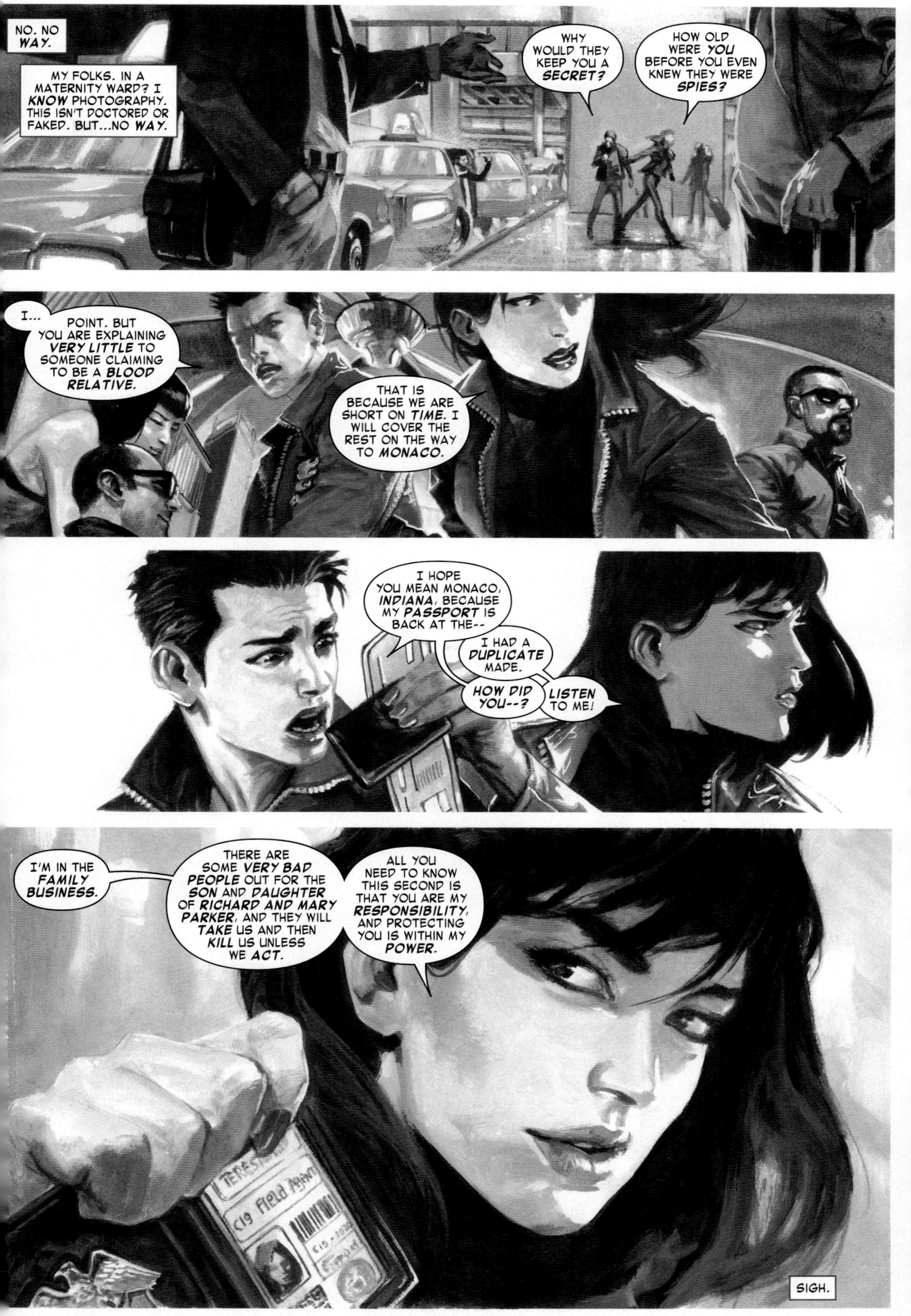

NO. NO WAY.
MY FOLKS. IN A MATERNITY WARD? I KNOW PHOTOGRAPHY. THIS ISN'T DOCTORED OR FAKED. BUT...NO WAY.
WHY WOULD THEY KEEP YOU A SECRET?
HOW OLD WERE YOU BEFORE YOU EVEN KNEW THEY WERE SPIES?
I... POINT. BUT YOU ARE EXPLAINING VERY LITTLE TO SOMEONE CLAIMING TO BE A BLOOD RELATIVE.
THAT IS BECAUSE WE ARE SHORT ON TIME. I WILL COVER THE REST ON THE WAY TO MONACO.
I HOPE YOU MEAN MONACO, INDIANA, BECAUSE MY PASSPORT IS BACK AT THE--
I HAD A DUPLICATE MADE.
HOW DID YOU--?
LISTEN TO ME!
I'M IN THE FAMILY BUSINESS.
THERE ARE SOME VERY BAD PEOPLE OUT FOR THE SON AND DAUGHTER OF RICHARD AND MARY PARKER, AND THEY WILL TAKE US AND THEN KILL US UNLESS WE ACT.
ALL YOU NEED TO KNOW THIS SECOND IS THAT YOU ARE MY RESPONSIBILITY, AND PROTECTING YOU IS WITHIN MY POWER.
SIGH.

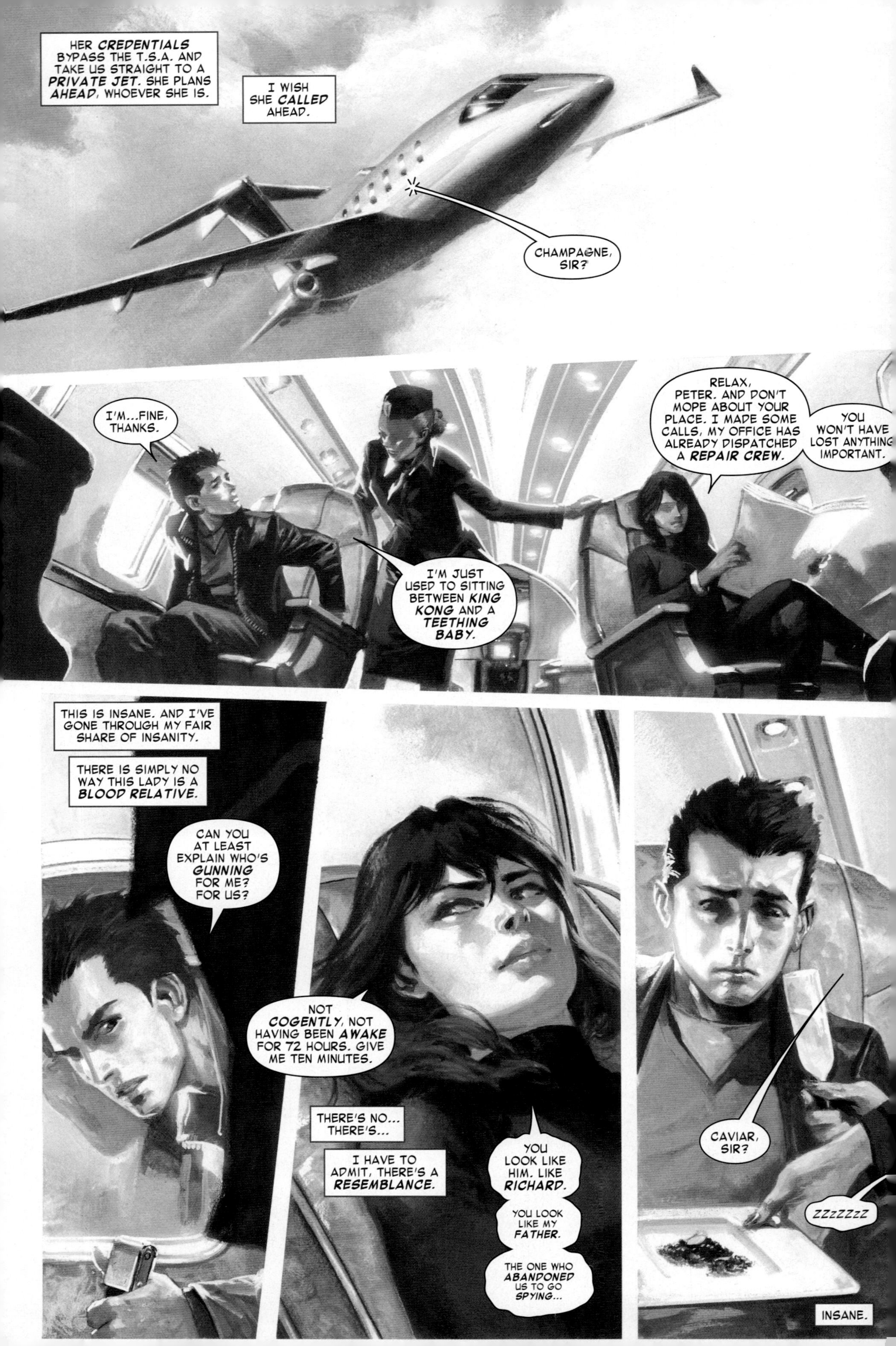
HER CREDENTIALS BYPASS THE T.S.A. AND TAKE US STRAIGHT TO A PRIVATE JET. SHE PLANS AHEAD, WHOEVER SHE IS.
I WISH SHE CALLED AHEAD.
CHAMPAGNE, SIR?
I'M...FINE, THANKS.
I'M JUST USED TO SITTING BETWEEN KING KONG AND A TEETHING BABY.
RELAX, PETER. AND DON'T MOPE ABOUT YOUR PLACE. I MADE SOME CALLS, MY OFFICE HAS ALREADY DISPATCHED A REPAIR CREW.
YOU WON'T HAVE LOST ANYTHING IMPORTANT.
THIS IS INSANE. AND I'VE GONE THROUGH MY FAIR SHARE OF INSANITY.
THERE IS SIMPLY NO WAY THIS LADY IS A BLOOD RELATIVE.
CAN YOU AT LEAST EXPLAIN WHO'S GUNNING FOR ME? FOR US?
NOT COGENTLY, NOT HAVING BEEN AWAKE FOR 72 HOURS. GIVE ME TEN MINUTES.
THERE'S NO... THERE'S...
I HAVE TO ADMIT, THERE'S A RESEMBLANCE.
YOU LOOK LIKE HIM. LIKE RICHARD.
YOU LOOK LIKE MY FATHER.
THE ONE WHO ABANDONED US TO GO SPYING...
CAVIAR, SIR?
ZZzZZzZ
INSANE.

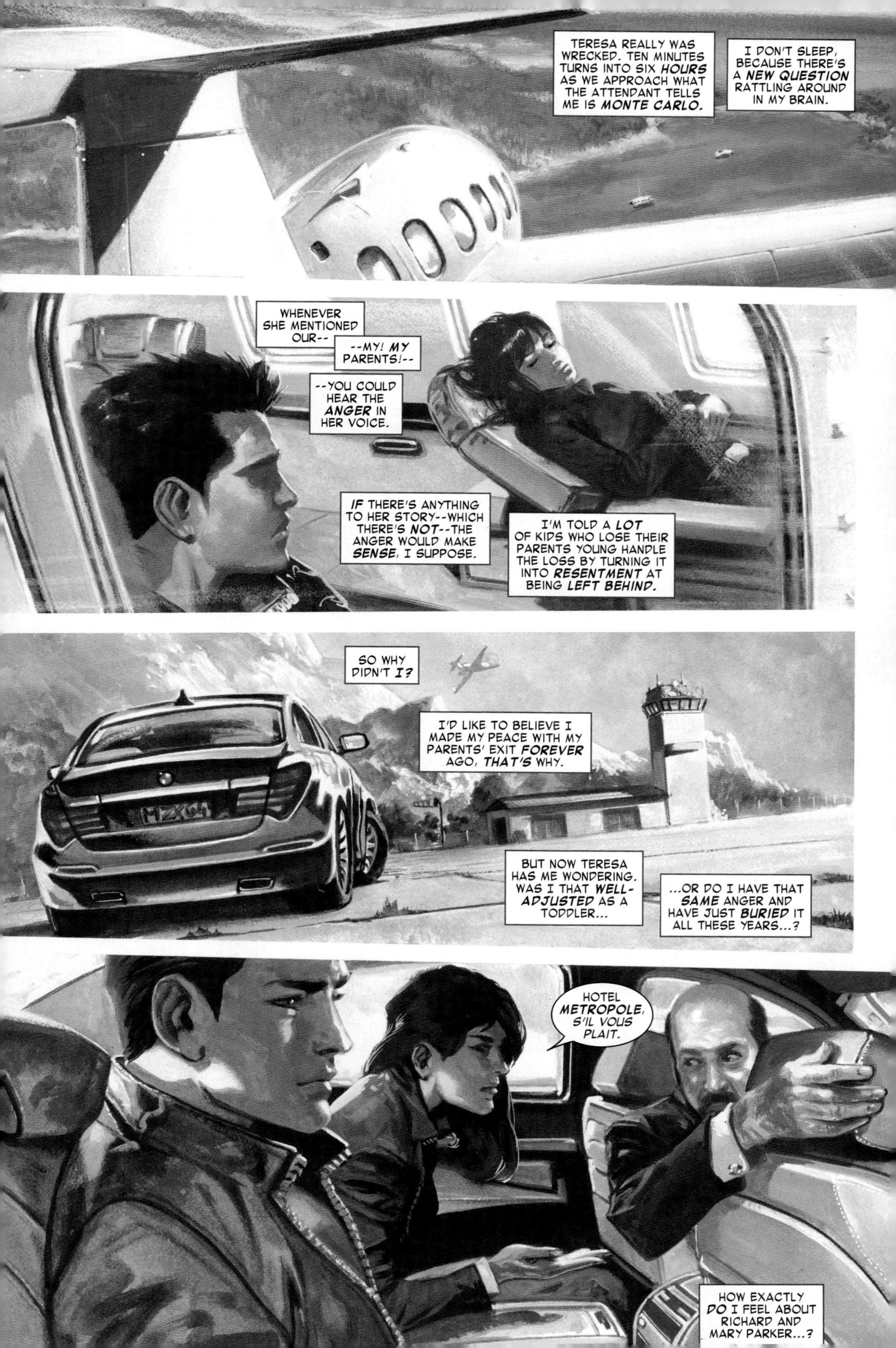
TERESA REALLY WAS WRECKED. TEN MINUTES TURNS INTO SIX *HOURS* AS WE APPROACH WHAT THE ATTENDANT TELLS ME IS *MONTE CARLO.*
I DON'T SLEEP, BECAUSE THERE'S A *NEW QUESTION* RATTLING AROUND IN MY BRAIN.
WHENEVER SHE MENTIONED OUR--
--MY! *MY* PARENTS!--
--YOU COULD HEAR THE *ANGER* IN HER VOICE.
IF THERE'S ANYTHING TO HER STORY--WHICH THERE'S *NOT*--THE ANGER WOULD MAKE *SENSE*, I SUPPOSE.
I'M TOLD A *LOT* OF KIDS WHO LOSE THEIR PARENTS YOUNG HANDLE THE LOSS BY TURNING IT INTO *RESENTMENT* AT BEING *LEFT BEHIND.*
SO WHY DIDN'T *I?*
I'D LIKE TO BELIEVE I MADE MY PEACE WITH MY PARENTS' EXIT *FOREVER* AGO, *THAT'S* WHY.
BUT NOW TERESA HAS ME WONDERING. WAS I THAT *WELL-ADJUSTED* AS A TODDLER...
...OR DO I HAVE THAT *SAME* ANGER AND HAVE JUST *BURIED* IT ALL THESE YEARS...?
HOTEL *METROPOLE*, S'IL VOUS PLAIT.
HOW EXACTLY *DO* I FEEL ABOUT RICHARD AND MARY PARKER...?

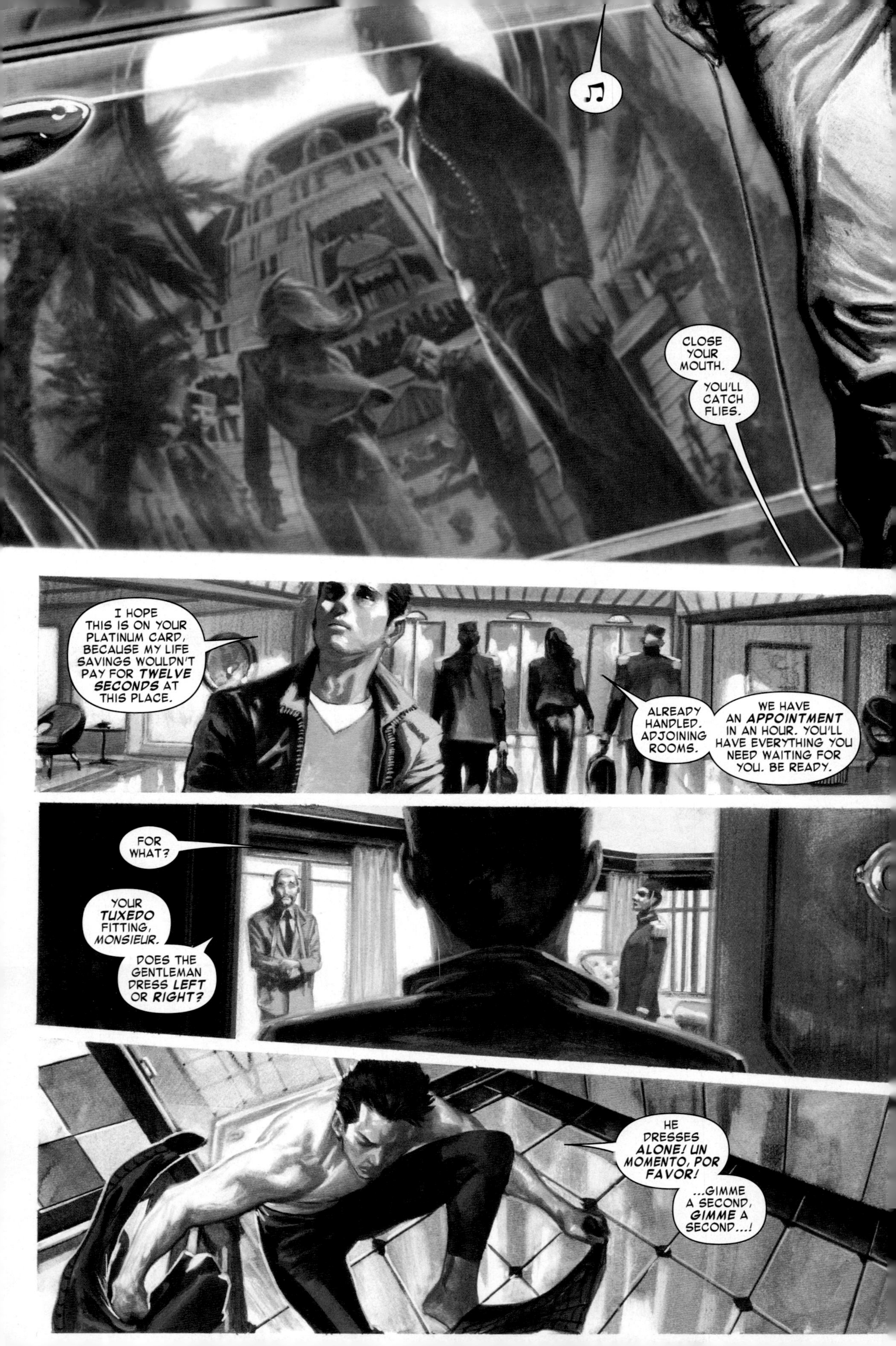
♫
CLOSE YOUR MOUTH.
YOU'LL CATCH FLIES.
I HOPE THIS IS ON YOUR PLATINUM CARD, BECAUSE MY LIFE SAVINGS WOULDN'T PAY FOR TWELVE SECONDS AT THIS PLACE.
ALREADY HANDLED. ADJOINING ROOMS.
WE HAVE AN APPOINTMENT IN AN HOUR. YOU'LL HAVE EVERYTHING YOU NEED WAITING FOR YOU. BE READY.
FOR WHAT?
YOUR TUXEDO FITTING, MONSIEUR.
DOES THE GENTLEMAN DRESS LEFT OR RIGHT?
HE DRESSES ALONE! UN MOMENTO, POR FAVOR!
...GIMME A SECOND, GIMME A SECOND...!

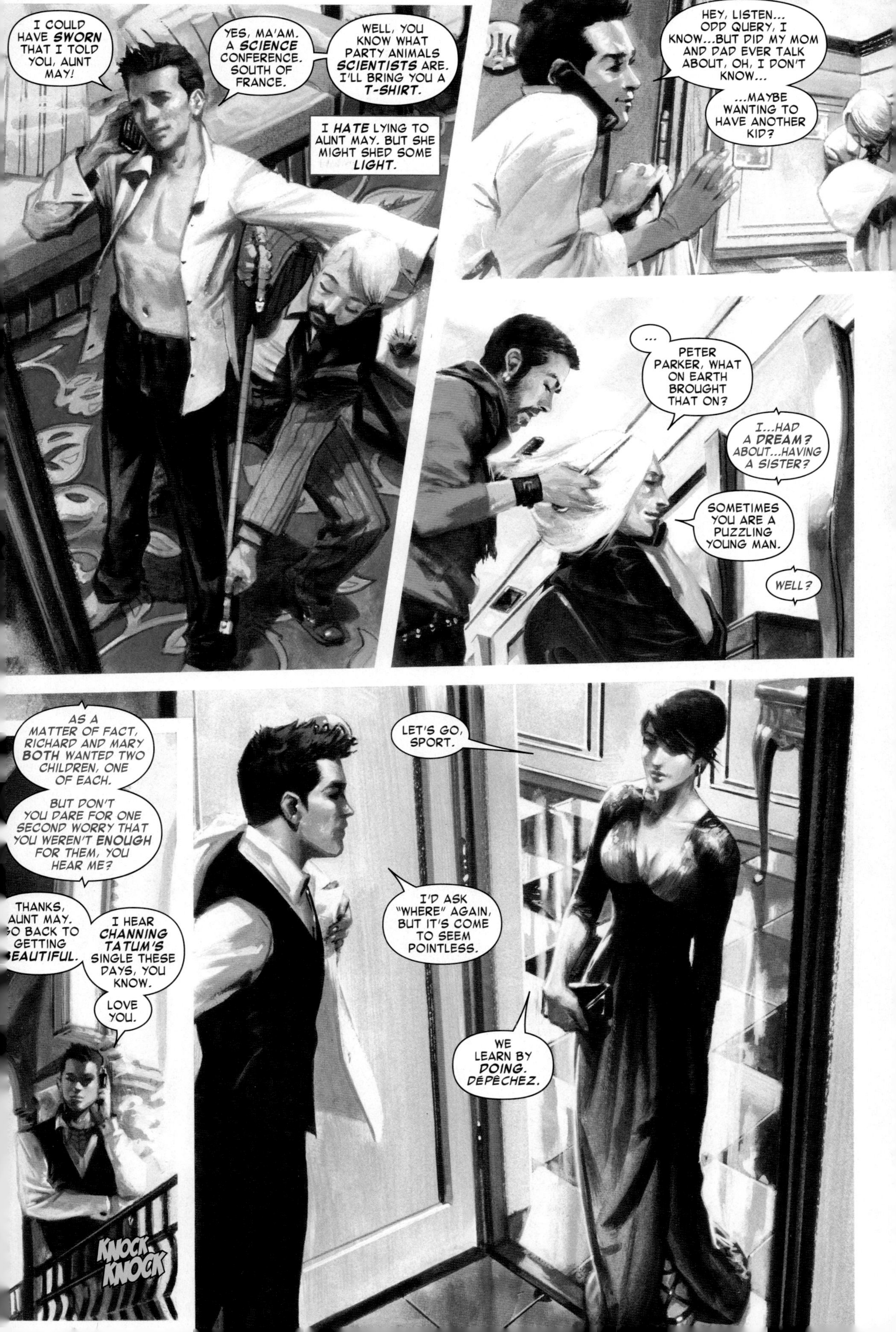

I COULD HAVE SWORN THAT I TOLD YOU, AUNT MAY!
YES, MA'AM. A SCIENCE CONFERENCE. SOUTH OF FRANCE.
WELL, YOU KNOW WHAT PARTY ANIMALS SCIENTISTS ARE. I'LL BRING YOU A T-SHIRT.
I HATE LYING TO AUNT MAY. BUT SHE MIGHT SHED SOME LIGHT.
HEY, LISTEN... ODD QUERY, I KNOW...BUT DID MY MOM AND DAD EVER TALK ABOUT, OH, I DON'T KNOW...
...MAYBE WANTING TO HAVE ANOTHER KID?
...
PETER PARKER, WHAT ON EARTH BROUGHT THAT ON?
I...HAD A DREAM? ABOUT...HAVING A SISTER?
SOMETIMES YOU ARE A PUZZLING YOUNG MAN.
WELL?
AS A MATTER OF FACT, RICHARD AND MARY BOTH WANTED TWO CHILDREN, ONE OF EACH.
BUT DON'T YOU DARE FOR ONE SECOND WORRY THAT YOU WEREN'T ENOUGH FOR THEM, YOU HEAR ME?
THANKS, AUNT MAY. GO BACK TO GETTING BEAUTIFUL.
I HEAR CHANNING TATUM'S SINGLE THESE DAYS, YOU KNOW.
LOVE YOU.
KNOCK KNOCK
LET'S GO, SPORT.
I'D ASK "WHERE" AGAIN, BUT IT'S COME TO SEEM POINTLESS.
WE LEARN BY DOING. DÉPÊCHEZ.

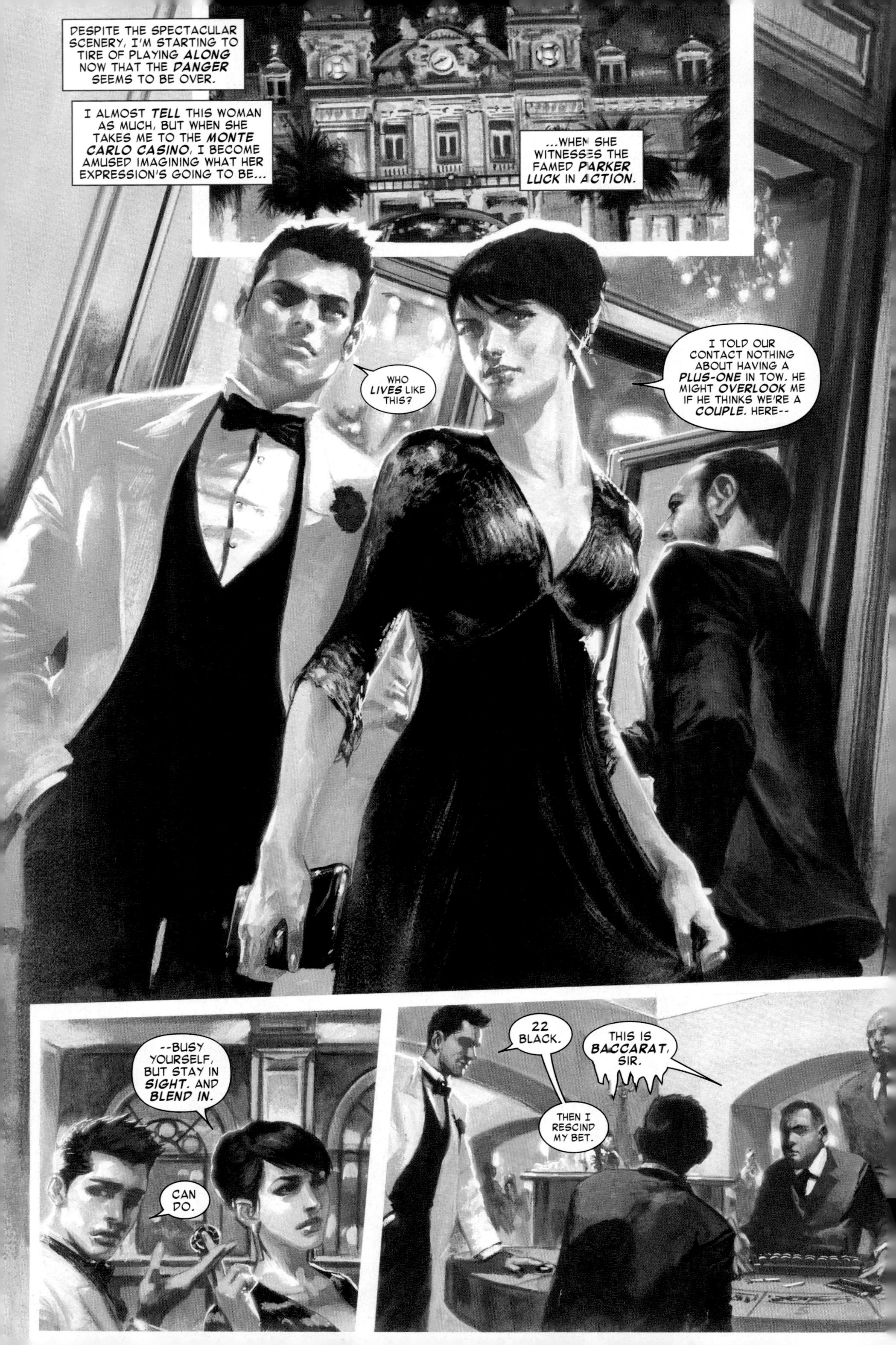
DESPITE THE SPECTACULAR SCENERY, I'M STARTING TO TIRE OF PLAYING ALONG NOW THAT THE DANGER SEEMS TO BE OVER.
I ALMOST TELL THIS WOMAN AS MUCH, BUT WHEN SHE TAKES ME TO THE MONTE CARLO CASINO, I BECOME AMUSED IMAGINING WHAT HER EXPRESSION'S GOING TO BE...
...WHEN SHE WITNESSES THE FAMED PARKER LUCK IN ACTION.
WHO LIVES LIKE THIS?
I TOLD OUR CONTACT NOTHING ABOUT HAVING A PLUS-ONE IN TOW. HE MIGHT OVERLOOK ME IF HE THINKS WE'RE A COUPLE. HERE--
--BUSY YOURSELF, BUT STAY IN SIGHT. AND BLEND IN.
CAN DO.
22 BLACK.
THIS IS BACCARAT, SIR.
THEN I RESCIND MY BET.

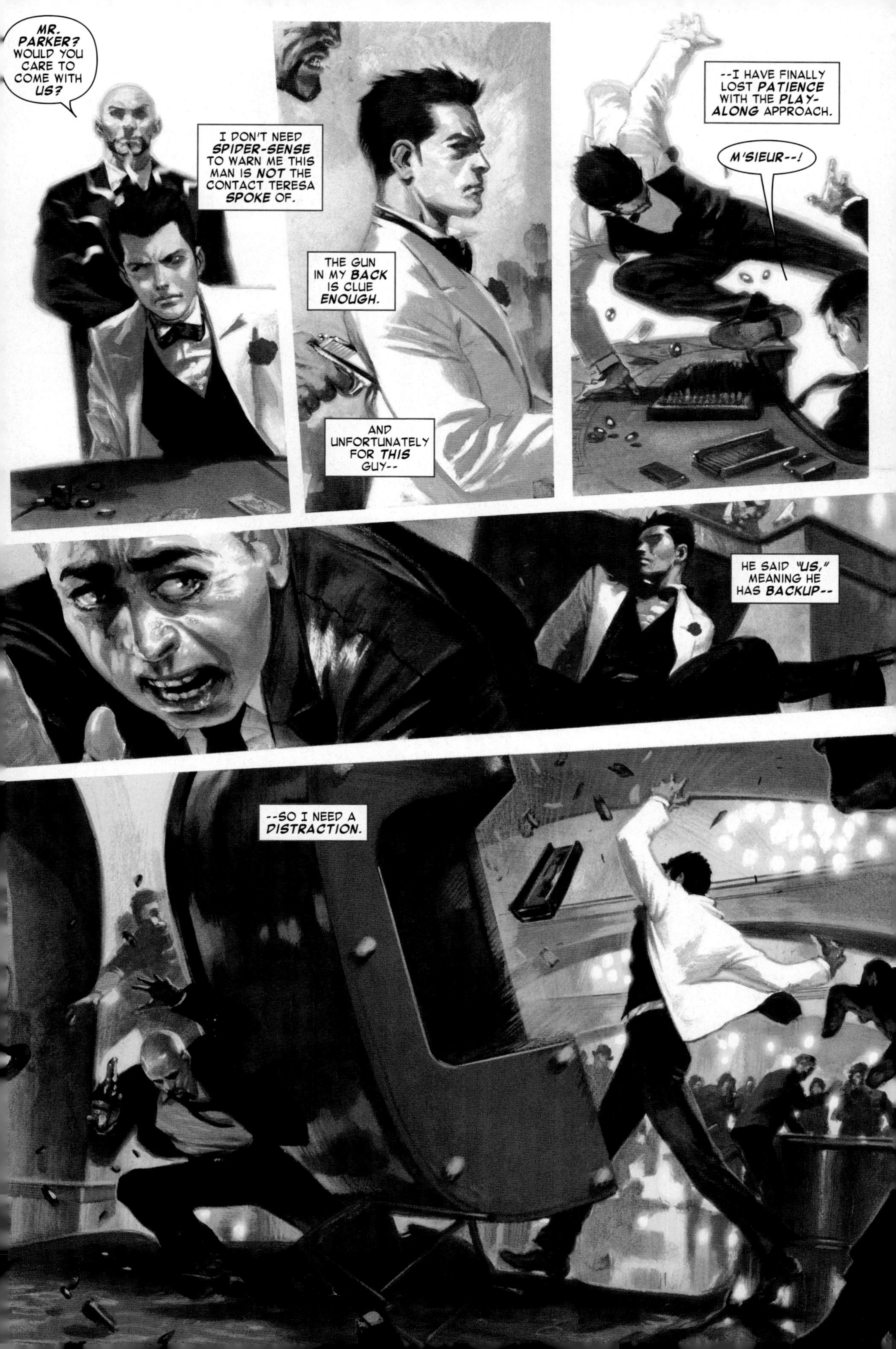

MR. PARKER? WOULD YOU CARE TO COME WITH US?
I DON'T NEED SPIDER-SENSE TO WARN ME THIS MAN IS NOT THE CONTACT TERESA SPOKE OF.
THE GUN IN MY BACK IS CLUE ENOUGH.
AND UNFORTUNATELY FOR THIS GUY--
--I HAVE FINALLY LOST PATIENCE WITH THE PLAY-ALONG APPROACH.
M'SIEUR--!
HE SAID "US," MEANING HE HAS BACKUP--
--SO I NEED A DISTRACTION.

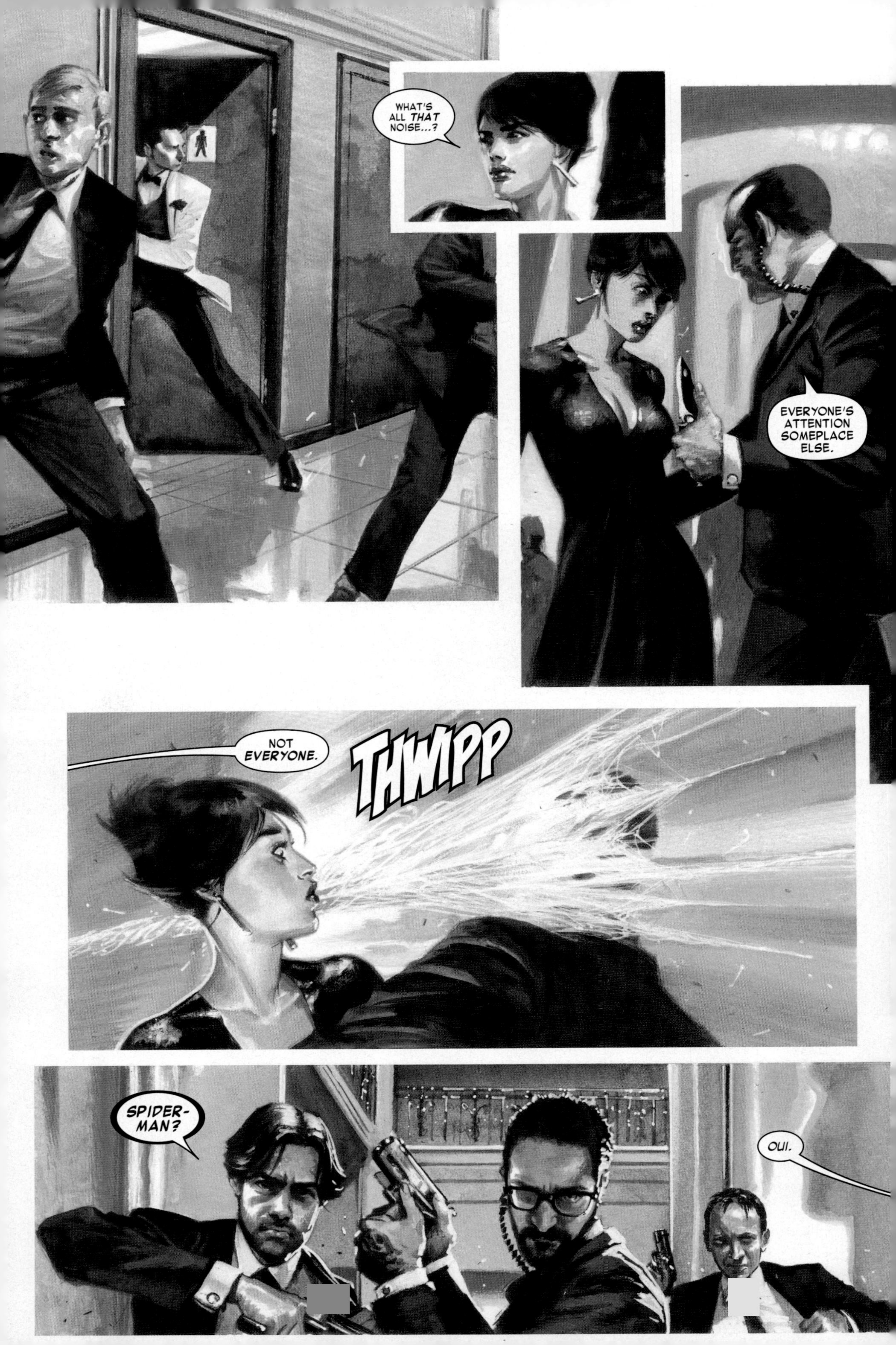
WHAT'S ALL THAT NOISE...?
EVERYONE'S ATTENTION SOMEPLACE ELSE.
NOT EVERYONE.
THWIPP
SPIDER-MAN?
OUI.

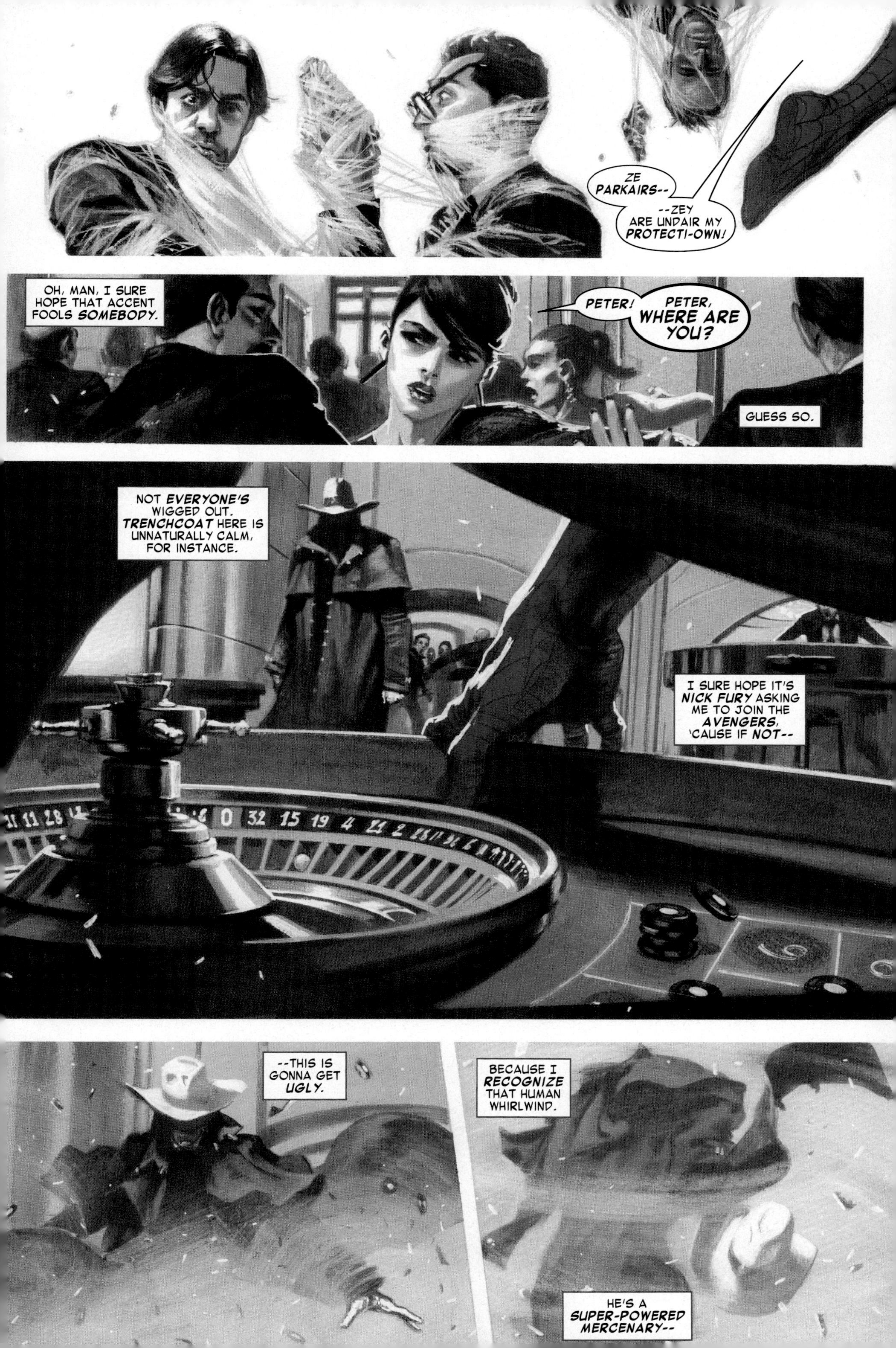

ZE PARKAIRS--
--ZEY ARE UNDAIR MY PROTECTI-OWN!
OH, MAN, I SURE HOPE THAT ACCENT FOOLS SOMEBODY.
PETER!
PETER, WHERE ARE YOU?
GUESS SO.
NOT EVERYONE'S WIGGED OUT. TRENCHCOAT HERE IS UNNATURALLY CALM, FOR INSTANCE.
I SURE HOPE IT'S NICK FURY ASKING ME TO JOIN THE AVENGERS, 'CAUSE IF NOT--
--THIS IS GONNA GET UGLY.
BECAUSE I RECOGNIZE THAT HUMAN WHIRLWIND.
HE'S A SUPER-POWERED MERCENARY--

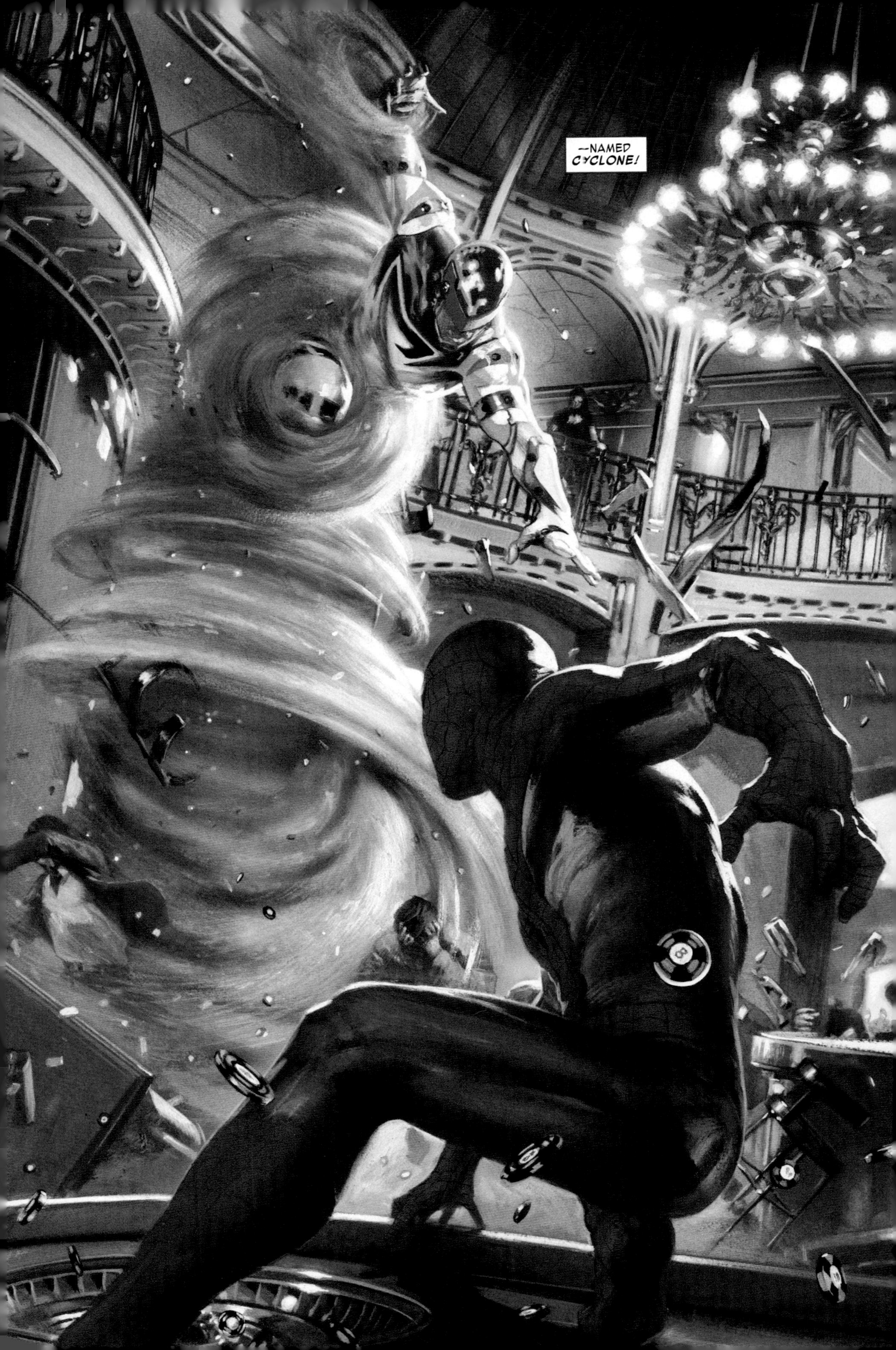
—NAMED CYCLONE!

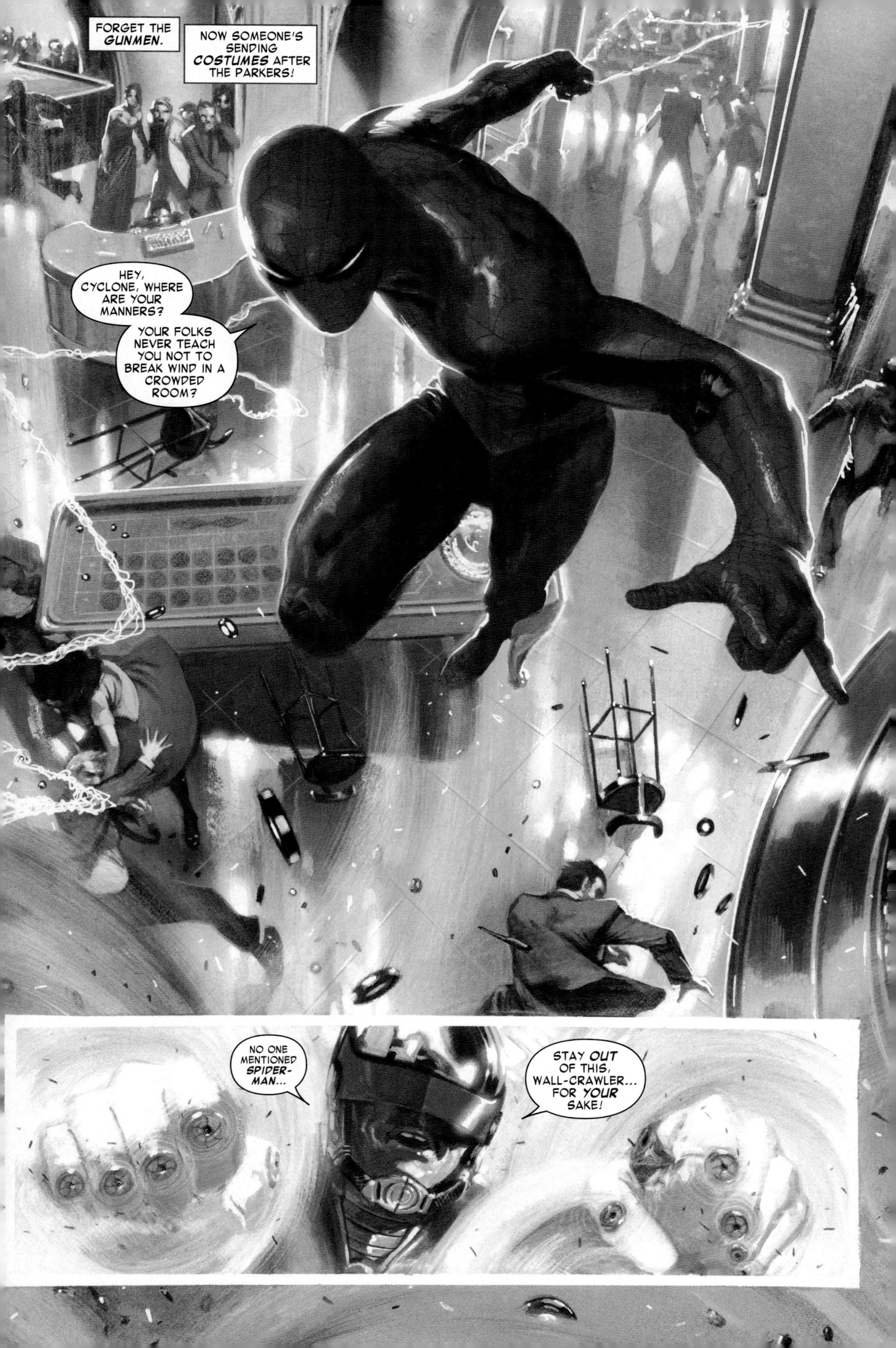
FORGET THE GUNMEN.
NOW SOMEONE'S SENDING COSTUMES AFTER THE PARKERS!
HEY, CYCLONE, WHERE ARE YOUR MANNERS?
YOUR FOLKS NEVER TEACH YOU NOT TO BREAK WIND IN A CROWDED ROOM?
NO ONE MENTIONED SPIDER-MAN...
STAY OUT OF THIS, WALL-CRAWLER... FOR YOUR SAKE!

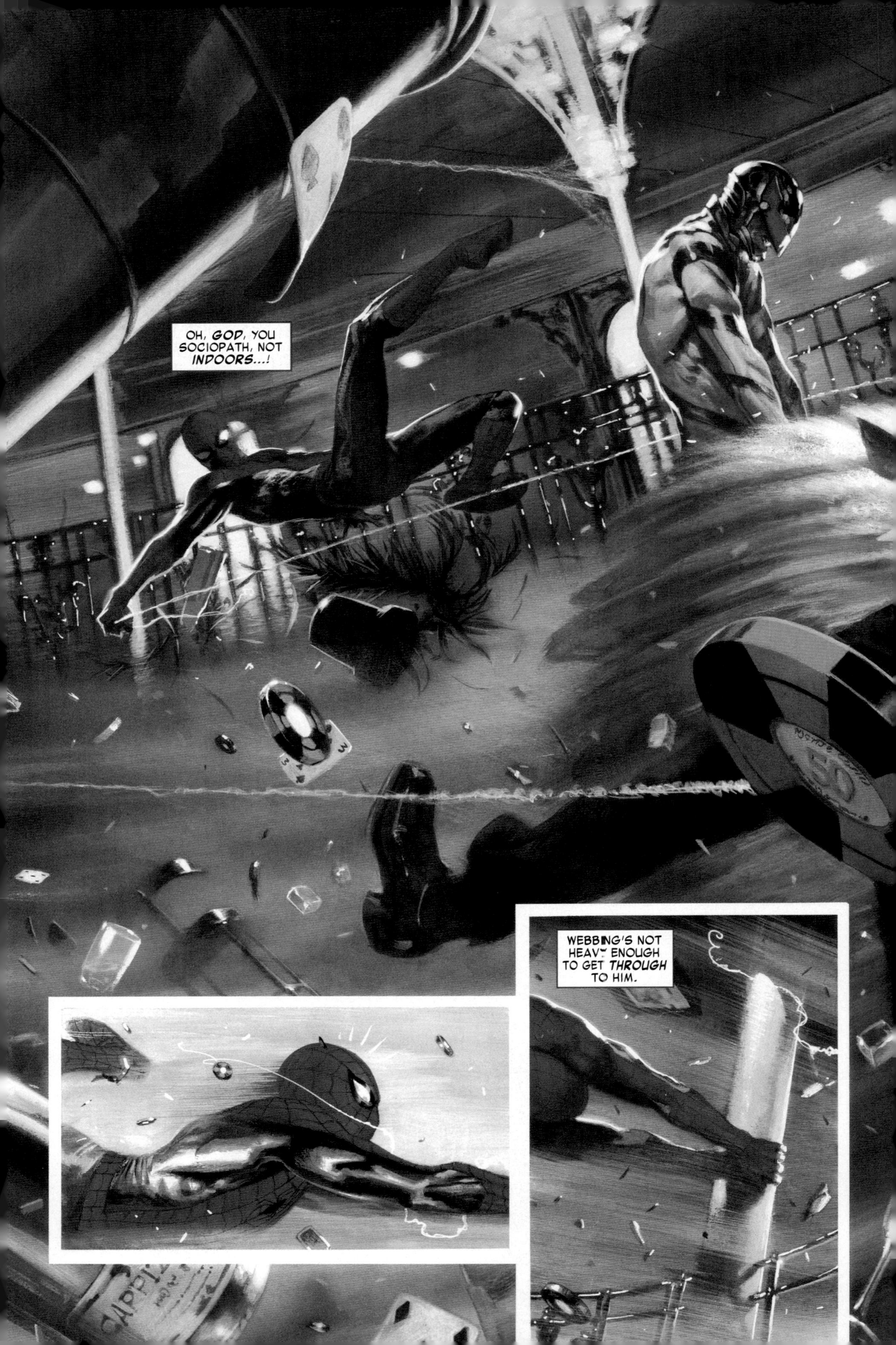
OH, *GOD*, YOU SOCIOPATH, NOT *INDOORS*...!
WEBBING'S NOT HEAVY ENOUGH TO GET *THROUGH* TO HIM.

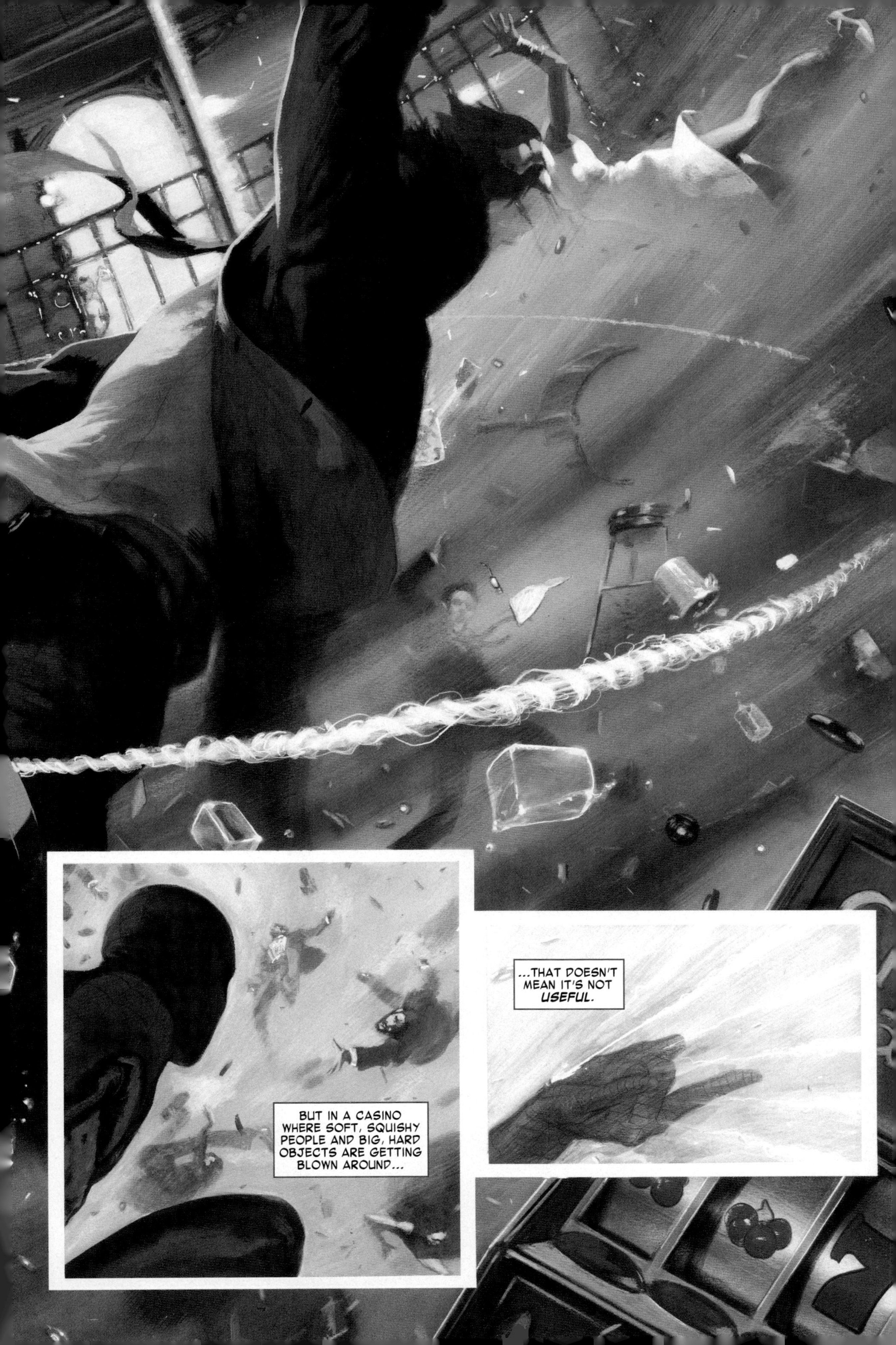
BUT IN A CASINO WHERE SOFT, SQUISHY PEOPLE AND BIG, HARD OBJECTS ARE GETTING BLOWN AROUND...
...THAT DOESN'T MEAN IT'S NOT *USEFUL*.

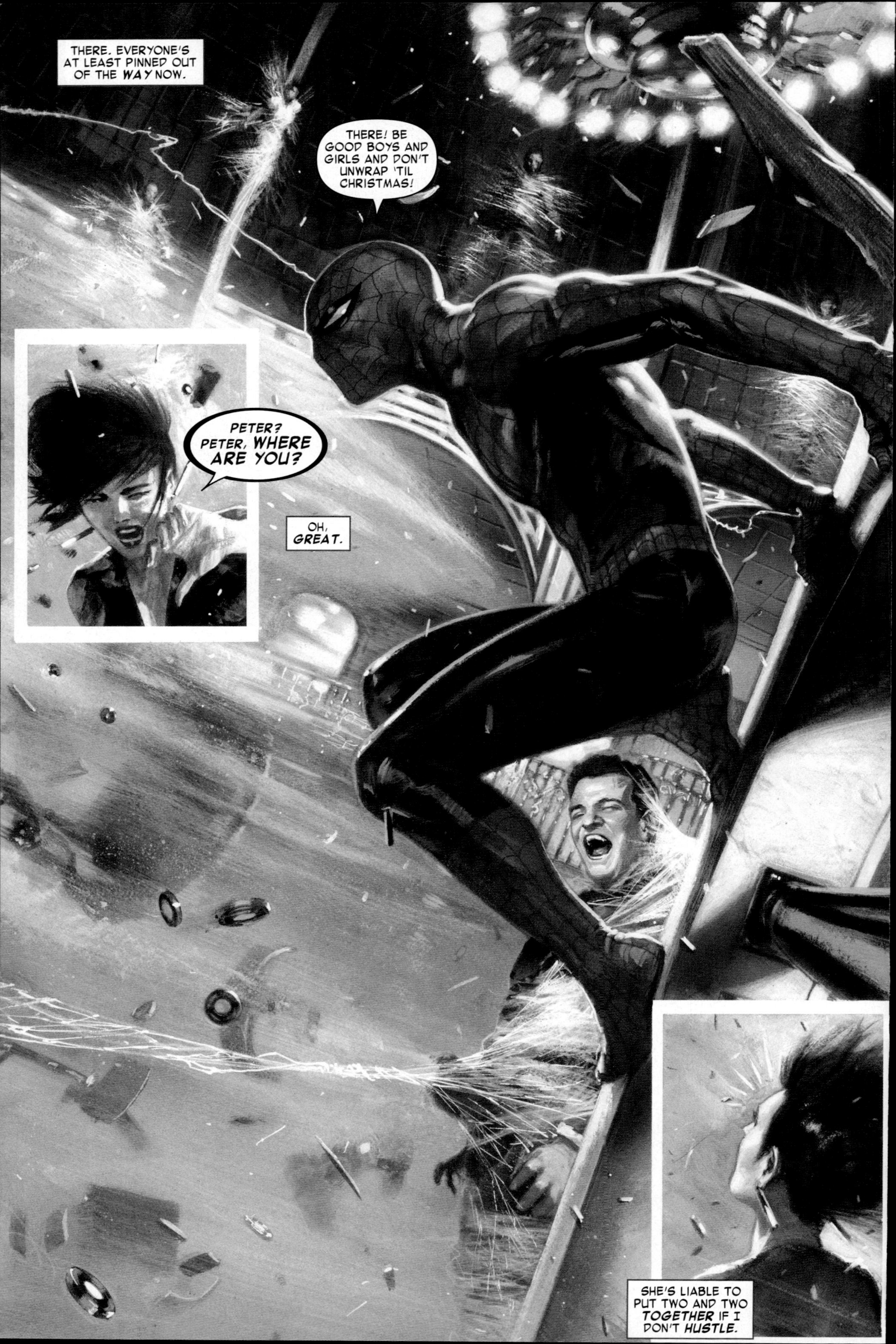
THERE. EVERYONE'S AT LEAST PINNED OUT OF THE WAY NOW.
THERE! BE GOOD BOYS AND GIRLS AND DON'T UNWRAP 'TIL CHRISTMAS!
PETER? PETER, WHERE ARE YOU?
OH, GREAT.
SHE'S LIABLE TO PUT TWO AND TWO TOGETHER IF I DON'T HUSTLE.

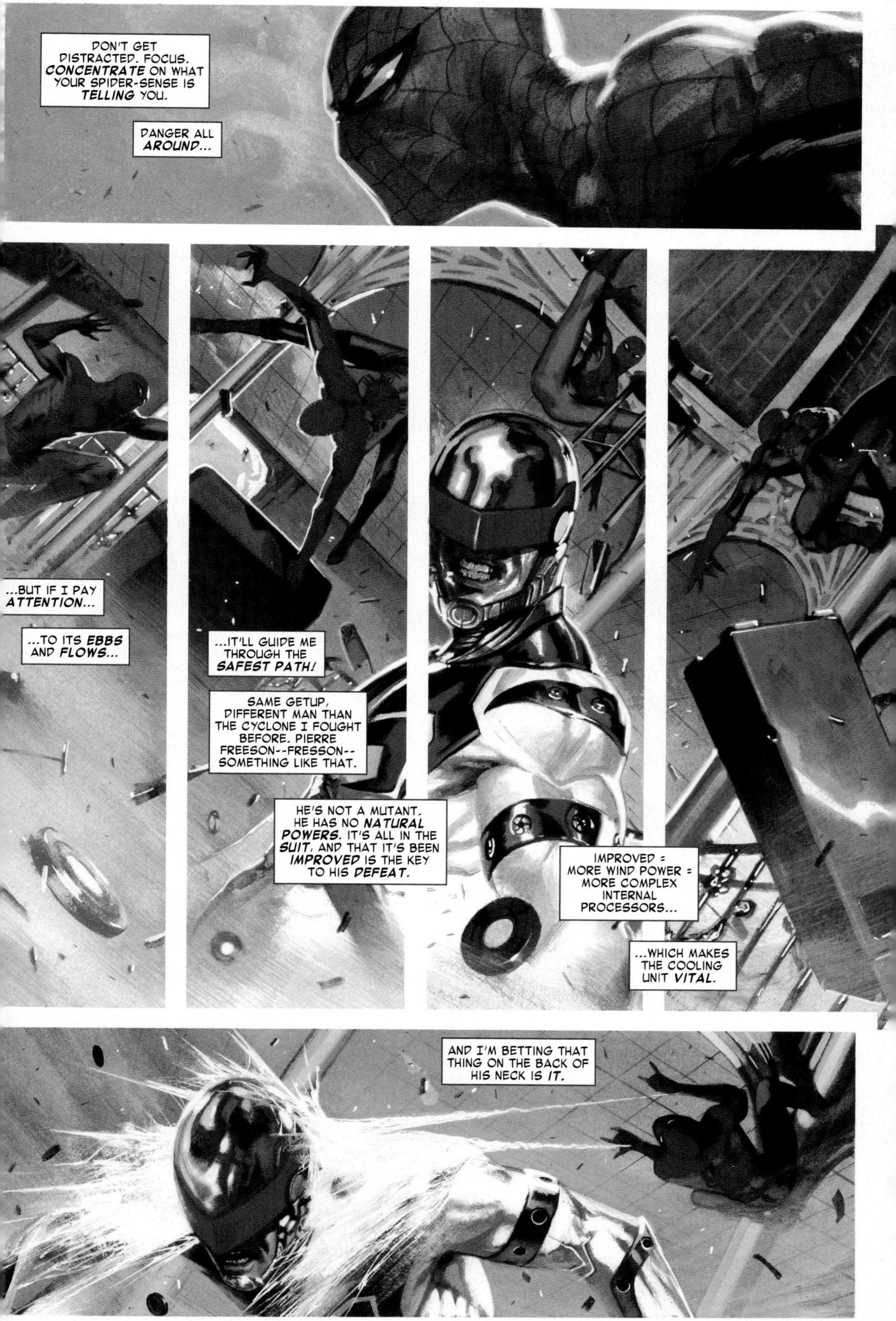
DON'T GET DISTRACTED. FOCUS. CONCENTRATE ON WHAT YOUR SPIDER-SENSE IS TELLING YOU.
DANGER ALL AROUND...
...BUT IF I PAY ATTENTION...
...TO ITS EBBS AND FLOWS...
...IT'LL GUIDE ME THROUGH THE SAFEST PATH!
SAME GETUP, DIFFERENT MAN THAN THE CYCLONE I FOUGHT BEFORE. PIERRE FREESON--FRESSON--SOMETHING LIKE THAT.
HE'S NOT A MUTANT. HE HAS NO NATURAL POWERS. IT'S ALL IN THE SUIT, AND THAT IT'S BEEN IMPROVED IS THE KEY TO HIS DEFEAT.
IMPROVED = MORE WIND POWER = MORE COMPLEX INTERNAL PROCESSORS...
...WHICH MAKES THE COOLING UNIT VITAL.
AND I'M BETTING THAT THING ON THE BACK OF HIS NECK IS IT.

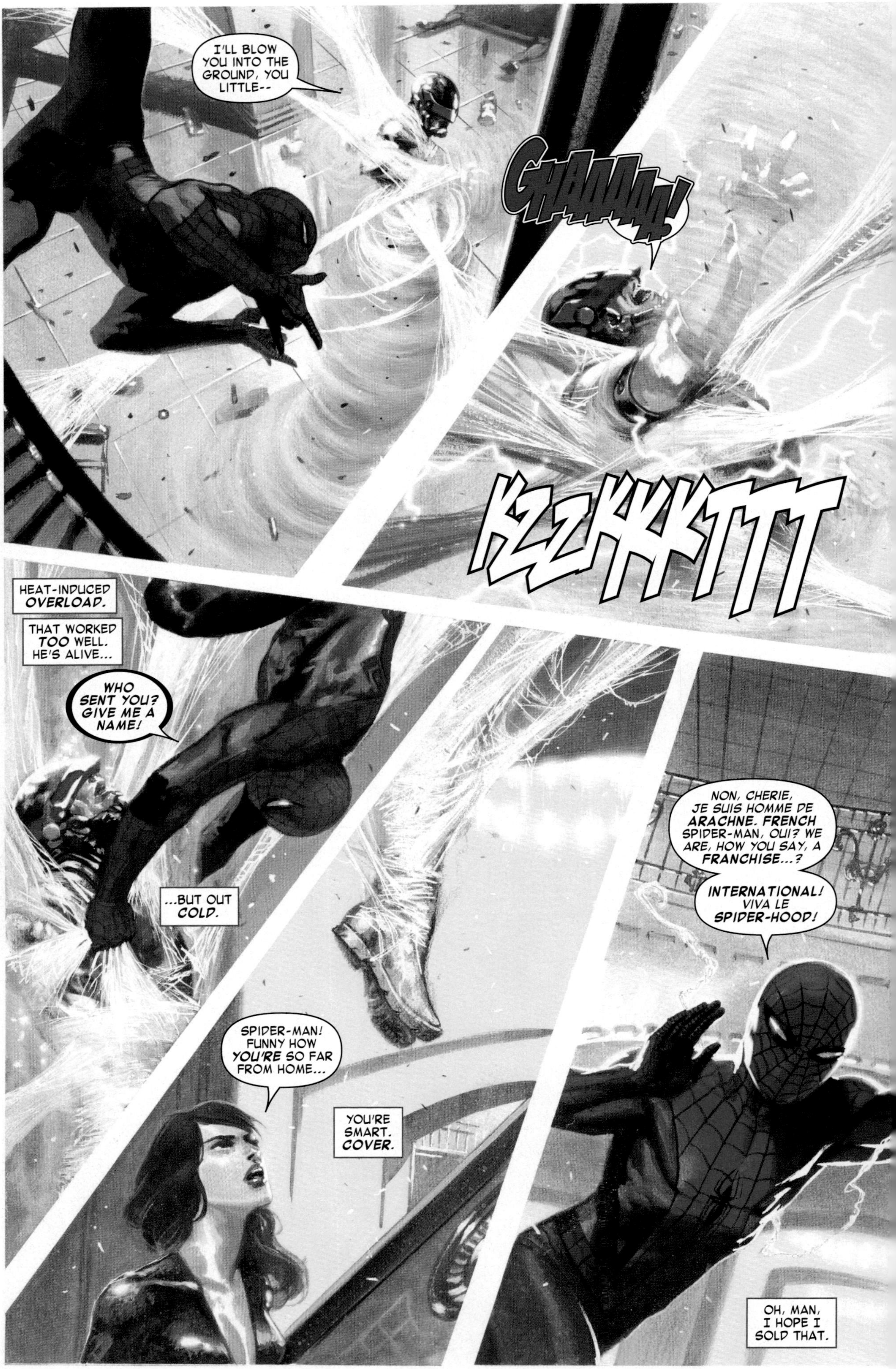

I'LL BLOW YOU INTO THE GROUND, YOU LITTLE--
GHAAAAAA!
KZZKKKTTTT
HEAT-INDUCED OVERLOAD.
THAT WORKED TOO WELL. HE'S ALIVE...
WHO SENT YOU? GIVE ME A NAME!
...BUT OUT COLD.
SPIDER-MAN! FUNNY HOW YOU'RE SO FAR FROM HOME...
YOU'RE SMART. COVER.
NON, CHERIE, JE SUIS HOMME DE ARACHNE. FRENCH SPIDER-MAN, OUI? WE ARE, HOW YOU SAY, A FRANCHISE...?
INTERNATIONAL! VIVA LE SPIDER-HOOD!
OH, MAN, I HOPE I SOLD THAT.

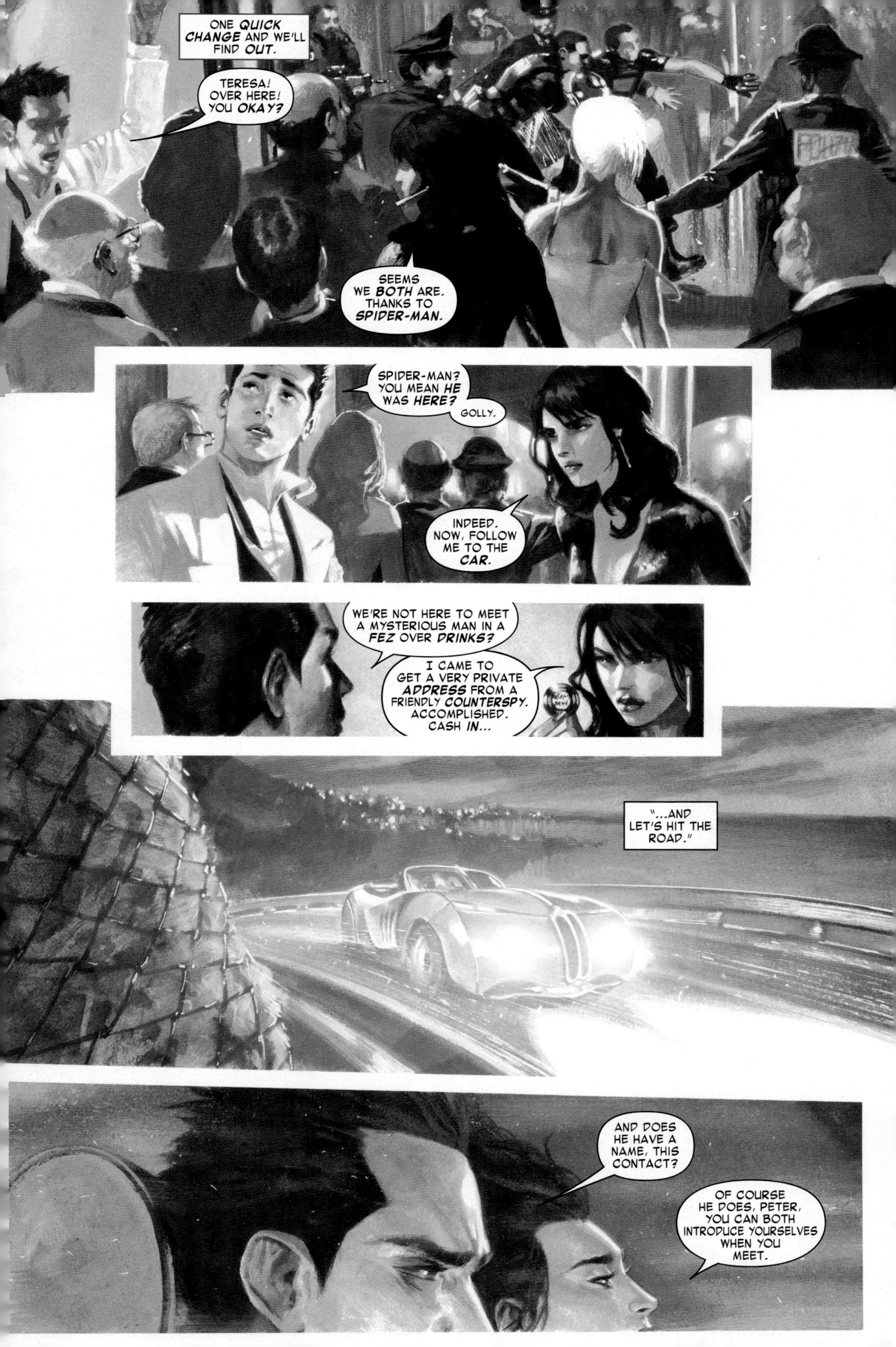
ONE QUICK CHANGE AND WE'LL FIND OUT.
TERESA! OVER HERE! YOU OKAY?
SEEMS WE BOTH ARE. THANKS TO SPIDER-MAN.
SPIDER-MAN? YOU MEAN HE WAS HERE?
GOLLY.
INDEED. NOW, FOLLOW ME TO THE CAR.
WE'RE NOT HERE TO MEET A MYSTERIOUS MAN IN A FEZ OVER DRINKS?
I CAME TO GET A VERY PRIVATE ADDRESS FROM A FRIENDLY COUNTERSPY. ACCOMPLISHED. CASH IN...
"...AND LET'S HIT THE ROAD."
AND DOES HE HAVE A NAME, THIS CONTACT?
OF COURSE HE DOES, PETER, YOU CAN BOTH INTRODUCE YOURSELVES WHEN YOU MEET.

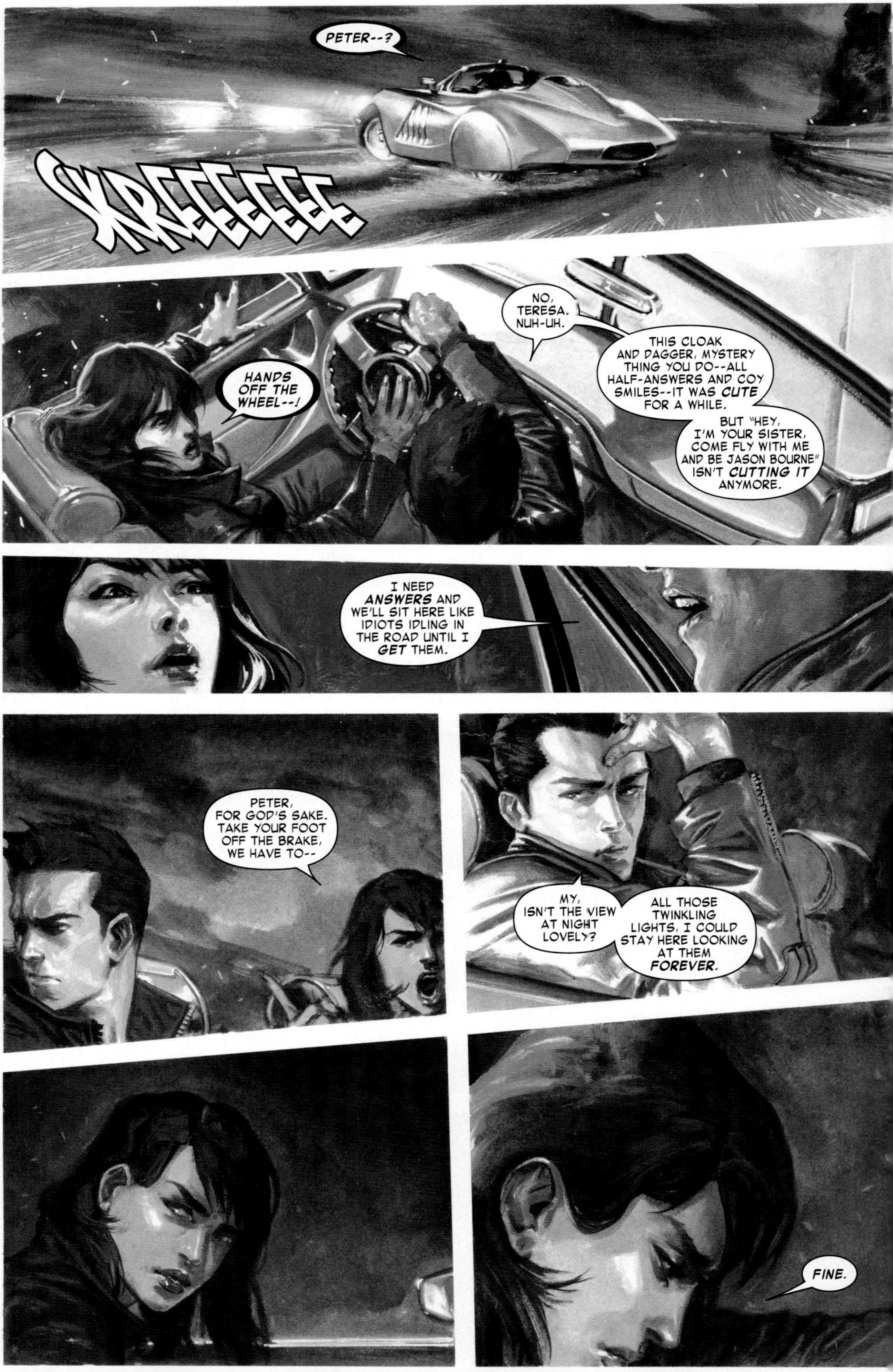
PETER--?
SKREEEEEEE
HANDS OFF THE WHEEL--!
NO, TERESA. NUH-UH.
THIS CLOAK AND DAGGER, MYSTERY THING YOU DO--ALL HALF-ANSWERS AND COY SMILES--IT WAS CUTE FOR A WHILE.
BUT "HEY, I'M YOUR SISTER, COME FLY WITH ME AND BE JASON BOURNE" ISN'T CUTTING IT ANYMORE.
I NEED ANSWERS AND WE'LL SIT HERE LIKE IDIOTS IDLING IN THE ROAD UNTIL I GET THEM.
PETER, FOR GOD'S SAKE. TAKE YOUR FOOT OFF THE BRAKE, WE HAVE TO--
MY, ISN'T THE VIEW AT NIGHT LOVELY?
ALL THOSE TWINKLING LIGHTS, I COULD STAY HERE LOOKING AT THEM FOREVER.
FINE.

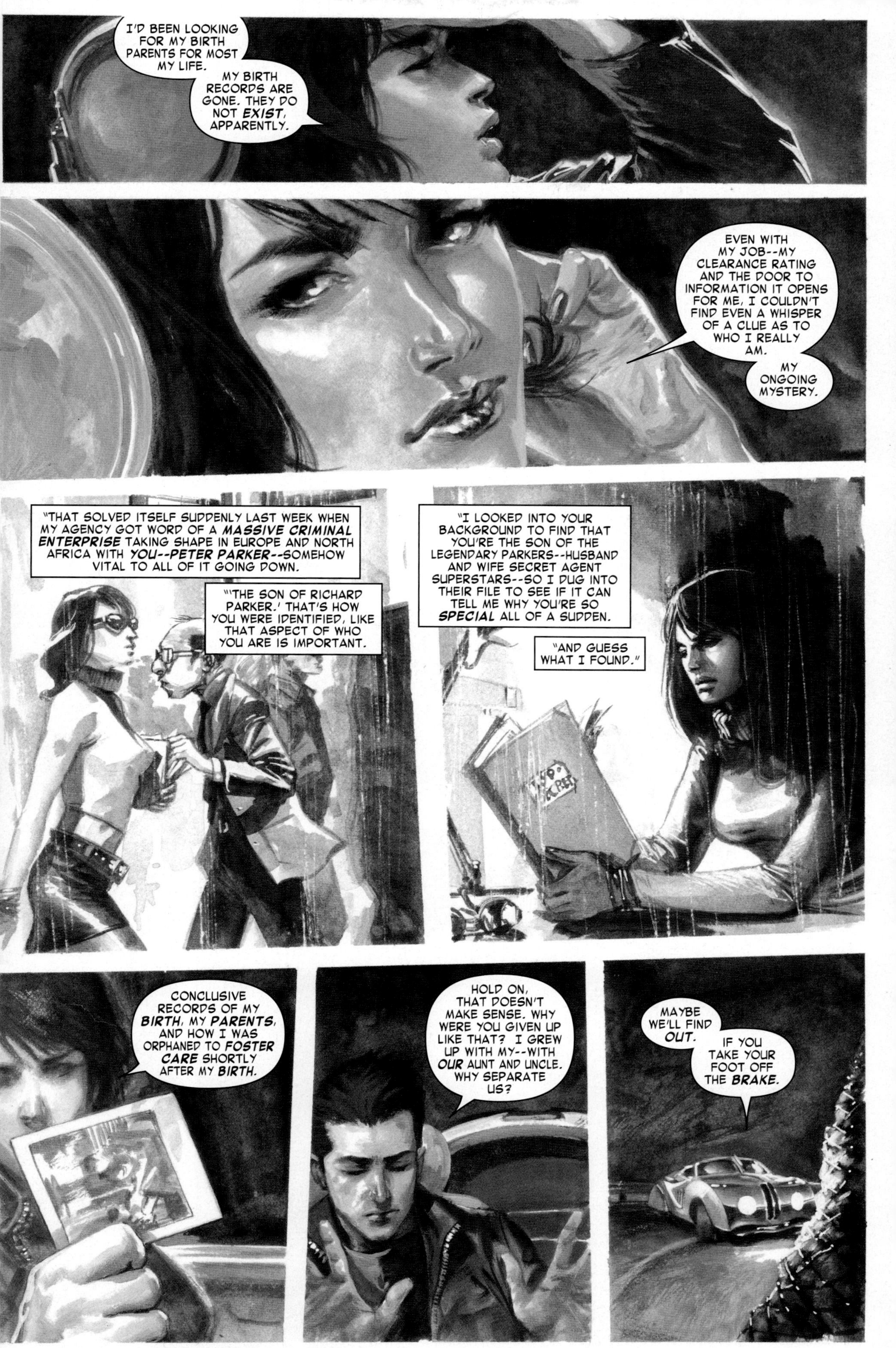
I'D BEEN LOOKING FOR MY BIRTH PARENTS FOR MOST MY LIFE.
MY BIRTH RECORDS ARE GONE. THEY DO NOT EXIST, APPARENTLY.
EVEN WITH MY JOB--MY CLEARANCE RATING AND THE DOOR TO INFORMATION IT OPENS FOR ME, I COULDN'T FIND EVEN A WHISPER OF A CLUE AS TO WHO I REALLY AM.
MY ONGOING MYSTERY.
"THAT SOLVED ITSELF SUDDENLY LAST WEEK WHEN MY AGENCY GOT WORD OF A MASSIVE CRIMINAL ENTERPRISE TAKING SHAPE IN EUROPE AND NORTH AFRICA WITH YOU--PETER PARKER--SOMEHOW VITAL TO ALL OF IT GOING DOWN.
"'THE SON OF RICHARD PARKER.' THAT'S HOW YOU WERE IDENTIFIED, LIKE THAT ASPECT OF WHO YOU ARE IS IMPORTANT.
"I LOOKED INTO YOUR BACKGROUND TO FIND THAT YOU'RE THE SON OF THE LEGENDARY PARKERS--HUSBAND AND WIFE SECRET AGENT SUPERSTARS--SO I DUG INTO THEIR FILE TO SEE IF IT CAN TELL ME WHY YOU'RE SO SPECIAL ALL OF A SUDDEN.
"AND GUESS WHAT I FOUND."
CONCLUSIVE RECORDS OF MY BIRTH, MY PARENTS, AND HOW I WAS ORPHANED TO FOSTER CARE SHORTLY AFTER MY BIRTH.
HOLD ON, THAT DOESN'T MAKE SENSE. WHY WERE YOU GIVEN UP LIKE THAT? I GREW UP WITH MY--WITH OUR AUNT AND UNCLE. WHY SEPARATE US?
MAYBE WE'LL FIND OUT.
IF YOU TAKE YOUR FOOT OFF THE BRAKE.

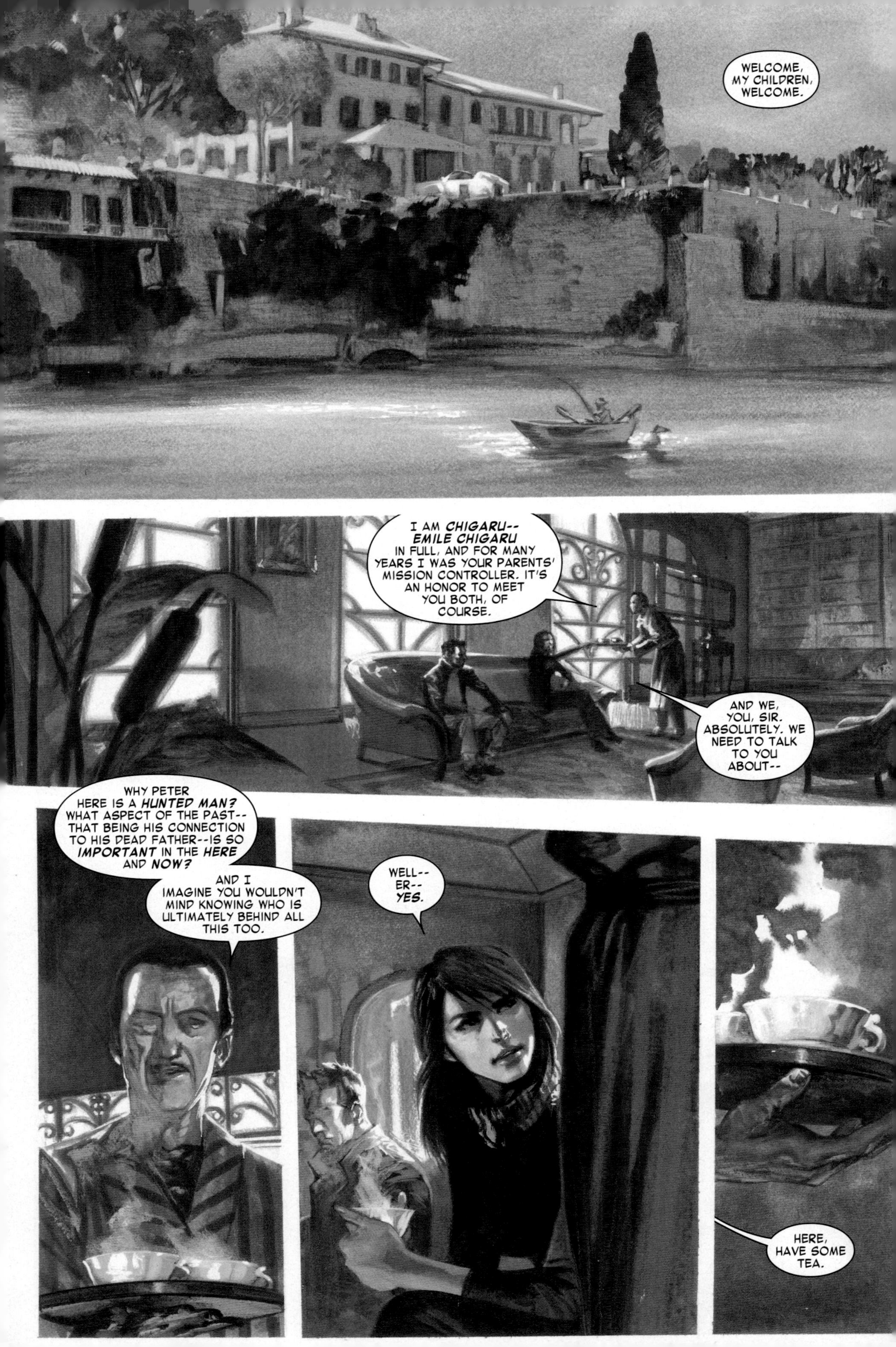
WELCOME, MY CHILDREN, WELCOME.
I AM CHIGARU-- EMILE CHIGARU IN FULL, AND FOR MANY YEARS I WAS YOUR PARENTS' MISSION CONTROLLER. IT'S AN HONOR TO MEET YOU BOTH, OF COURSE.
AND WE, YOU, SIR. ABSOLUTELY. WE NEED TO TALK TO YOU ABOUT--
WHY PETER HERE IS A HUNTED MAN? WHAT ASPECT OF THE PAST-- THAT BEING HIS CONNECTION TO HIS DEAD FATHER--IS SO IMPORTANT IN THE HERE AND NOW?
AND I IMAGINE YOU WOULDN'T MIND KNOWING WHO IS ULTIMATELY BEHIND ALL THIS TOO.
WELL-- ER-- YES.
HERE, HAVE SOME TEA.

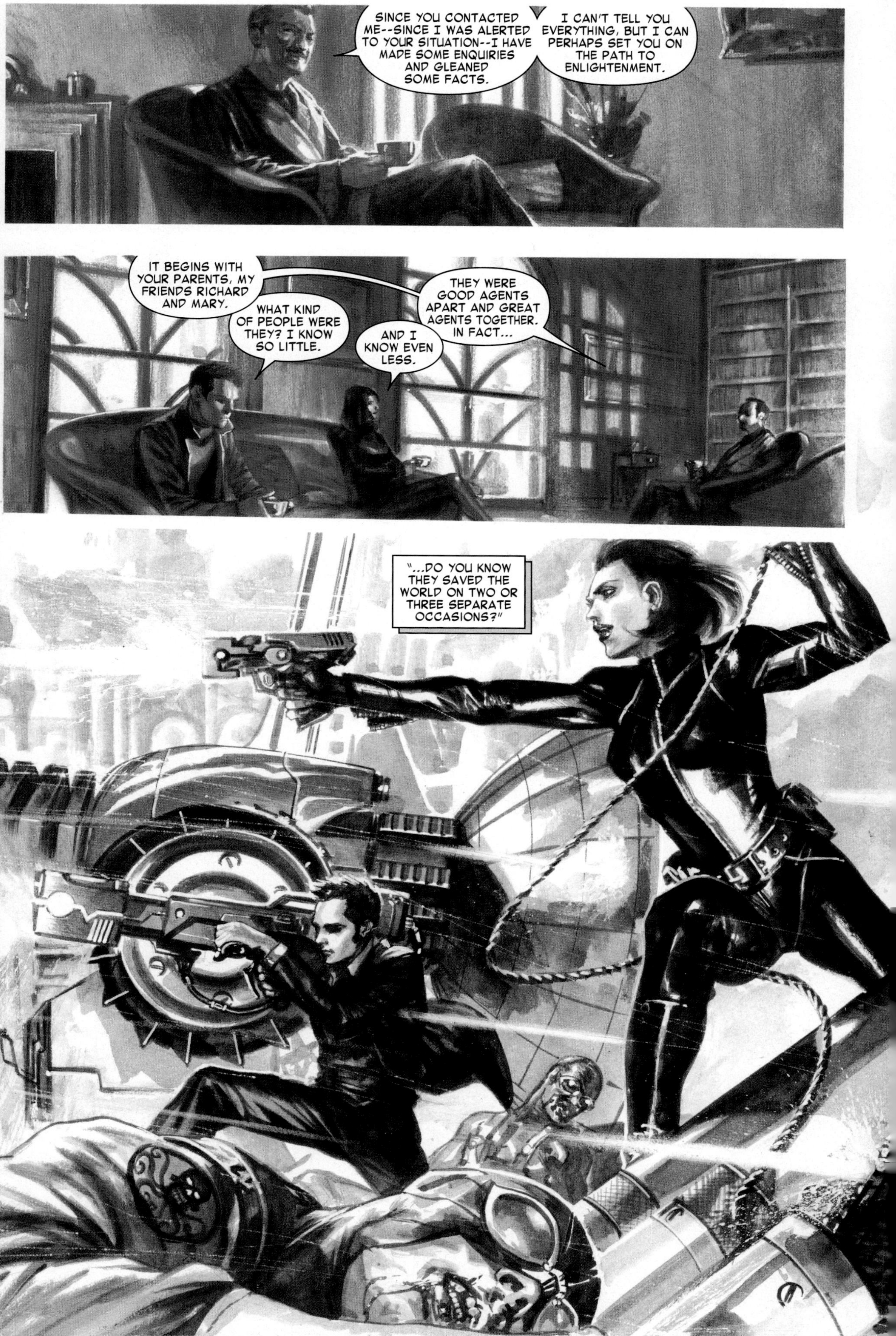
SINCE YOU CONTACTED ME--SINCE I WAS ALERTED TO YOUR SITUATION--I HAVE MADE SOME ENQUIRIES AND GLEANED SOME FACTS.
I CAN'T TELL YOU EVERYTHING, BUT I CAN PERHAPS SET YOU ON THE PATH TO ENLIGHTENMENT.
IT BEGINS WITH YOUR PARENTS, MY FRIENDS RICHARD AND MARY.
WHAT KIND OF PEOPLE WERE THEY? I KNOW SO LITTLE.
AND I KNOW EVEN LESS.
THEY WERE GOOD AGENTS APART AND GREAT AGENTS TOGETHER. IN FACT...
"...DO YOU KNOW THEY SAVED THE WORLD ON TWO OR THREE SEPARATE OCCASIONS?"

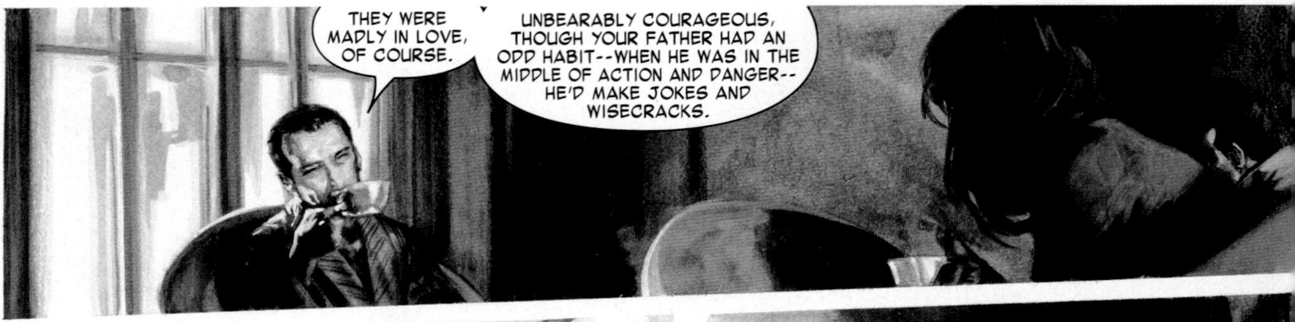
THEY WERE MADLY IN LOVE, OF COURSE.
UNBEARABLY COURAGEOUS, THOUGH YOUR FATHER HAD AN ODD HABIT--WHEN HE WAS IN THE MIDDLE OF ACTION AND DANGER--HE'D MAKE JOKES AND WISECRACKS.

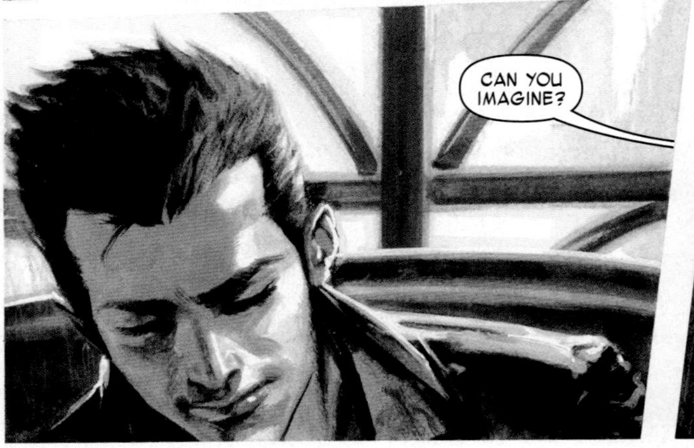
CAN YOU IMAGINE?

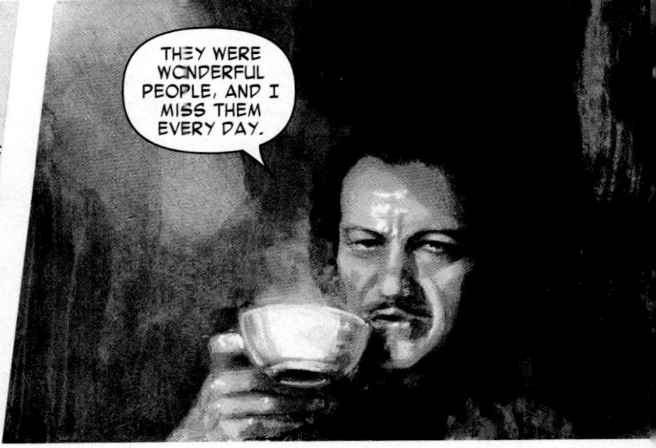
THEY WERE WONDERFUL PEOPLE, AND I MISS THEM EVERY DAY.

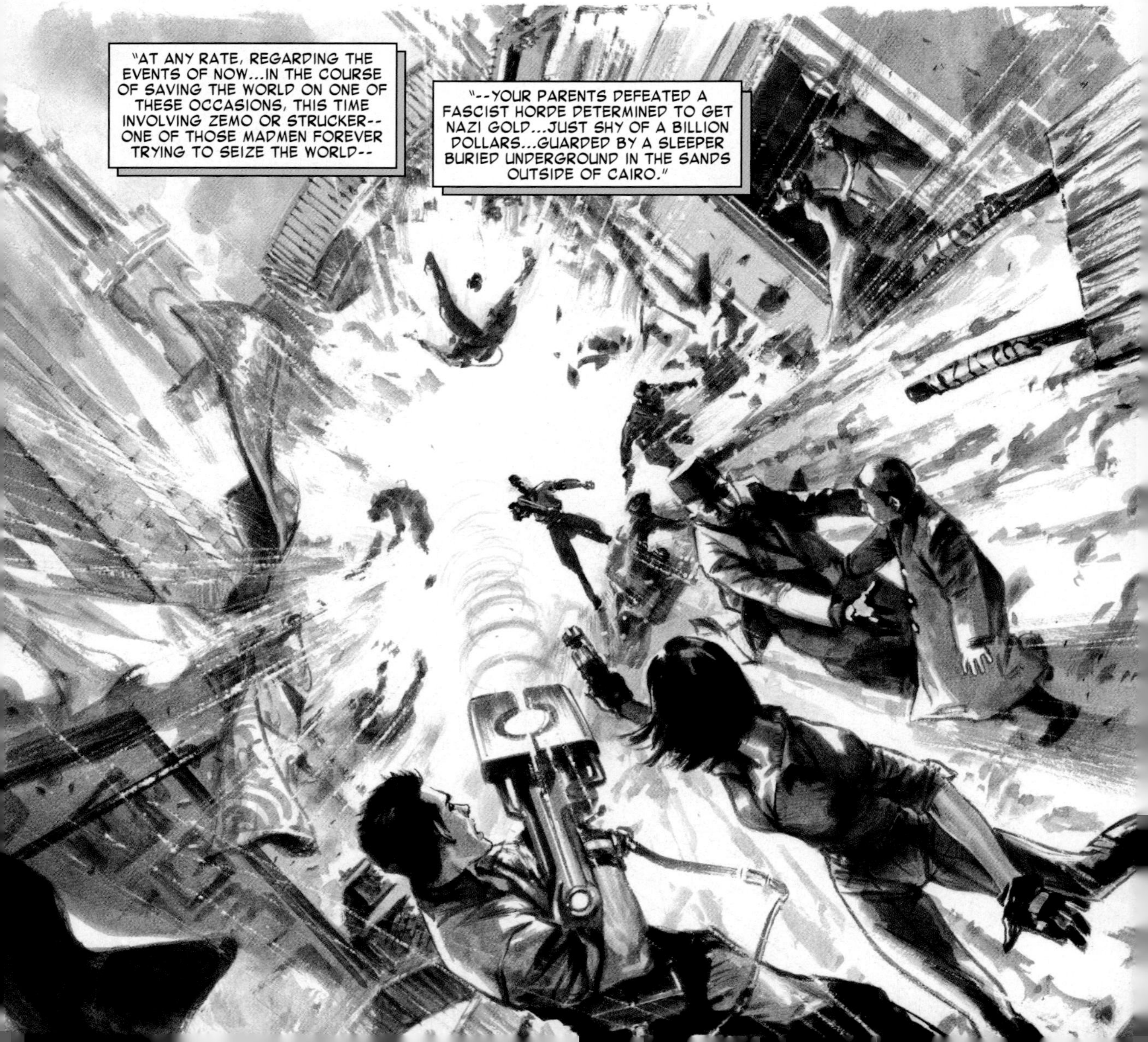
"AT ANY RATE, REGARDING THE EVENTS OF NOW...IN THE COURSE OF SAVING THE WORLD ON ONE OF THESE OCCASIONS, THIS TIME INVOLVING ZEMO OR STRUCKER--ONE OF THOSE MADMEN FOREVER TRYING TO SEIZE THE WORLD--
"--YOUR PARENTS DEFEATED A FASCIST HORDE DETERMINED TO GET NAZI GOLD...JUST SHY OF A BILLION DOLLARS...GUARDED BY A SLEEPER BURIED UNDERGROUND IN THE SANDS OUTSIDE OF CAIRO."

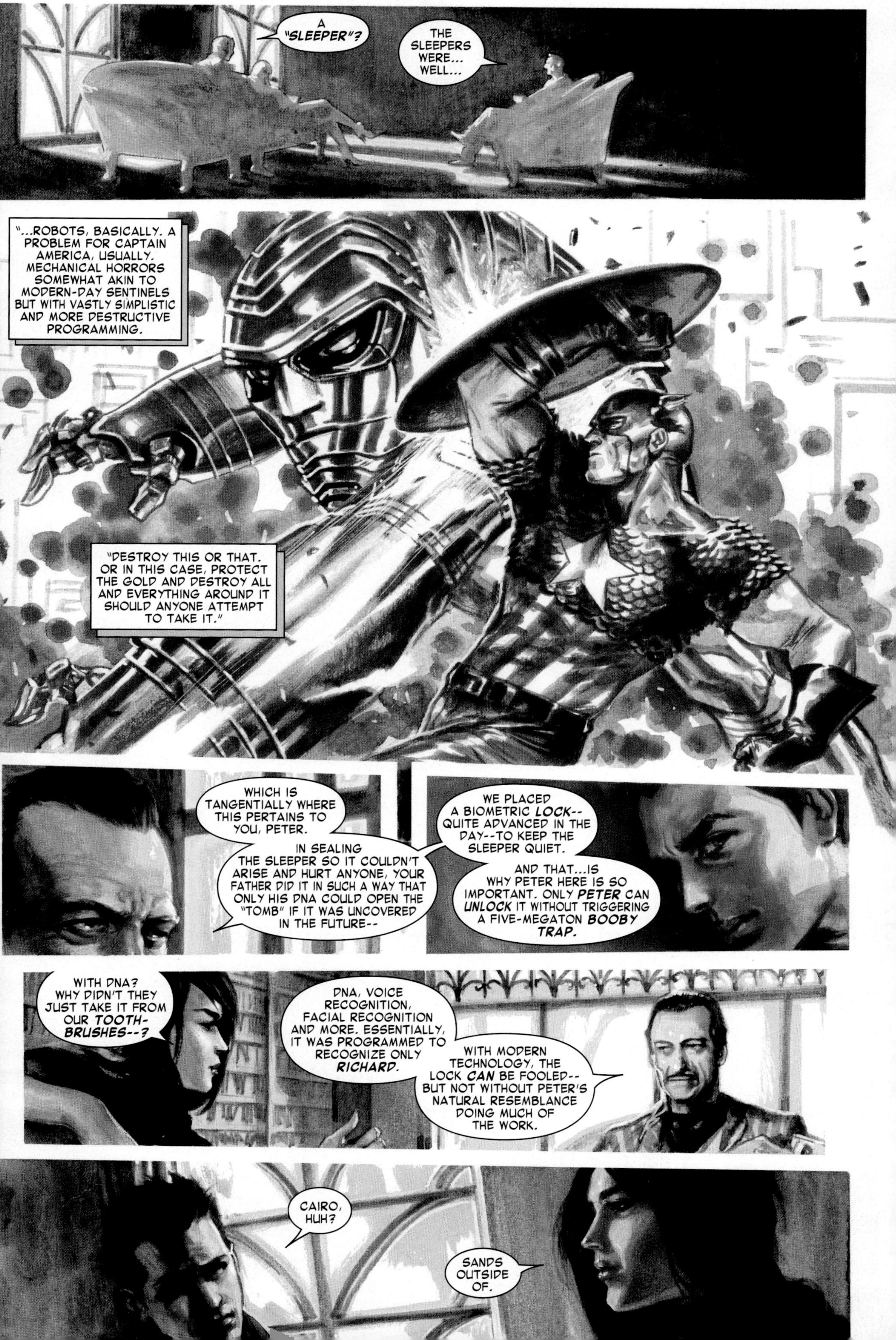
A "SLEEPER"?
THE SLEEPERS WERE... WELL...
"...ROBOTS, BASICALLY. A PROBLEM FOR CAPTAIN AMERICA, USUALLY. MECHANICAL HORRORS SOMEWHAT AKIN TO MODERN-DAY SENTINELS BUT WITH VASTLY SIMPLISTIC AND MORE DESTRUCTIVE PROGRAMMING.
"DESTROY THIS OR THAT. OR IN THIS CASE, PROTECT THE GOLD AND DESTROY ALL AND EVERYTHING AROUND IT SHOULD ANYONE ATTEMPT TO TAKE IT."
WHICH IS TANGENTIALLY WHERE THIS PERTAINS TO YOU, PETER.
IN SEALING THE SLEEPER SO IT COULDN'T ARISE AND HURT ANYONE, YOUR FATHER DID IT IN SUCH A WAY THAT ONLY HIS DNA COULD OPEN THE "TOMB" IF IT WAS UNCOVERED IN THE FUTURE--
WE PLACED A BIOMETRIC LOCK-- QUITE ADVANCED IN THE DAY--TO KEEP THE SLEEPER QUIET.
AND THAT...IS WHY PETER HERE IS SO IMPORTANT. ONLY PETER CAN UNLOCK IT WITHOUT TRIGGERING A FIVE-MEGATON BOOBY TRAP.
WITH DNA? WHY DIDN'T THEY JUST TAKE IT FROM OUR TOOTH-BRUSHES--?
DNA, VOICE RECOGNITION, FACIAL RECOGNITION AND MORE. ESSENTIALLY, IT WAS PROGRAMMED TO RECOGNIZE ONLY RICHARD.
WITH MODERN TECHNOLOGY, THE LOCK CAN BE FOOLED-- BUT NOT WITHOUT PETER'S NATURAL RESEMBLANCE DOING MUCH OF THE WORK.
CAIRO, HUH?
SANDS OUTSIDE OF.

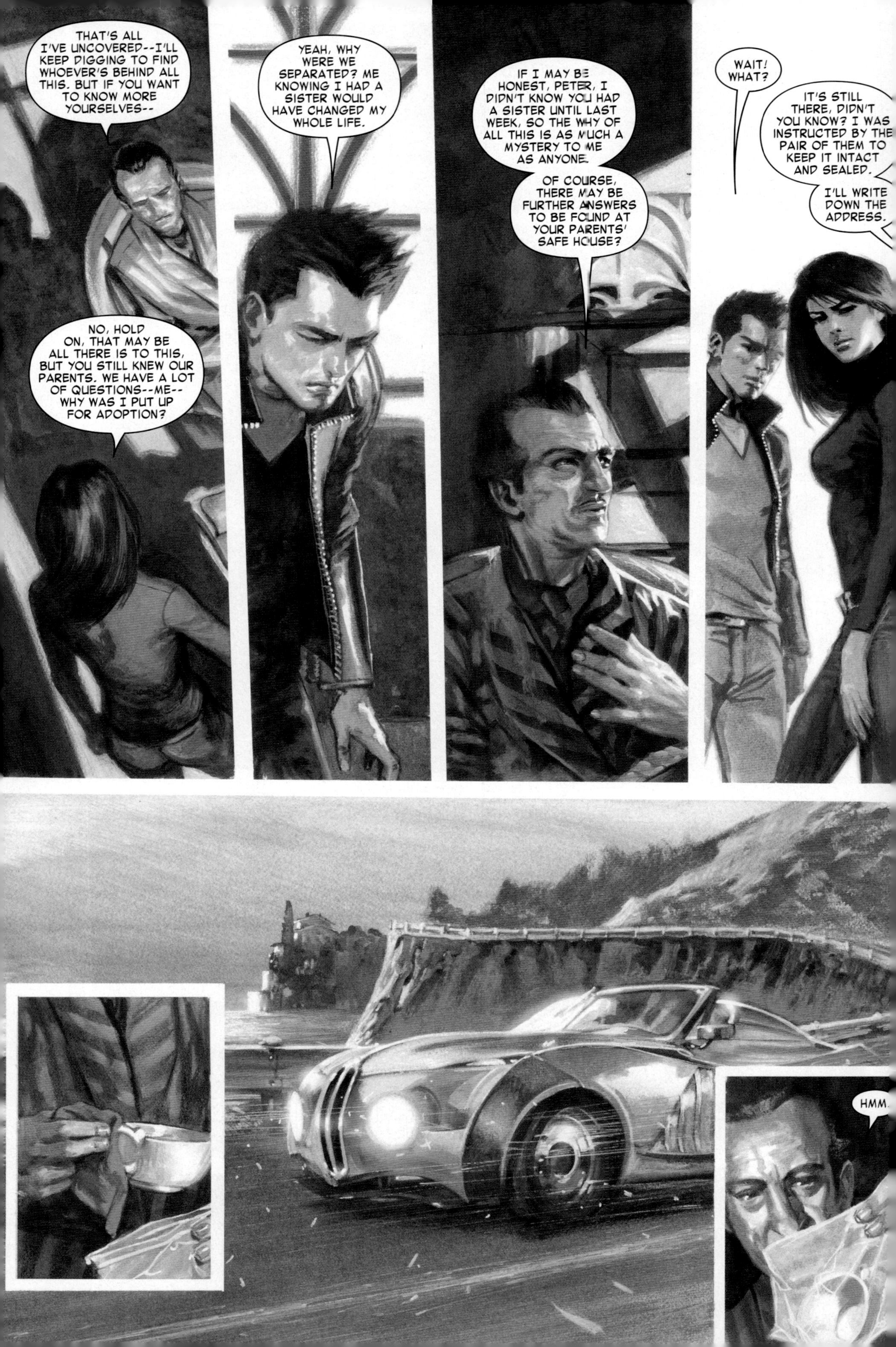
THAT'S ALL I'VE UNCOVERED--I'LL KEEP DIGGING TO FIND WHOEVER'S BEHIND ALL THIS. BUT IF YOU WANT TO KNOW MORE YOURSELVES--
NO, HOLD ON, THAT MAY BE ALL THERE IS TO THIS, BUT YOU STILL KNEW OUR PARENTS. WE HAVE A LOT OF QUESTIONS--ME-- WHY WAS I PUT UP FOR ADOPTION?
YEAH, WHY WERE WE SEPARATED? ME KNOWING I HAD A SISTER WOULD HAVE CHANGED MY WHOLE LIFE.
IF I MAY BE HONEST, PETER, I DIDN'T KNOW YOU HAD A SISTER UNTIL LAST WEEK, SO THE WHY OF ALL THIS IS AS MUCH A MYSTERY TO ME AS ANYONE.
OF COURSE, THERE MAY BE FURTHER ANSWERS TO BE FOUND AT YOUR PARENTS' SAFE HOUSE?
WAIT! WHAT?
IT'S STILL THERE, DIDN'T YOU KNOW? I WAS INSTRUCTED BY THE PAIR OF THEM TO KEEP IT INTACT AND SEALED.
I'LL WRITE DOWN THE ADDRESS.
HMM.

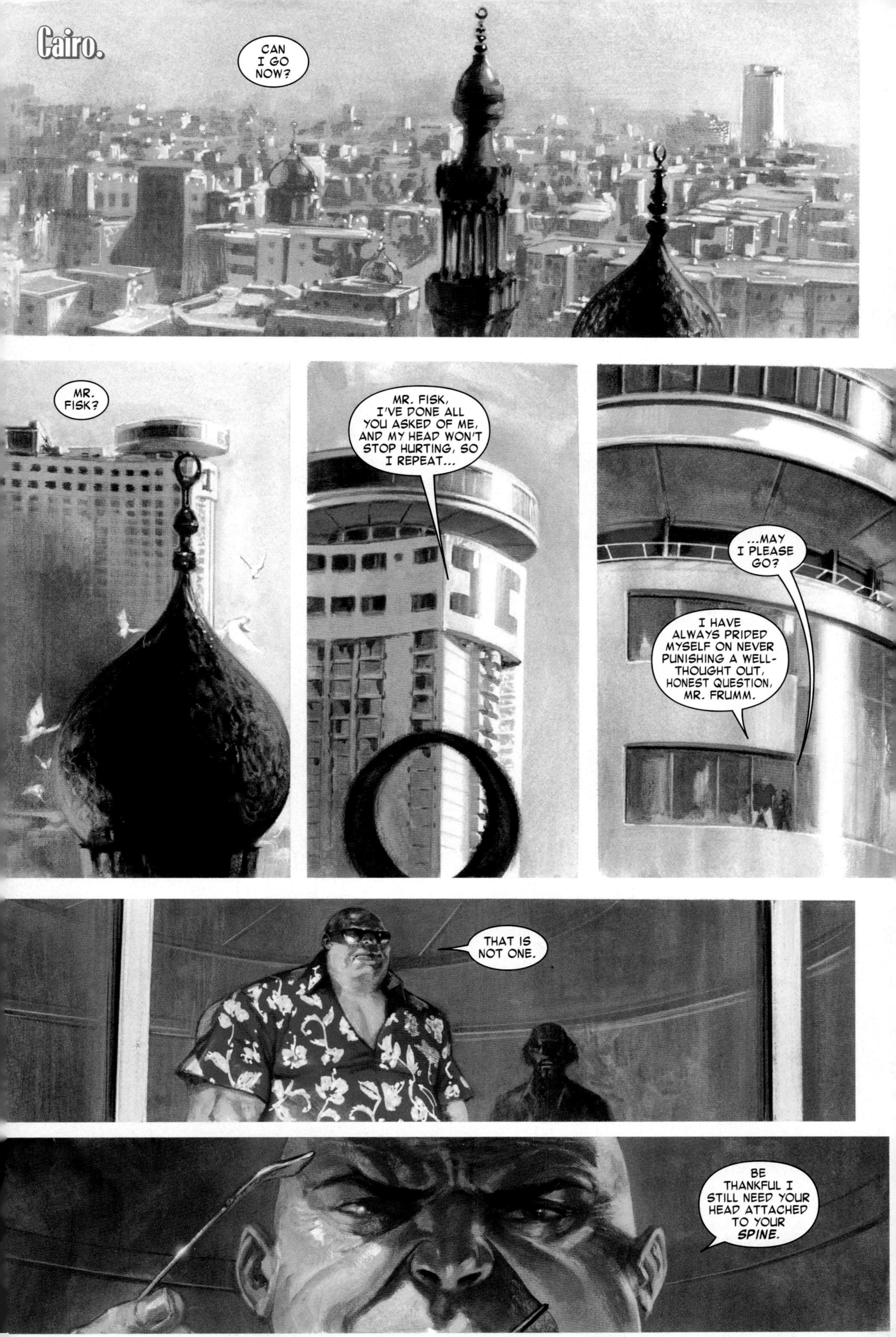
Cairo.
CAN I GO NOW?
MR. FISK?
MR. FISK, I'VE DONE ALL YOU ASKED OF ME, AND MY HEAD WON'T STOP HURTING, SO I REPEAT...
...MAY I PLEASE GO?
I HAVE ALWAYS PRIDED MYSELF ON NEVER PUNISHING A WELL-THOUGHT OUT, HONEST QUESTION, MR. FRUMM.
THAT IS NOT ONE.
BE THANKFUL I STILL NEED YOUR HEAD ATTACHED TO YOUR SPINE.

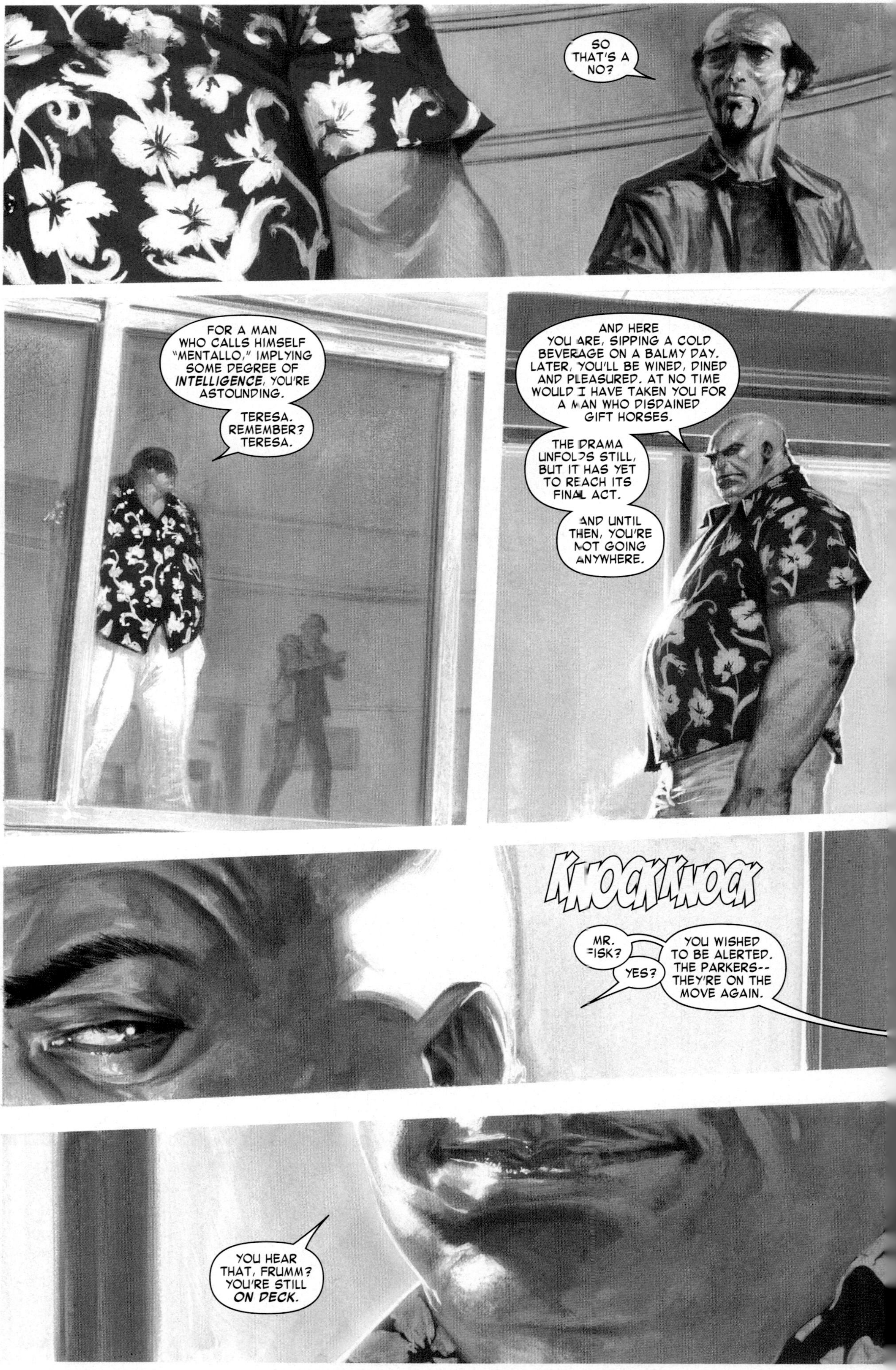
SO THAT'S A NO?
FOR A MAN WHO CALLS HIMSELF "MENTALLO," IMPLYING SOME DEGREE OF INTELLIGENCE, YOU'RE ASTOUNDING.
TERESA. REMEMBER? TERESA.
AND HERE YOU ARE, SIPPING A COLD BEVERAGE ON A BALMY DAY. LATER, YOU'LL BE WINED, DINED AND PLEASURED. AT NO TIME WOULD I HAVE TAKEN YOU FOR A MAN WHO DISDAINED GIFT HORSES.
THE DRAMA UNFOLDS STILL, BUT IT HAS YET TO REACH ITS FINAL ACT.
AND UNTIL THEN, YOU'RE NOT GOING ANYWHERE.
KNOCK KNOCK
MR. FISK?
YES?
YOU WISHED TO BE ALERTED. THE PARKERS-- THEY'RE ON THE MOVE AGAIN.
YOU HEAR THAT, FRUMM? YOU'RE STILL ON DECK.

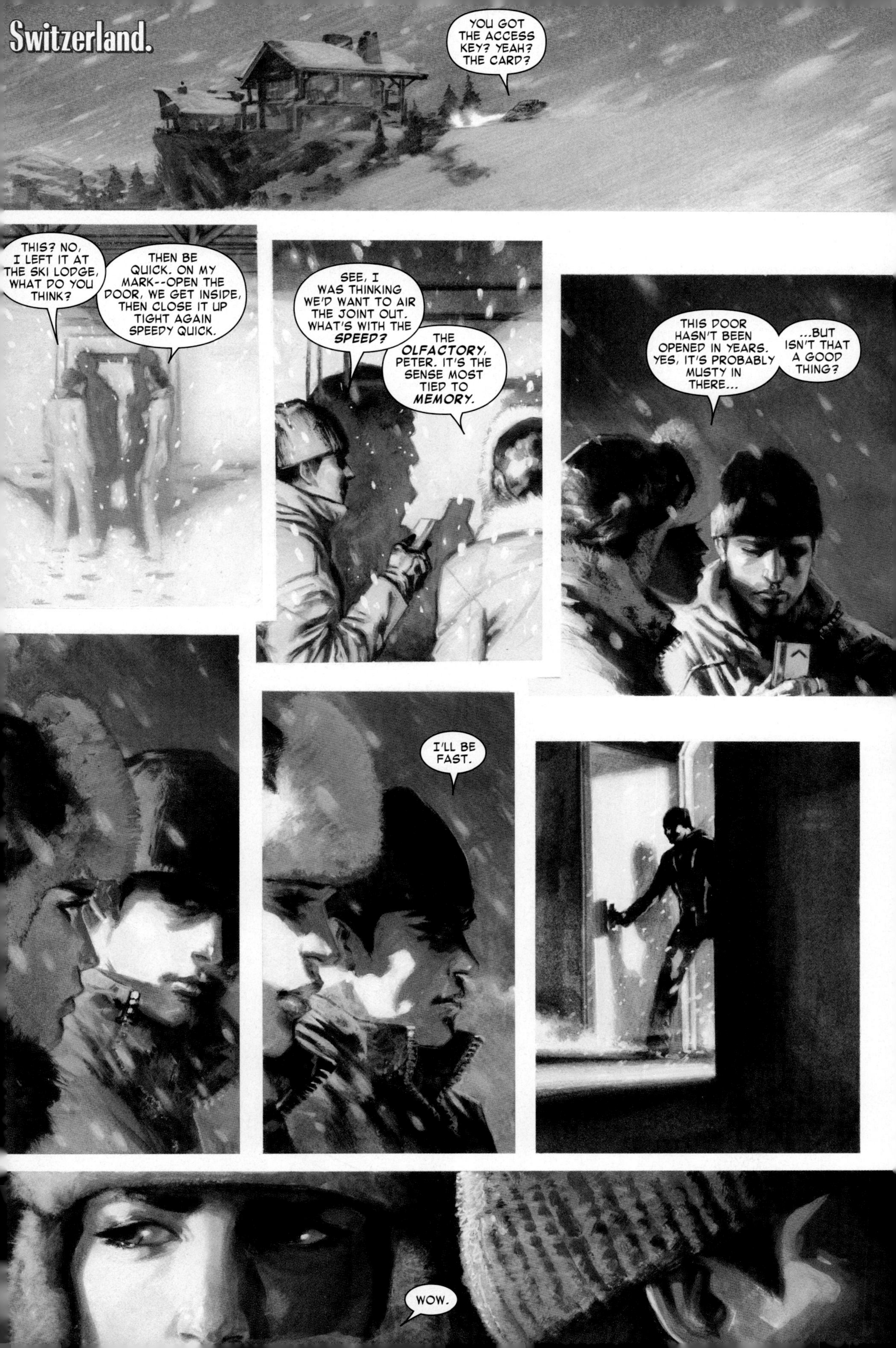
Switzerland.
YOU GOT THE ACCESS KEY? YEAH? THE CARD?
THIS? NO, I LEFT IT AT THE SKI LODGE, WHAT DO YOU THINK?
THEN BE QUICK. ON MY MARK--OPEN THE DOOR, WE GET INSIDE, THEN CLOSE IT UP TIGHT AGAIN SPEEDY QUICK.
SEE, I WAS THINKING WE'D WANT TO AIR THE JOINT OUT. WHAT'S WITH THE SPEED?
THE OLFACTORY, PETER. IT'S THE SENSE MOST TIED TO MEMORY.
THIS DOOR HASN'T BEEN OPENED IN YEARS. YES, IT'S PROBABLY MUSTY IN THERE...
...BUT ISN'T THAT A GOOD THING?
I'LL BE FAST.
WOW.

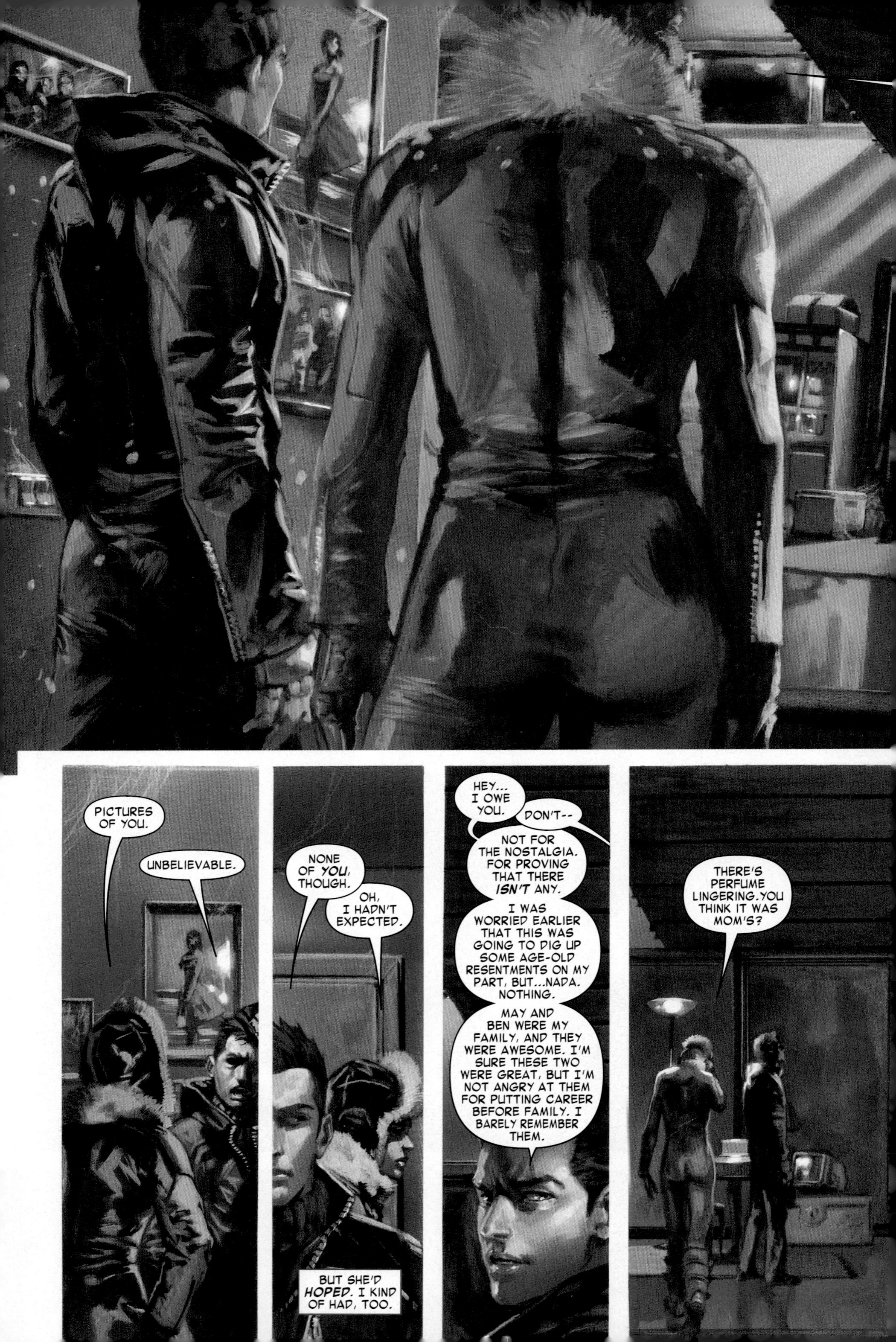
PICTURES OF YOU.
UNBELIEVABLE.
NONE OF YOU, THOUGH.
OH, I HADN'T EXPECTED.
BUT SHE'D HOPED. I KIND OF HAD, TOO.
HEY... I OWE YOU.
DON'T--
NOT FOR THE NOSTALGIA. FOR PROVING THAT THERE ISN'T ANY.
I WAS WORRIED EARLIER THAT THIS WAS GOING TO DIG UP SOME AGE-OLD RESENTMENTS ON MY PART, BUT...NADA. NOTHING.
MAY AND BEN WERE MY FAMILY, AND THEY WERE AWESOME. I'M SURE THESE TWO WERE GREAT, BUT I'M NOT ANGRY AT THEM FOR PUTTING CAREER BEFORE FAMILY. I BARELY REMEMBER THEM.
THERE'S PERFUME LINGERING. YOU THINK IT WAS MOM'S?

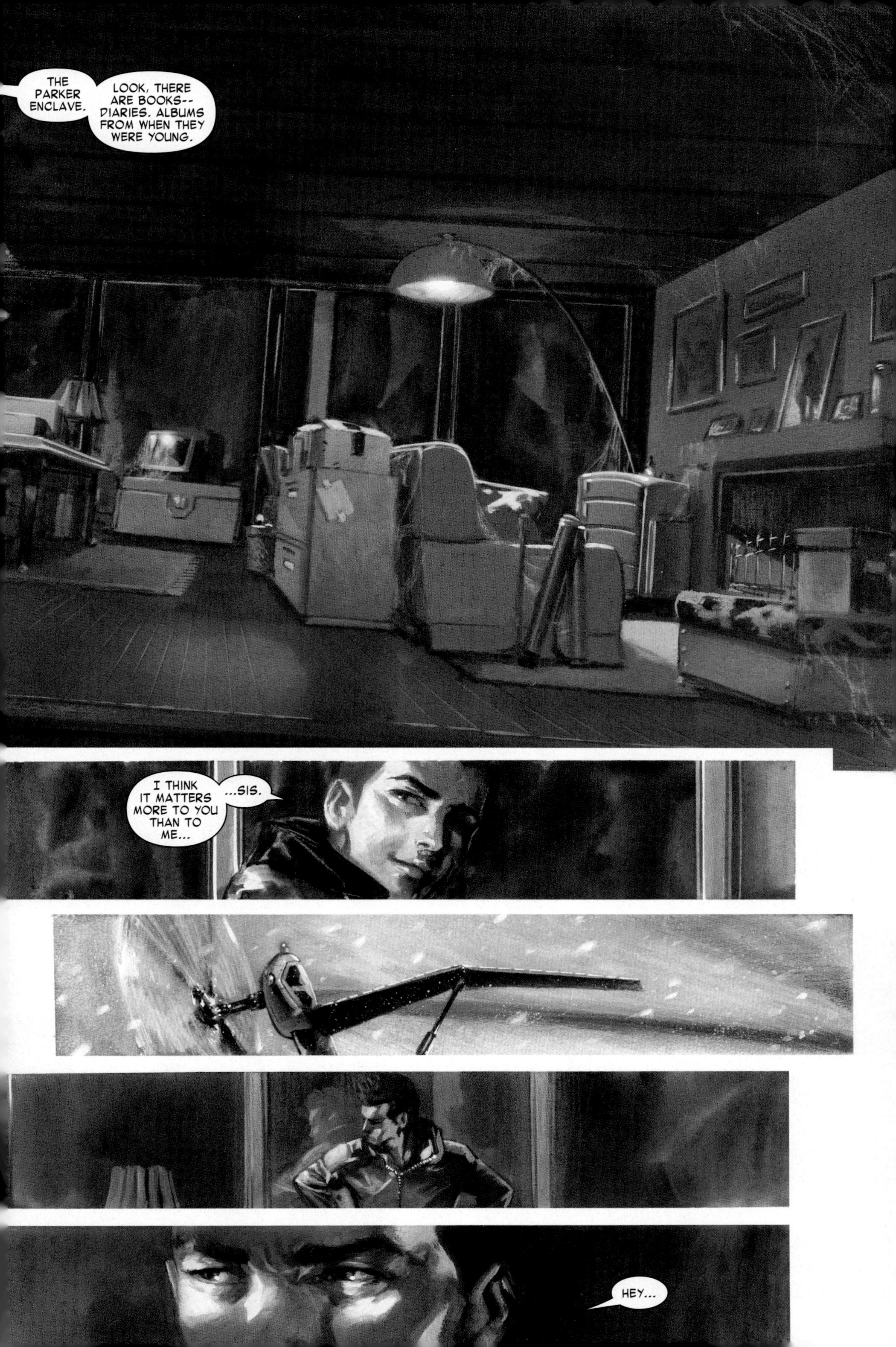
THE PARKER ENCLAVE.
LOOK, THERE ARE BOOKS-- DIARIES. ALBUMS FROM WHEN THEY WERE YOUNG.
I THINK IT MATTERS MORE TO YOU THAN TO ME...
...SIS.
HEY...

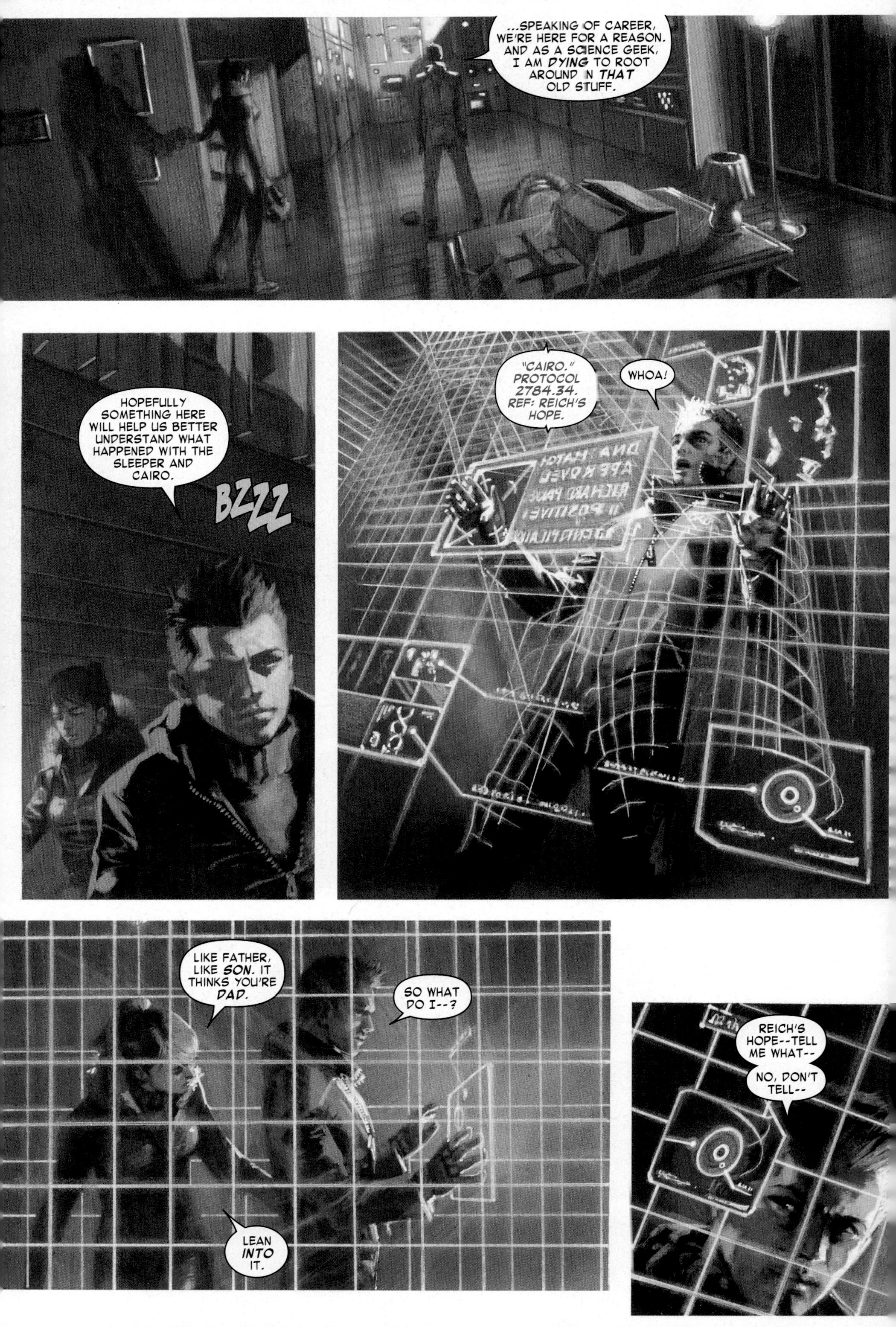
...SPEAKING OF CAREER, WE'RE HERE FOR A REASON. AND AS A SCIENCE GEEK, I AM *DYING* TO ROOT AROUND IN *THAT* OLD STUFF.
HOPEFULLY SOMETHING HERE WILL HELP US BETTER UNDERSTAND WHAT HAPPENED WITH THE SLEEPER AND CAIRO.
BZZZ
"CAIRO." PROTOCOL 2784.34. REF: REICH'S HOPE.
WHOA!
LIKE FATHER, LIKE *SON*. IT THINKS YOU'RE *DAD*.
SO WHAT DO I--?
LEAN *INTO* IT.
REICH'S HOPE--TELL ME WHAT--
NO, DON'T TELL--

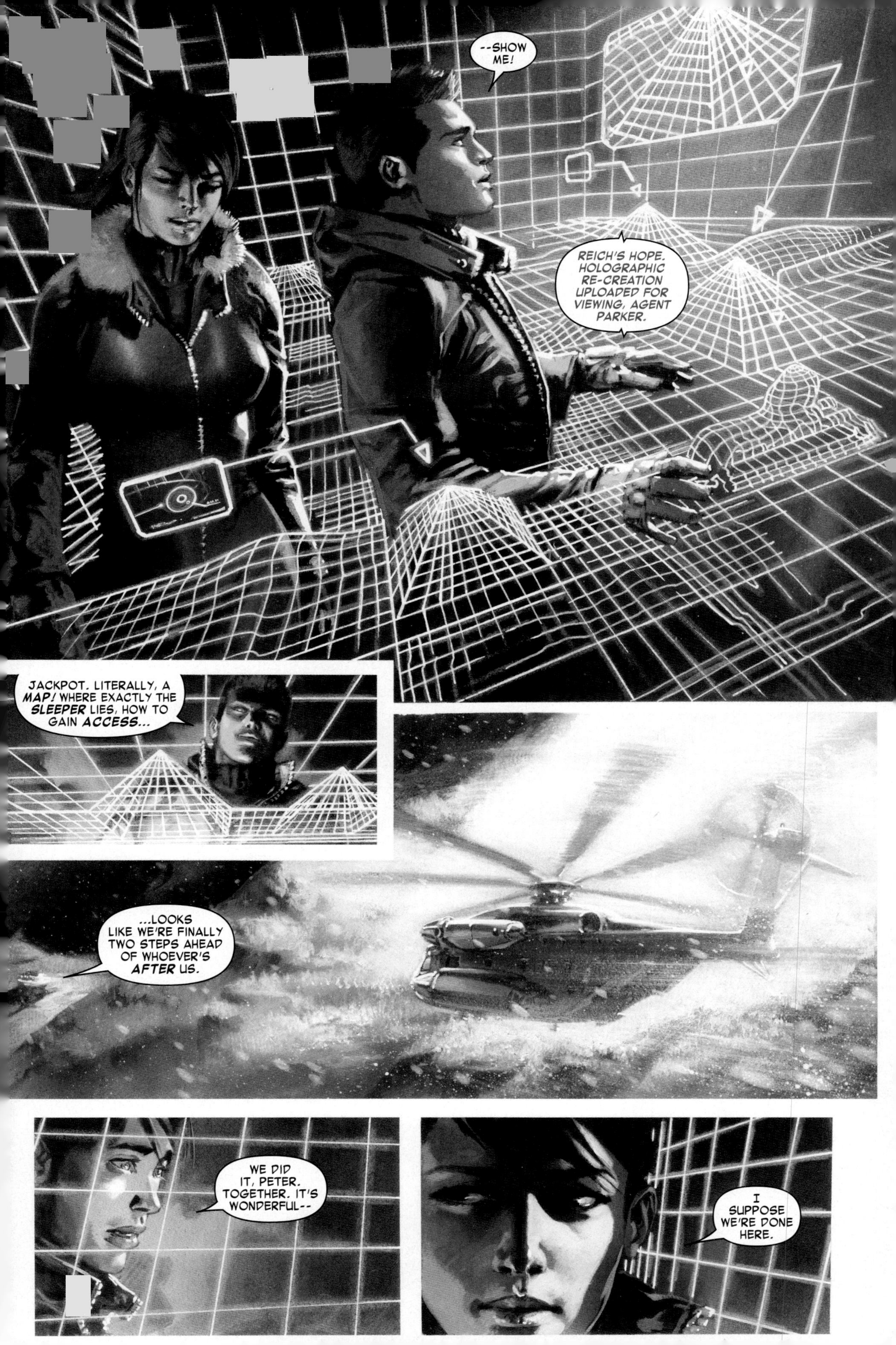
--SHOW ME!
REICH'S HOPE. HOLOGRAPHIC RE-CREATION UPLOADED FOR VIEWING, AGENT PARKER.
JACKPOT. LITERALLY, A MAP! WHERE EXACTLY THE SLEEPER LIES, HOW TO GAIN ACCESS...
...LOOKS LIKE WE'RE FINALLY TWO STEPS AHEAD OF WHOEVER'S AFTER US.
WE DID IT, PETER. TOGETHER. IT'S WONDERFUL--
I SUPPOSE WE'RE DONE HERE.

RELAX. WE CAN SPARE A MINUTE OR--

WRONG AGAIN.

SPIDER-SENSES, GOING CRAZY. ZERO TO *LIGHT SPEED* IN NO TIME.

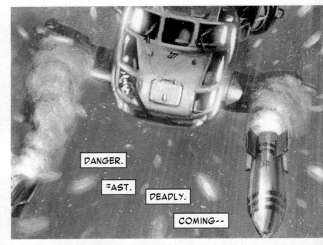

DANGER.

FAST.

DEADLY.

COMING--

TERESA!

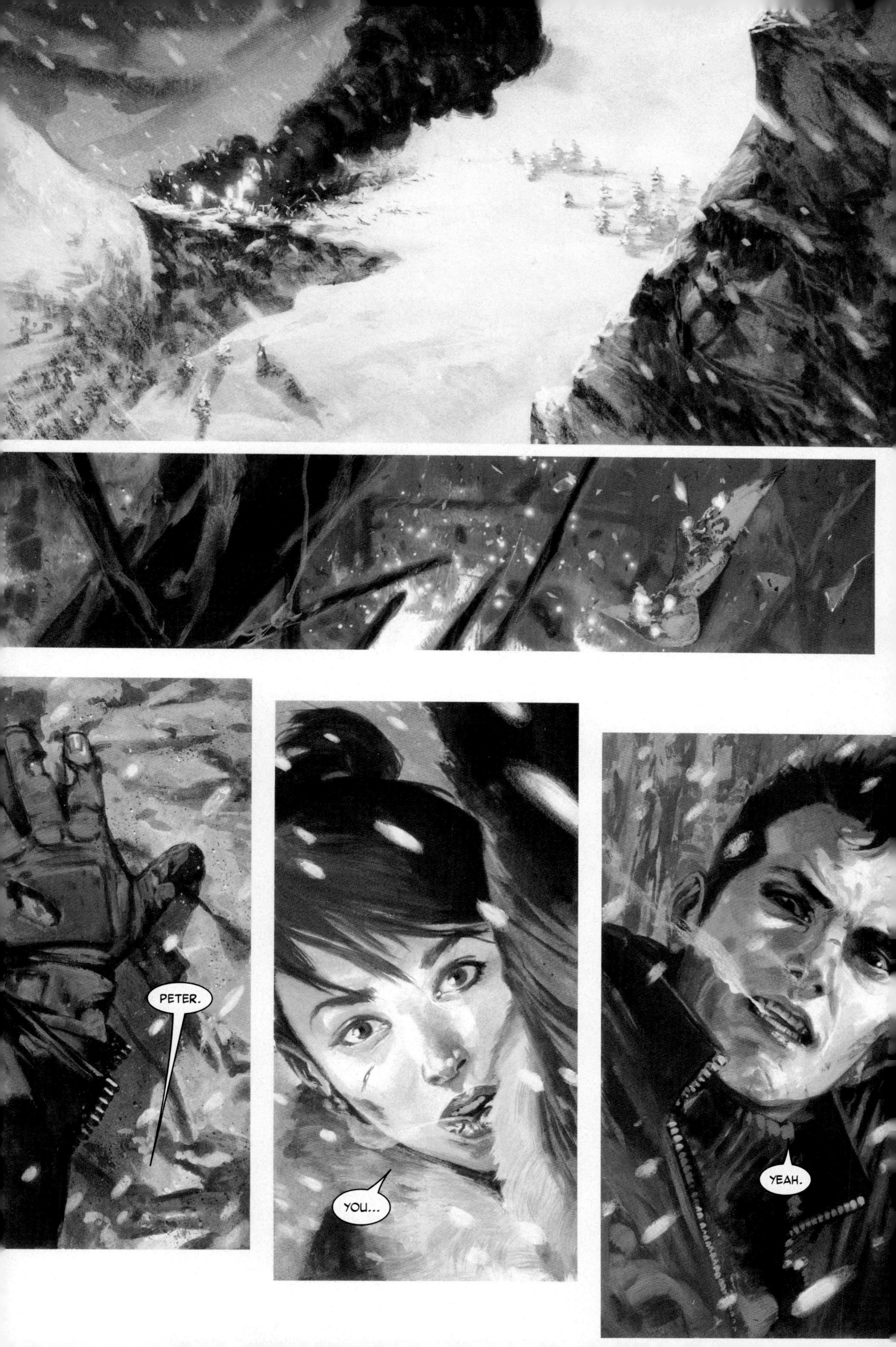
PETER.
YOU...
YEAH.

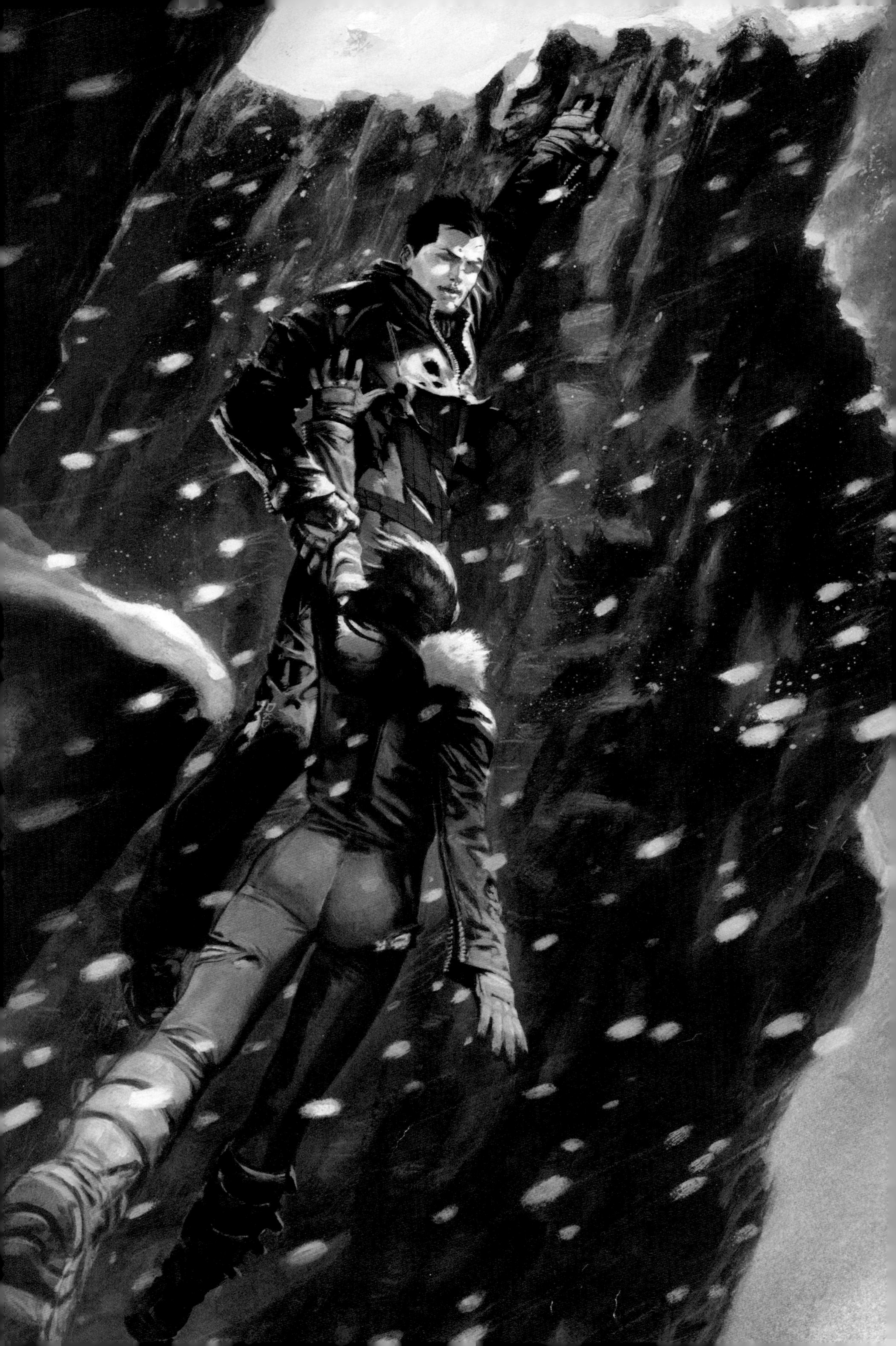

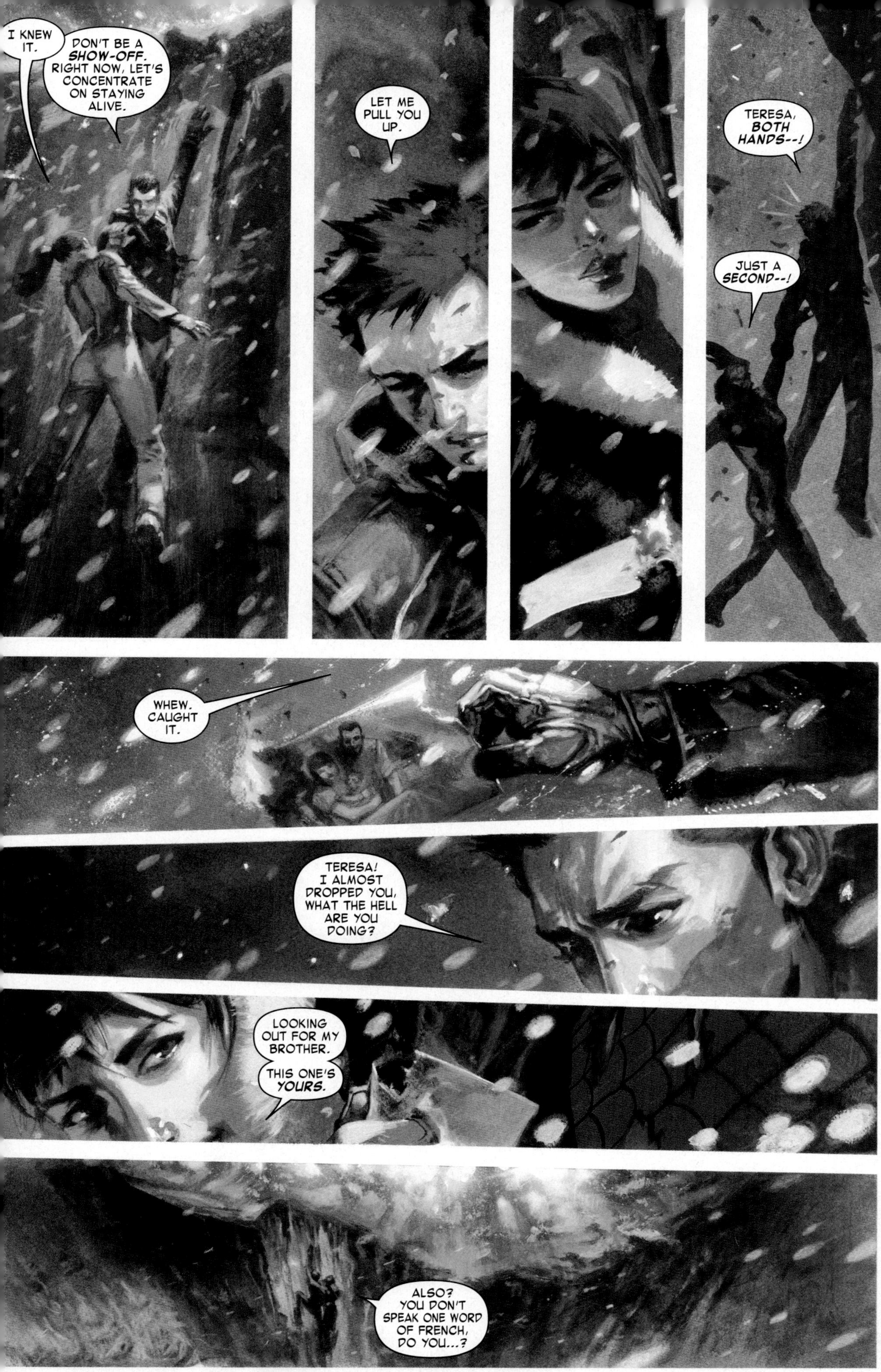
I KNEW IT.
DON'T BE A SHOW-OFF. RIGHT NOW, LET'S CONCENTRATE ON STAYING ALIVE.
LET ME PULL YOU UP.
TERESA, BOTH HANDS--!
JUST A SECOND--!
WHEW. CAUGHT IT.
TERESA! I ALMOST DROPPED YOU, WHAT THE HELL ARE YOU DOING?
LOOKING OUT FOR MY BROTHER.
THIS ONE'S YOURS.
ALSO? YOU DON'T SPEAK ONE WORD OF FRENCH, DO YOU...?

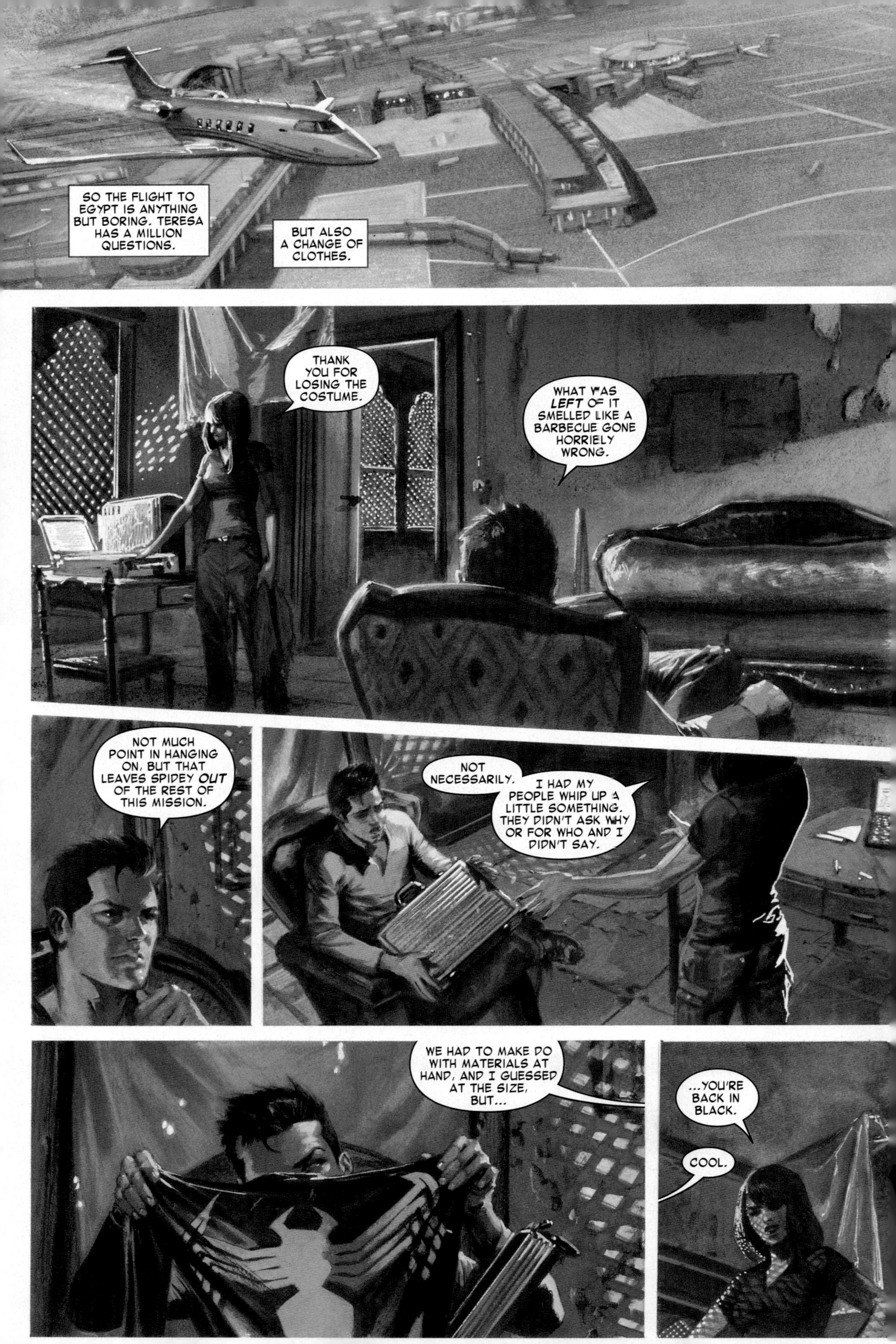
SO THE FLIGHT TO EGYPT IS ANYTHING BUT BORING. TERESA HAS A MILLION QUESTIONS.
BUT ALSO A CHANGE OF CLOTHES.
THANK YOU FOR LOSING THE COSTUME.
WHAT WAS LEFT OF IT SMELLED LIKE A BARBECUE GONE HORRIELY WRONG.
NOT MUCH POINT IN HANGING ON, BUT THAT LEAVES SPIDEY OUT OF THE REST OF THIS MISSION.
NOT NECESSARILY.
I HAD MY PEOPLE WHIP UP A LITTLE SOMETHING. THEY DIDN'T ASK WHY OR FOR WHO AND I DIDN'T SAY.
WE HAD TO MAKE DO WITH MATERIALS AT HAND, AND I GUESSED AT THE SIZE, BUT...
...YOU'RE BACK IN BLACK.
COOL.

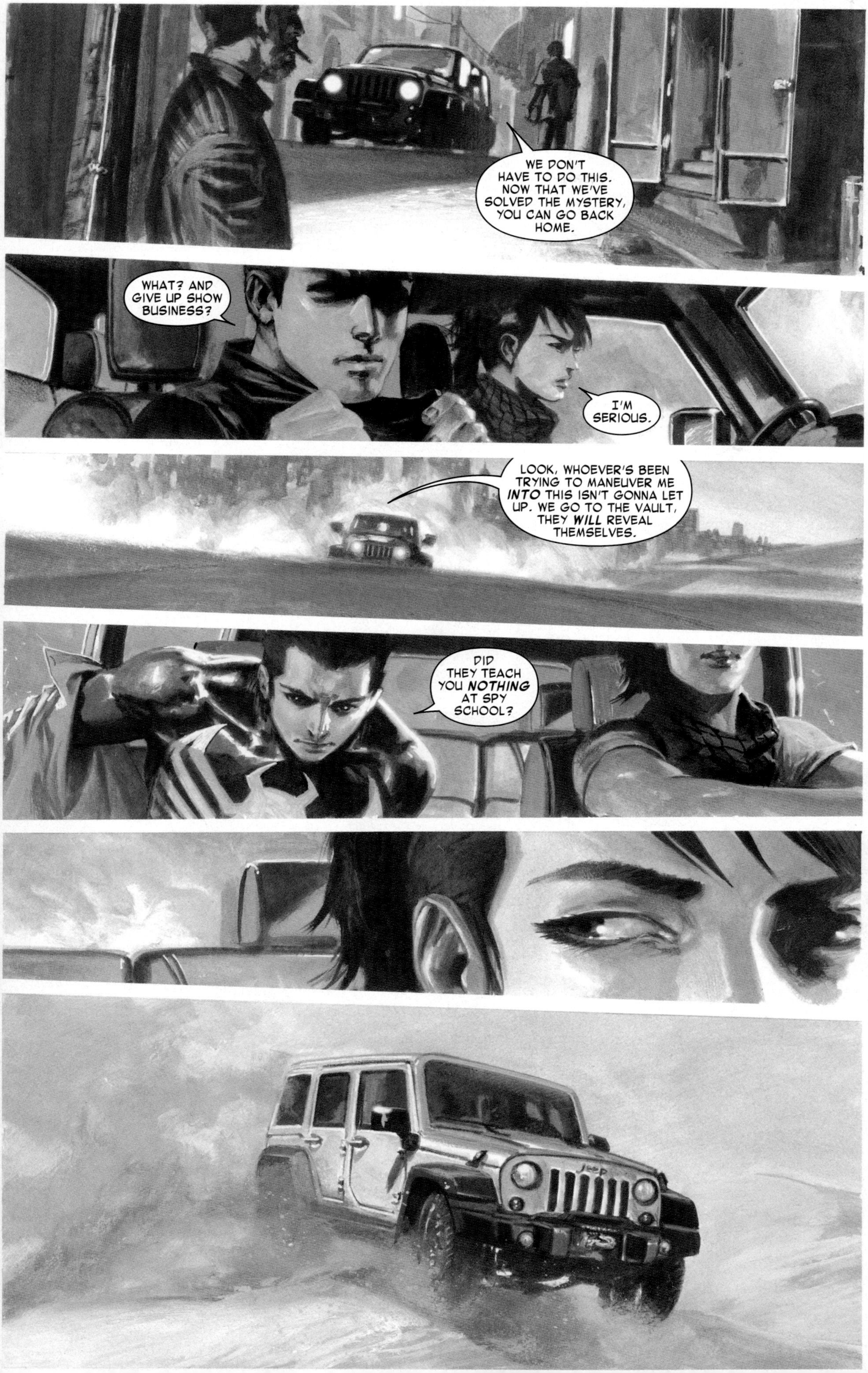
WE DON'T HAVE TO DO THIS. NOW THAT WE'VE SOLVED THE MYSTERY, YOU CAN GO BACK HOME.
WHAT? AND GIVE UP SHOW BUSINESS?
I'M SERIOUS.
LOOK, WHOEVER'S BEEN TRYING TO MANEUVER ME *INTO* THIS ISN'T GONNA LET UP. WE GO TO THE VAULT, THEY *WILL* REVEAL THEMSELVES.
DID THEY TEACH YOU *NOTHING* AT SPY SCHOOL?

THIS WAS THE SPOT ON THE MAP.

NOT MUCH LEFT.

WHY DON'T YOU GET DRESSED FOR WORK? USE YOUR SPIDER E.S.P. OR SOMETHING?

NAH, IT DOESN'T WORK LIKE THAT. BESIDES, WE DON'T NEED IT.

I'VE BEEN DOING THIS A LONG TIME...

...AND I KNOW THERE'S ALWAYS MORE TO FIND, MAYBE...

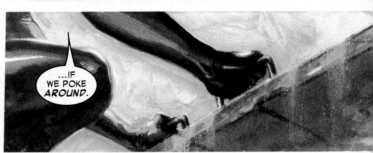

...IF WE POKE AROUND.

SPIDER-SENSE BUZZING A BIT. YOU GET THE LOCKPICKS READY, JUST IN CASE...

GOING DOWN...

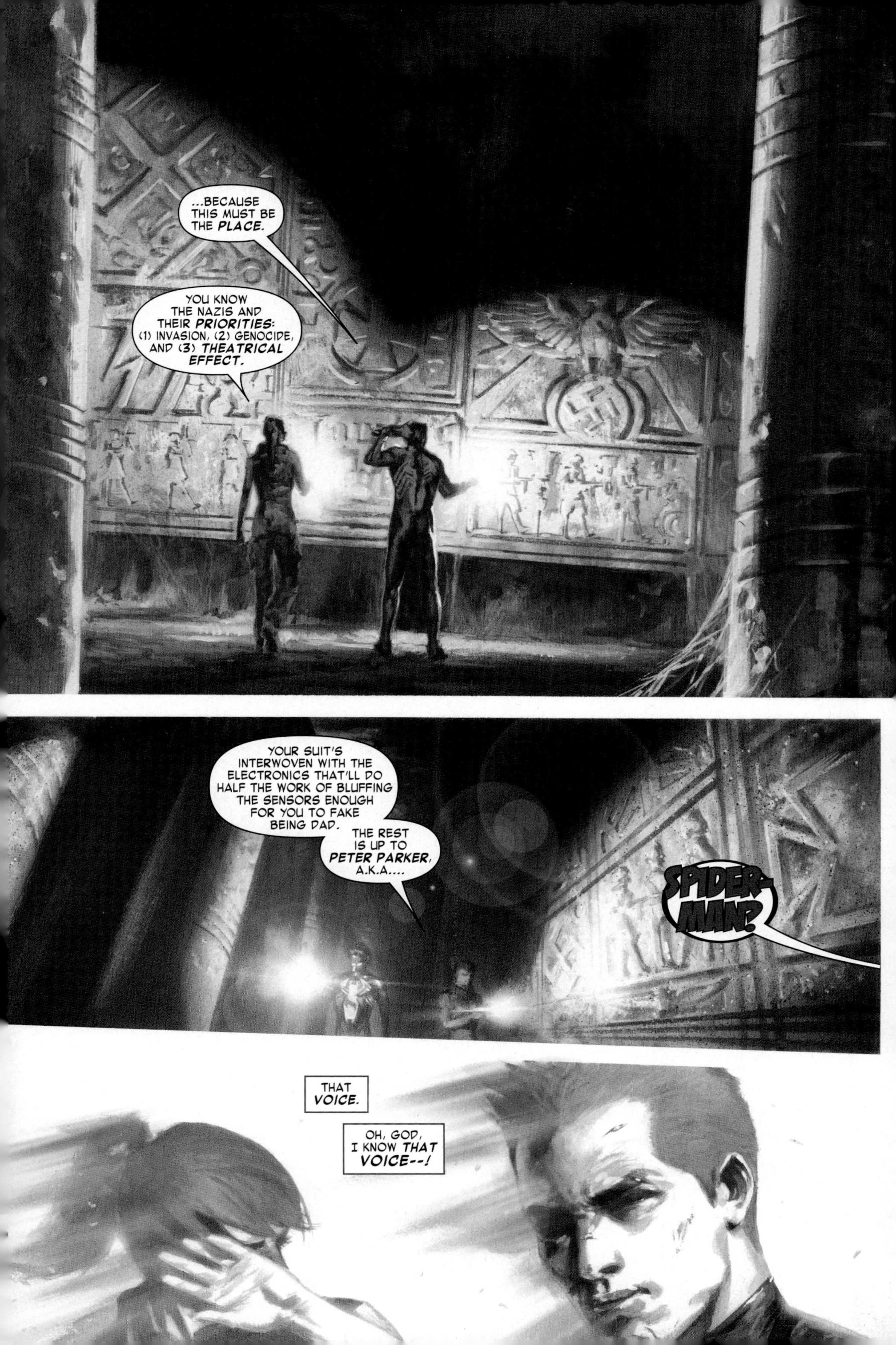
...BECAUSE THIS MUST BE THE PLACE.
YOU KNOW THE NAZIS AND THEIR PRIORITIES: (1) INVASION, (2) GENOCIDE, AND (3) THEATRICAL EFFECT.
YOUR SUIT'S INTERWOVEN WITH THE ELECTRONICS THAT'LL DO HALF THE WORK OF BLUFFING THE SENSORS ENOUGH FOR YOU TO FAKE BEING DAD.
THE REST IS UP TO PETER PARKER, A.K.A....
SPIDER-MAN?
THAT VOICE.
OH, GOD, I KNOW THAT VOICE--!

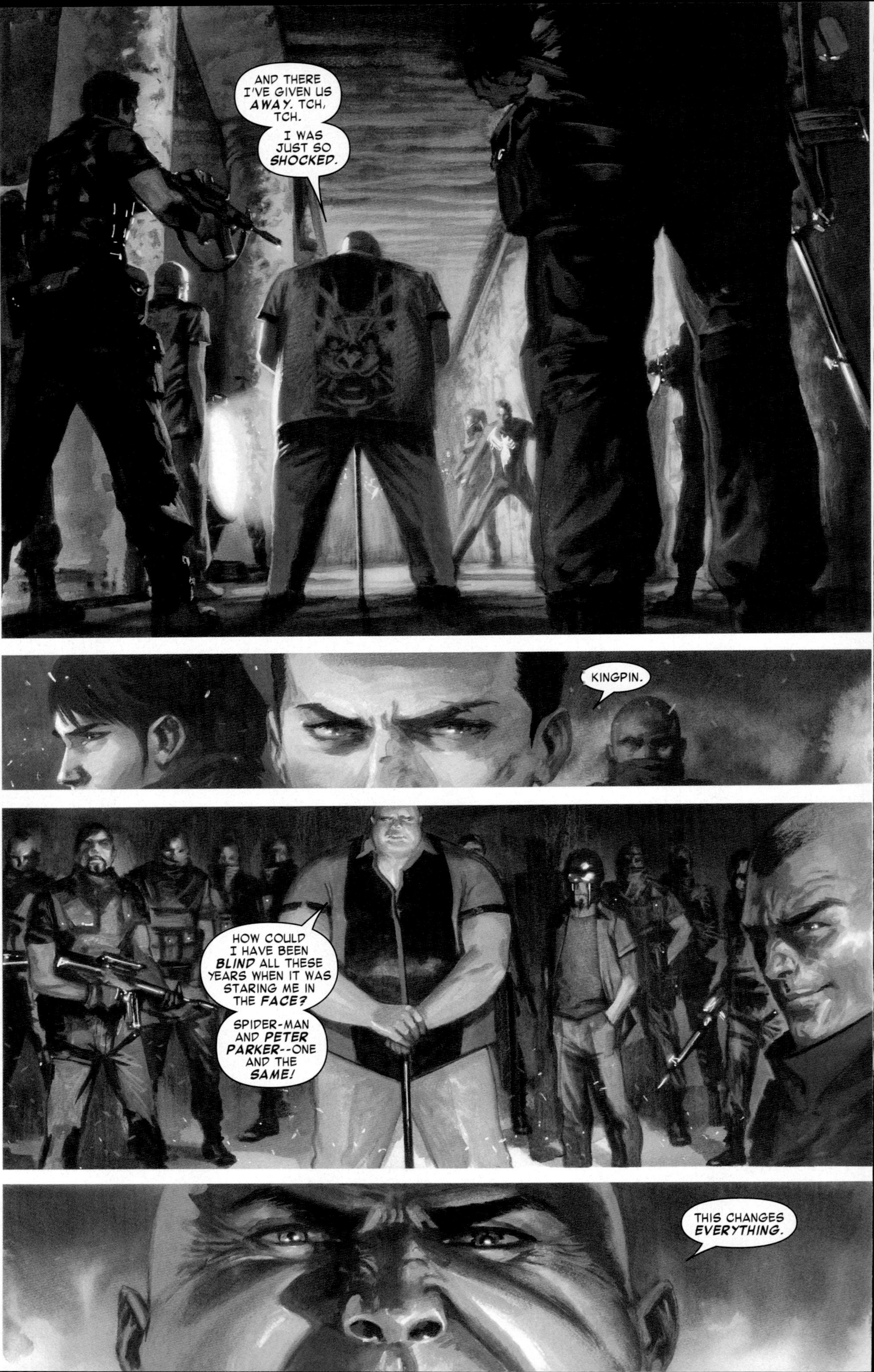

AND THERE I'VE GIVEN US AWAY. TCH, TCH.
I WAS JUST SO SHOCKED.
KINGPIN.
HOW COULD I HAVE BEEN BLIND ALL THESE YEARS WHEN IT WAS STARING ME IN THE FACE?
SPIDER-MAN AND PETER PARKER--ONE AND THE SAME!
THIS CHANGES EVERYTHING.

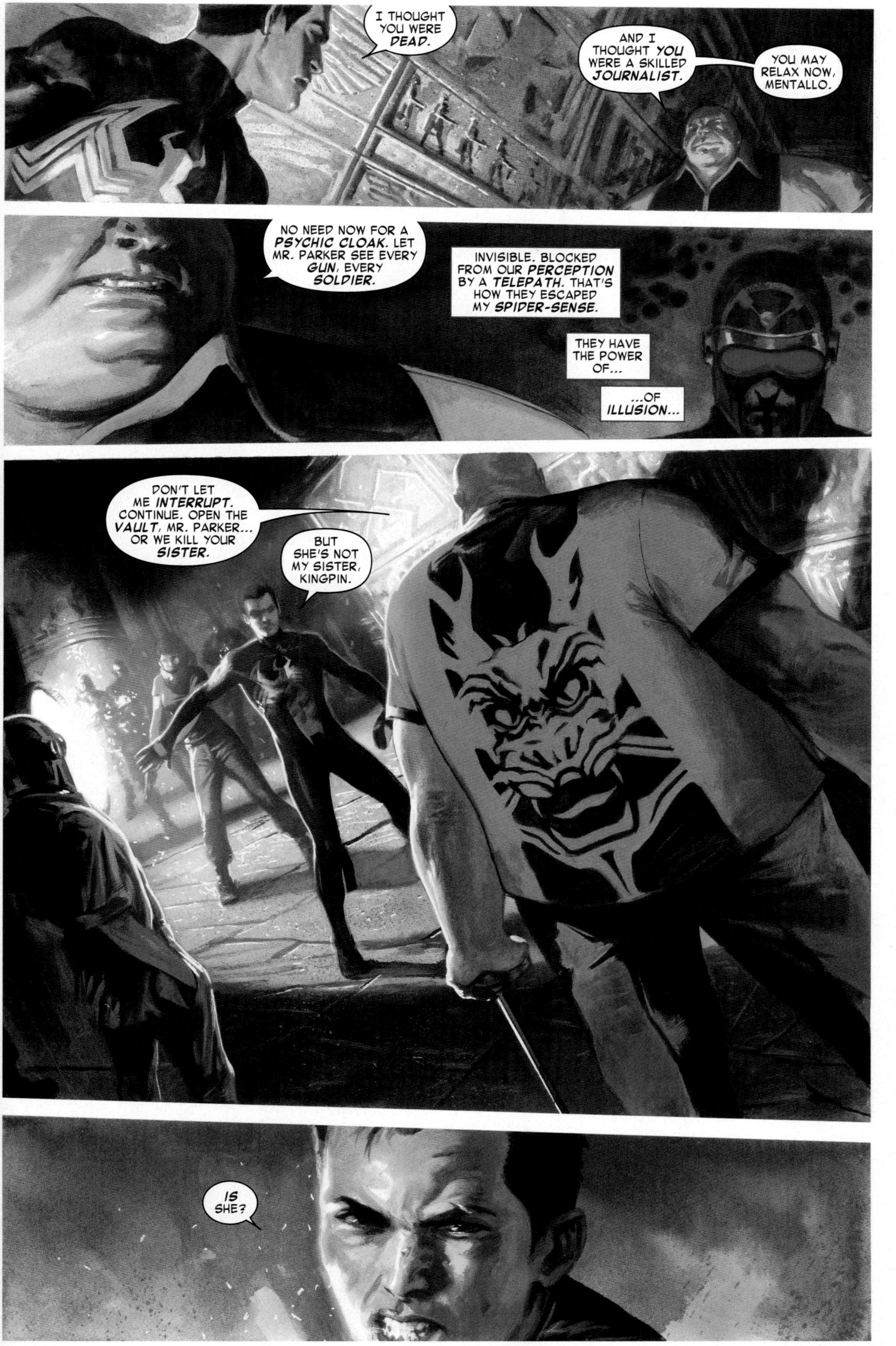
I THOUGHT YOU WERE *DEAD*.
AND I THOUGHT *YOU* WERE A SKILLED *JOURNALIST*.
YOU MAY RELAX NOW, MENTALLO.
NO NEED NOW FOR A *PSYCHIC CLOAK*. LET MR. PARKER SEE EVERY *GUN*, EVERY *SOLDIER*.
INVISIBLE. BLOCKED FROM OUR *PERCEPTION* BY A *TELEPATH*. THAT'S HOW THEY ESCAPED MY *SPIDER-SENSE*.
THEY HAVE THE POWER OF...
...OF *ILLUSION*...
DON'T LET ME *INTERRUPT*. CONTINUE. OPEN THE *VAULT*, MR. PARKER... OR WE KILL YOUR *SISTER*.
BUT SHE'S NOT MY SISTER, KINGPIN.
IS SHE?

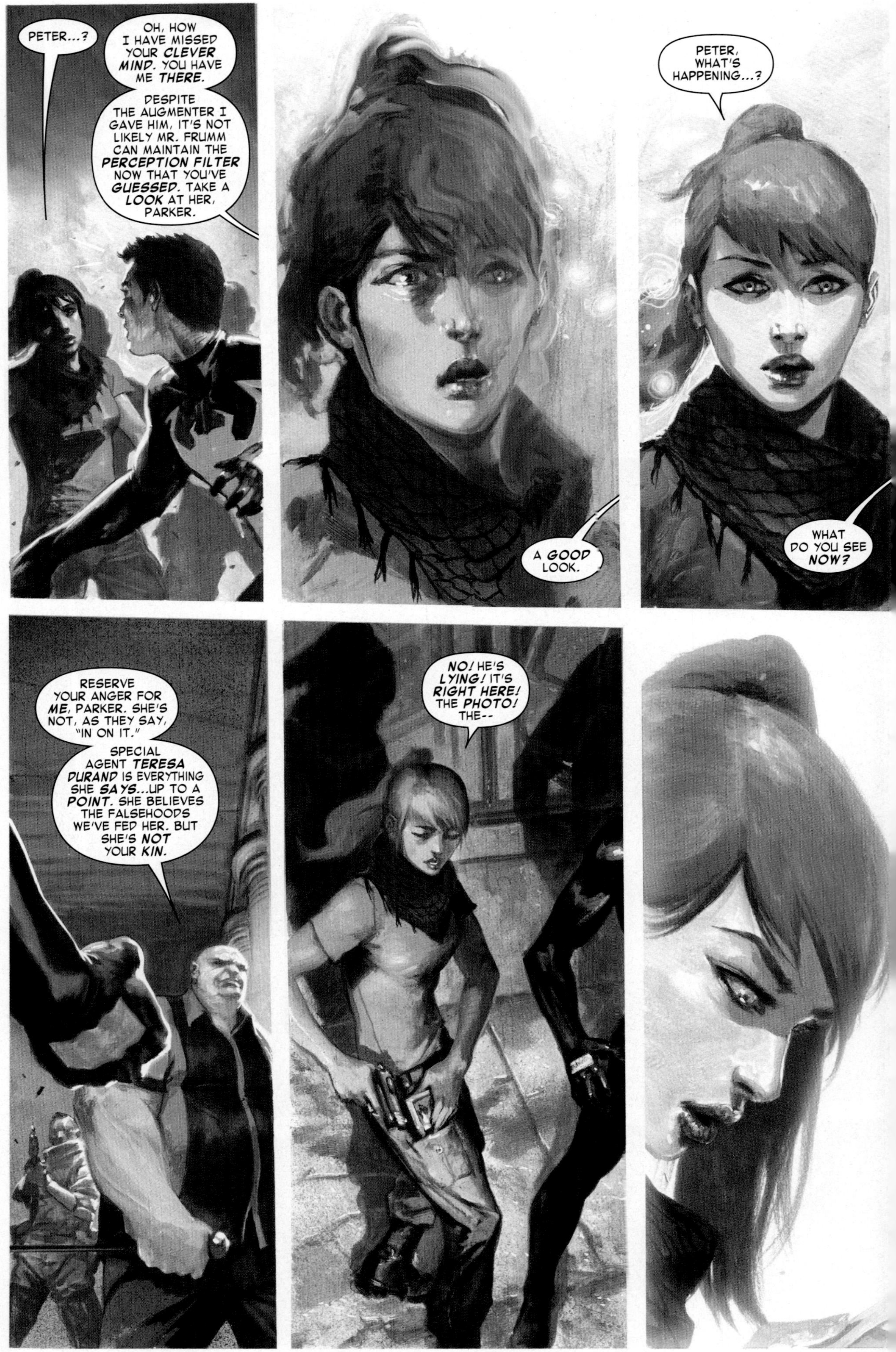
PETER...?
OH, HOW I HAVE MISSED YOUR CLEVER MIND. YOU HAVE ME THERE.
DESPITE THE AUGMENTER I GAVE HIM, IT'S NOT LIKELY MR. FRUMM CAN MAINTAIN THE PERCEPTION FILTER NOW THAT YOU'VE GUESSED. TAKE A LOOK AT HER, PARKER.
A GOOD LOOK.
PETER, WHAT'S HAPPENING...?
WHAT DO YOU SEE NOW?
RESERVE YOUR ANGER FOR ME, PARKER. SHE'S NOT, AS THEY SAY, "IN ON IT."
SPECIAL AGENT TERESA DURAND IS EVERYTHING SHE SAYS...UP TO A POINT. SHE BELIEVES THE FALSEHOODS WE'VE FED HER. BUT SHE'S NOT YOUR KIN.
NO! HE'S LYING! IT'S RIGHT HERE! THE PHOTO! THE--

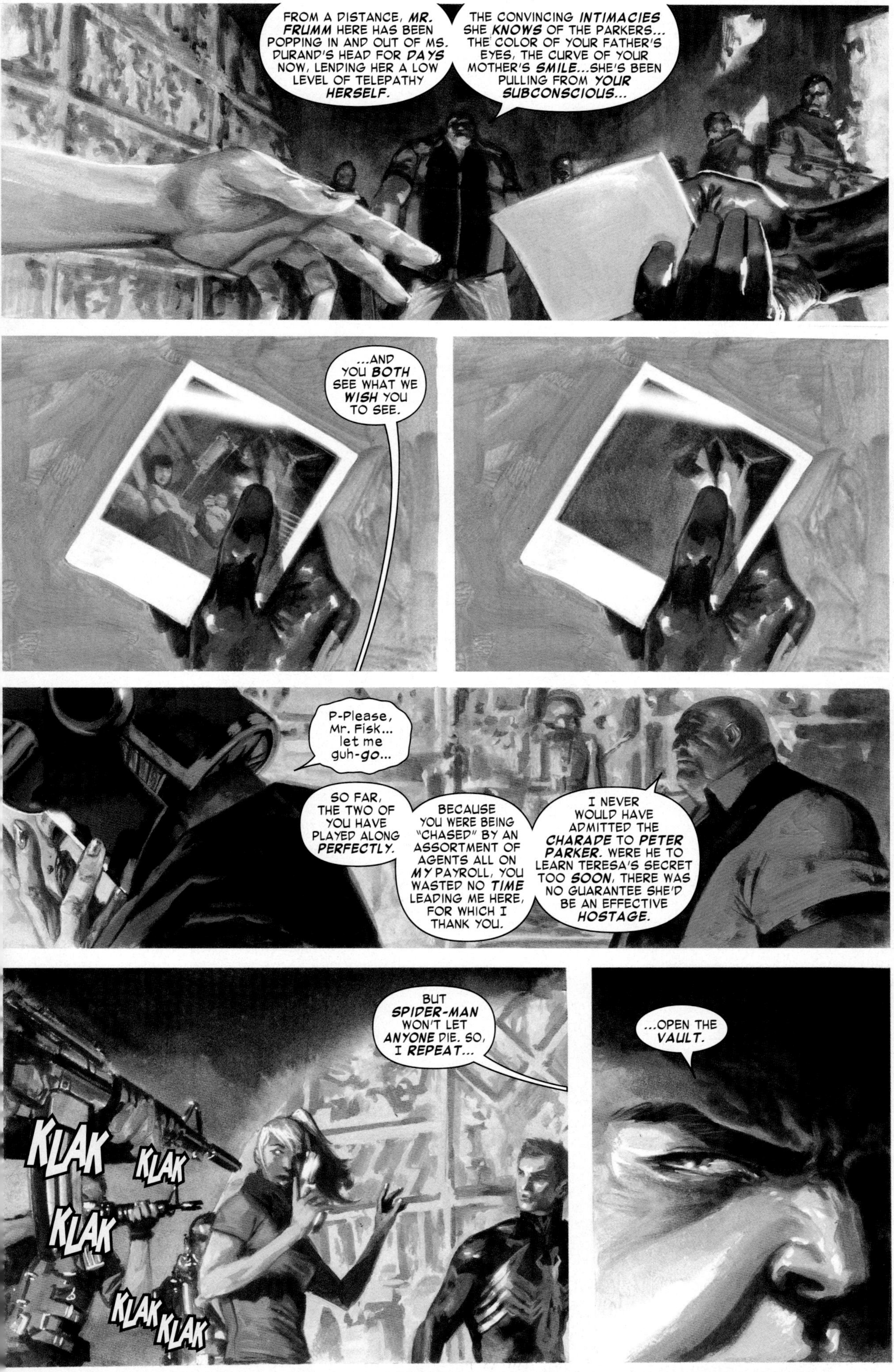
FROM A DISTANCE, MR. FRUMM HERE HAS BEEN POPPING IN AND OUT OF MS. DURAND'S HEAD FOR DAYS NOW, LENDING HER A LOW LEVEL OF TELEPATHY HERSELF.
THE CONVINCING INTIMACIES SHE KNOWS OF THE PARKERS... THE COLOR OF YOUR FATHER'S EYES, THE CURVE OF YOUR MOTHER'S SMILE...SHE'S BEEN PULLING FROM YOUR SUBCONSCIOUS...
...AND YOU BOTH SEE WHAT WE WISH YOU TO SEE.
P-Please, Mr. Fisk... let me guh-go...
SO FAR, THE TWO OF YOU HAVE PLAYED ALONG PERFECTLY.
BECAUSE YOU WERE BEING "CHASED" BY AN ASSORTMENT OF AGENTS ALL ON MY PAYROLL, YOU WASTED NO TIME LEADING ME HERE, FOR WHICH I THANK YOU.
I NEVER WOULD HAVE ADMITTED THE CHARADE TO PETER PARKER. WERE HE TO LEARN TERESA'S SECRET TOO SOON, THERE WAS NO GUARANTEE SHE'D BE AN EFFECTIVE HOSTAGE.
BUT SPIDER-MAN WON'T LET ANYONE DIE. SO, I REPEAT...
KLAK
KLAK
KLAK
KLAK KLAK
...OPEN THE VAULT.

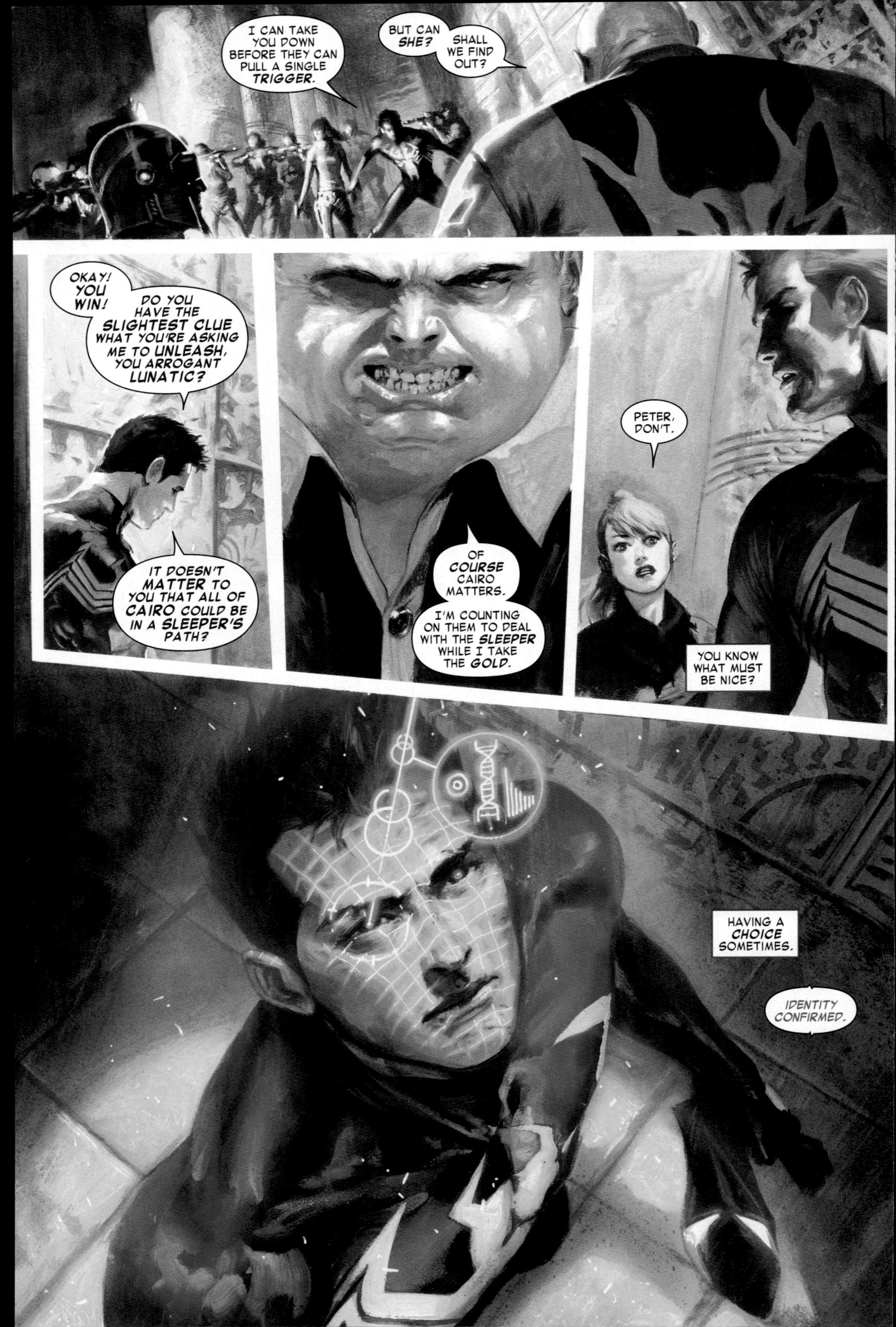
I CAN TAKE YOU DOWN BEFORE THEY CAN PULL A SINGLE TRIGGER.
BUT CAN SHE?
SHALL WE FIND OUT?
OKAY! YOU WIN!
DO YOU HAVE THE SLIGHTEST CLUE WHAT YOU'RE ASKING ME TO UNLEASH, YOU ARROGANT LUNATIC?
IT DOESN'T MATTER TO YOU THAT ALL OF CAIRO COULD BE IN A SLEEPER'S PATH?
OF COURSE CAIRO MATTERS.
I'M COUNTING ON THEM TO DEAL WITH THE SLEEPER WHILE I TAKE THE GOLD.
PETER, DON'T.
YOU KNOW WHAT MUST BE NICE?
HAVING A CHOICE SOMETIMES.
IDENTITY CONFIRMED.

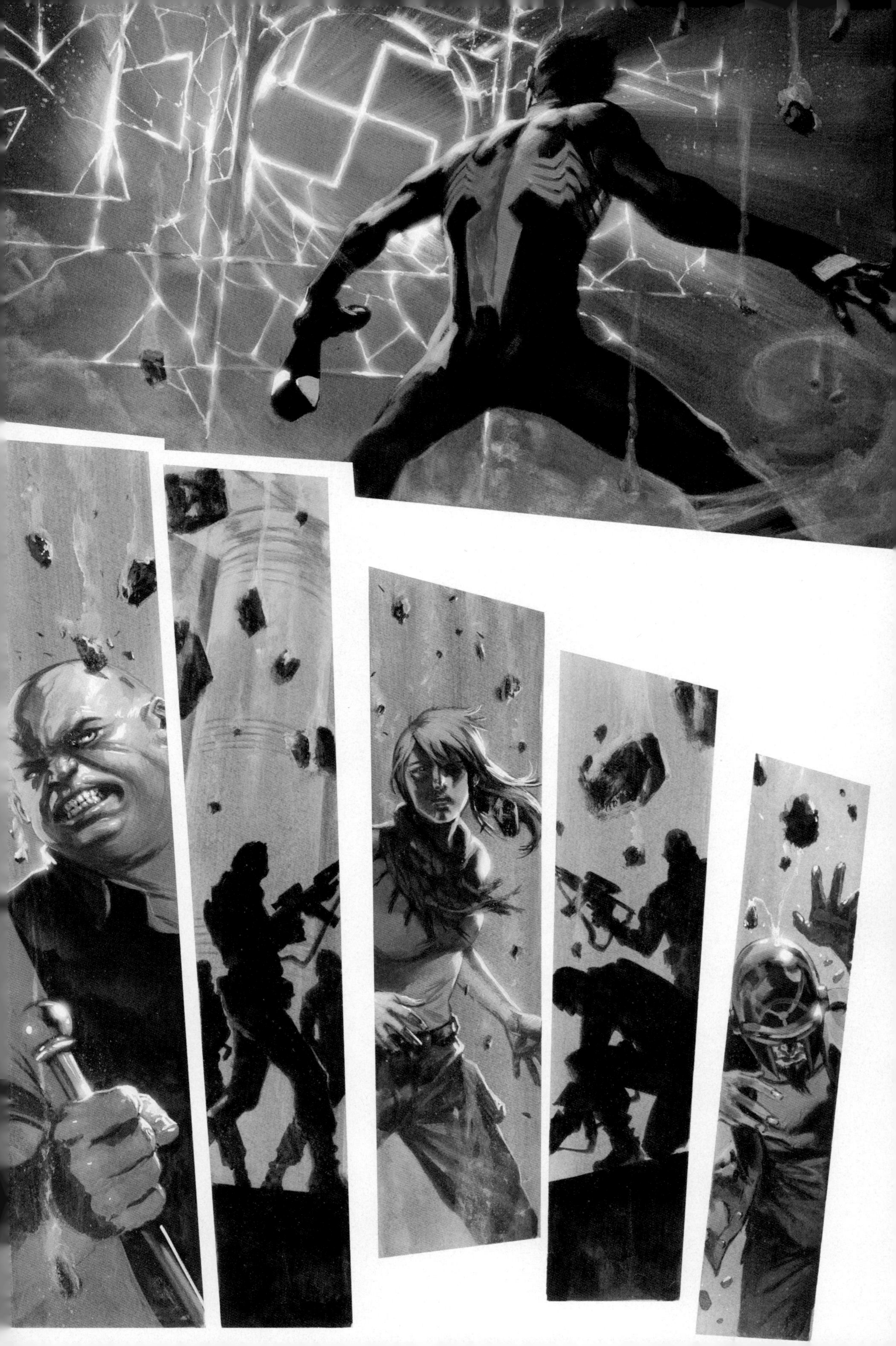

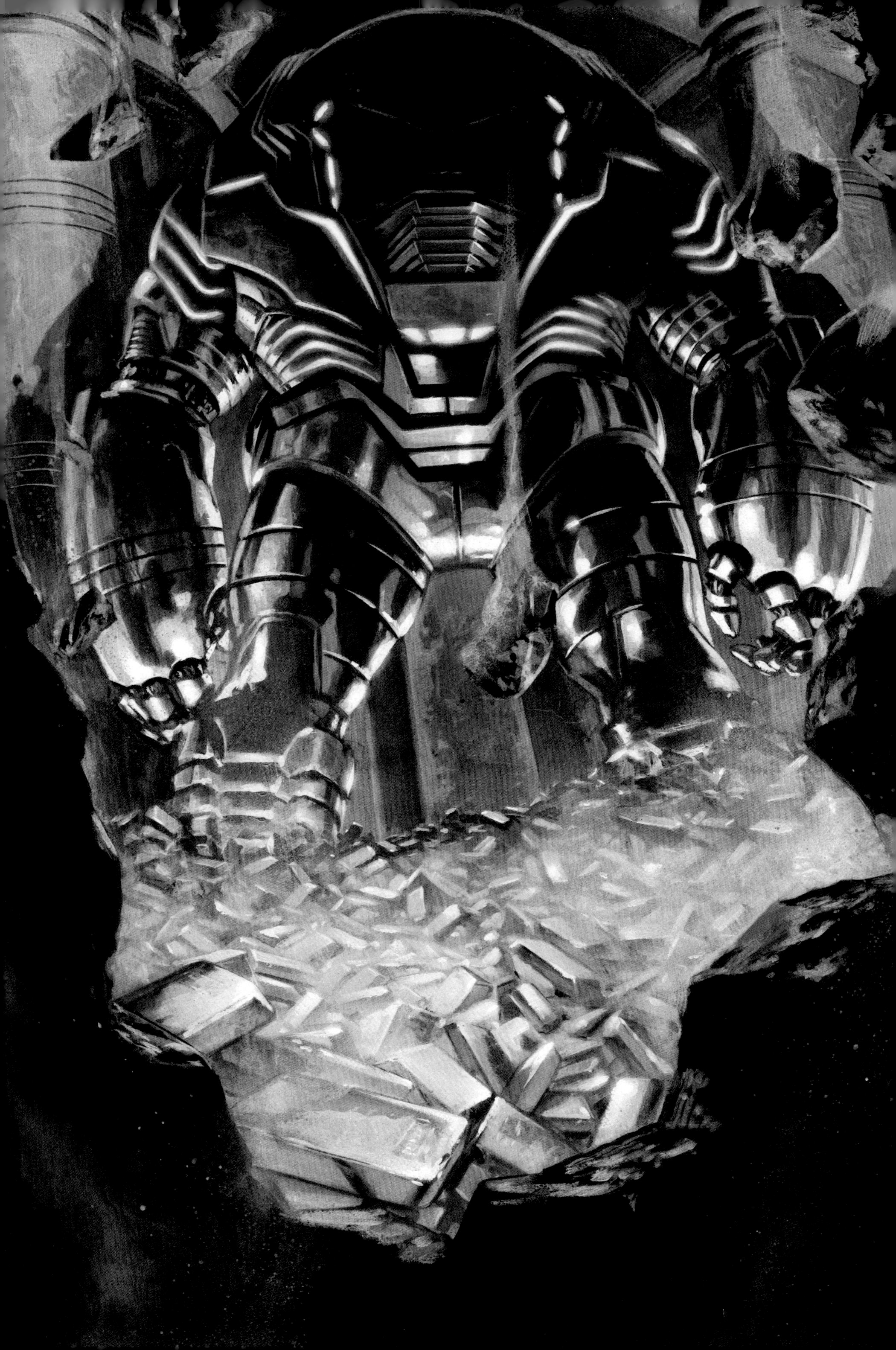

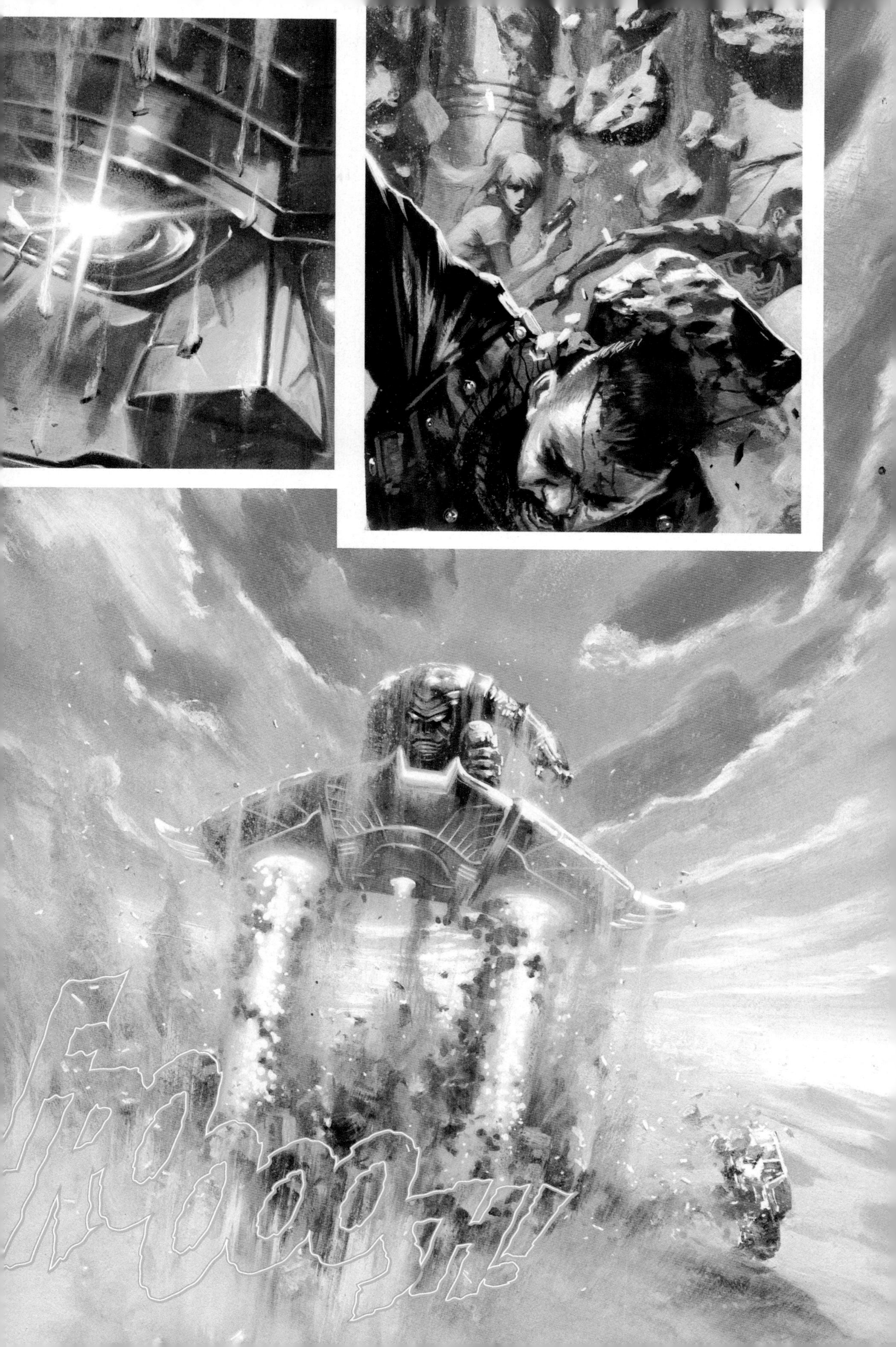

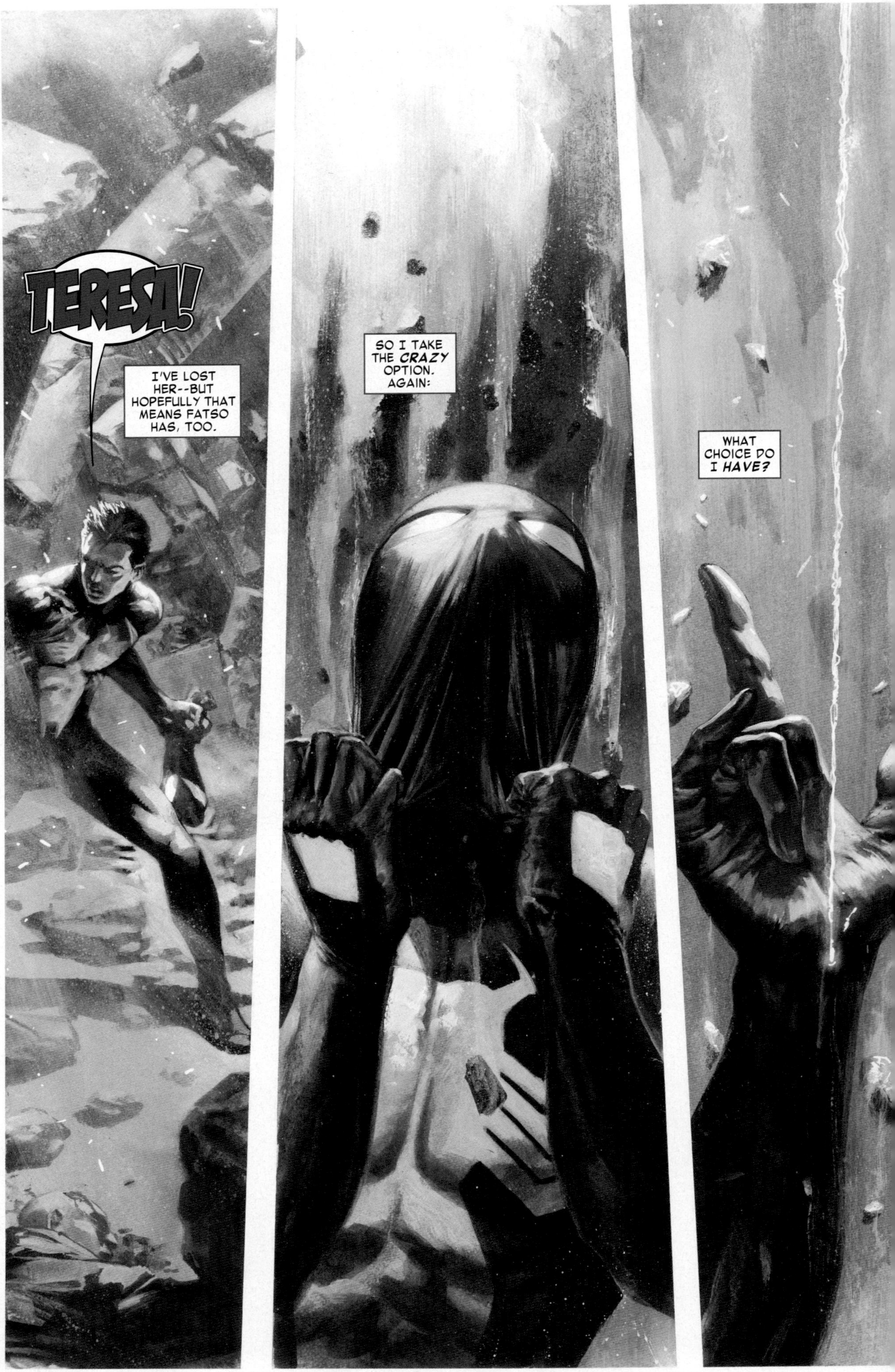
TERESA!
I'VE LOST HER--BUT HOPEFULLY THAT MEANS FATSO HAS, TOO.
SO I TAKE THE CRAZY OPTION. AGAIN:
WHAT CHOICE DO I HAVE?

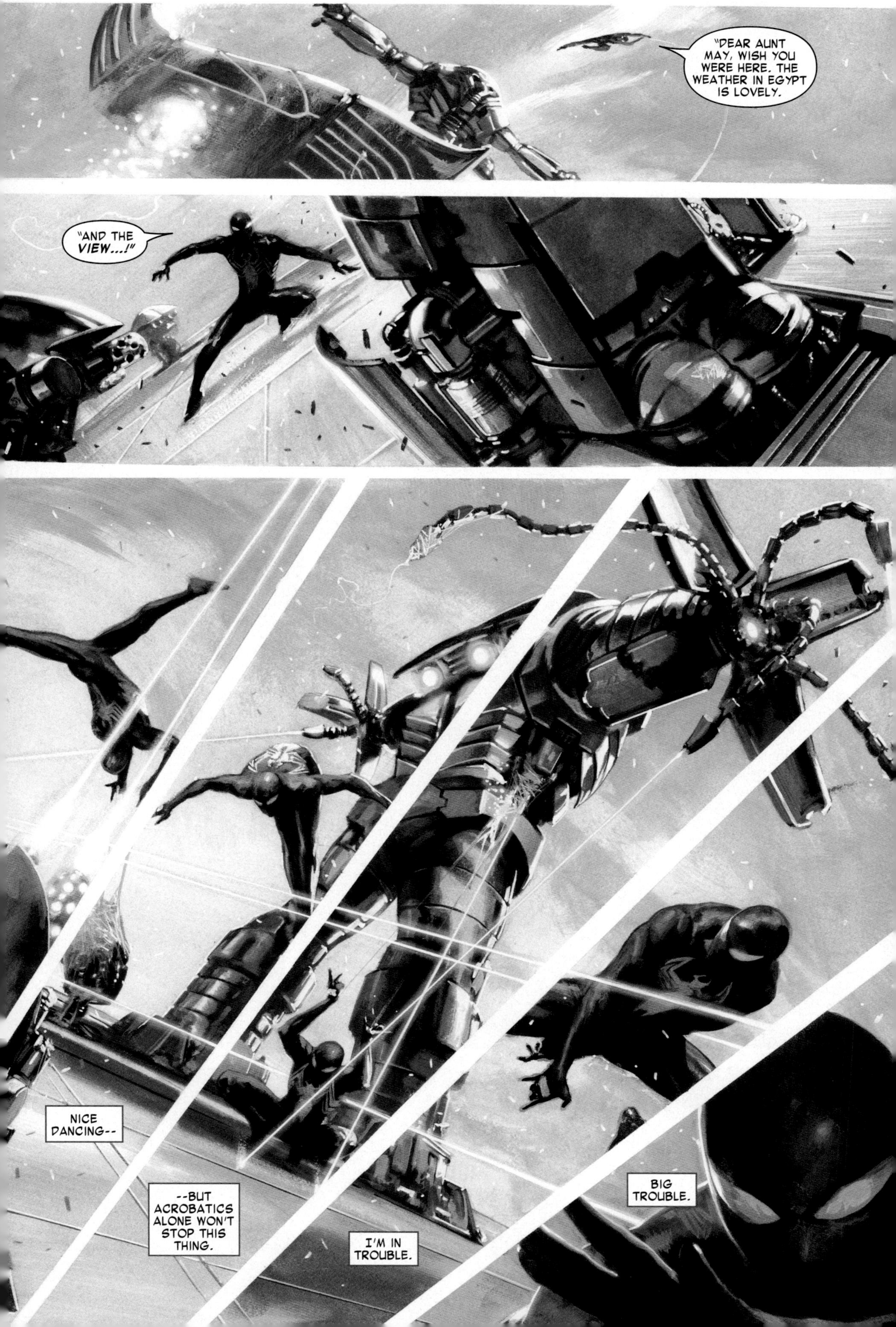
"DEAR AUNT MAY, WISH YOU WERE HERE. THE WEATHER IN EGYPT IS LOVELY.
"AND THE *VIEW*...!"
NICE DANCING--
--BUT ACROBATICS ALONE WON'T STOP THIS THING.
I'M IN TROUBLE.
BIG TROUBLE.

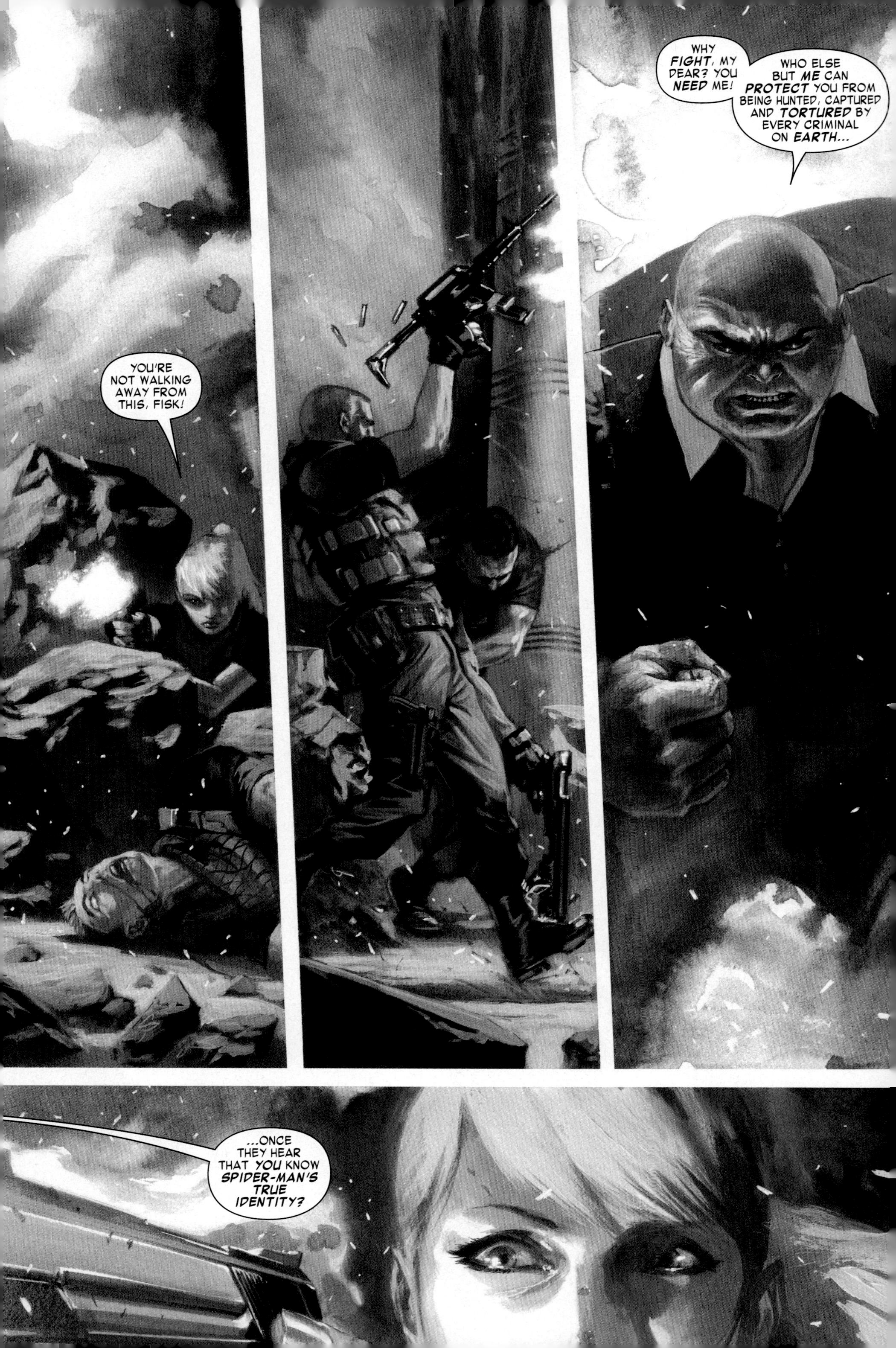
YOU'RE NOT WALKING AWAY FROM THIS, FISK!
WHY FIGHT, MY DEAR? YOU NEED ME!
WHO ELSE BUT ME CAN PROTECT YOU FROM BEING HUNTED, CAPTURED AND TORTURED BY EVERY CRIMINAL ON EARTH...
...ONCE THEY HEAR THAT YOU KNOW SPIDER-MAN'S TRUE IDENTITY?

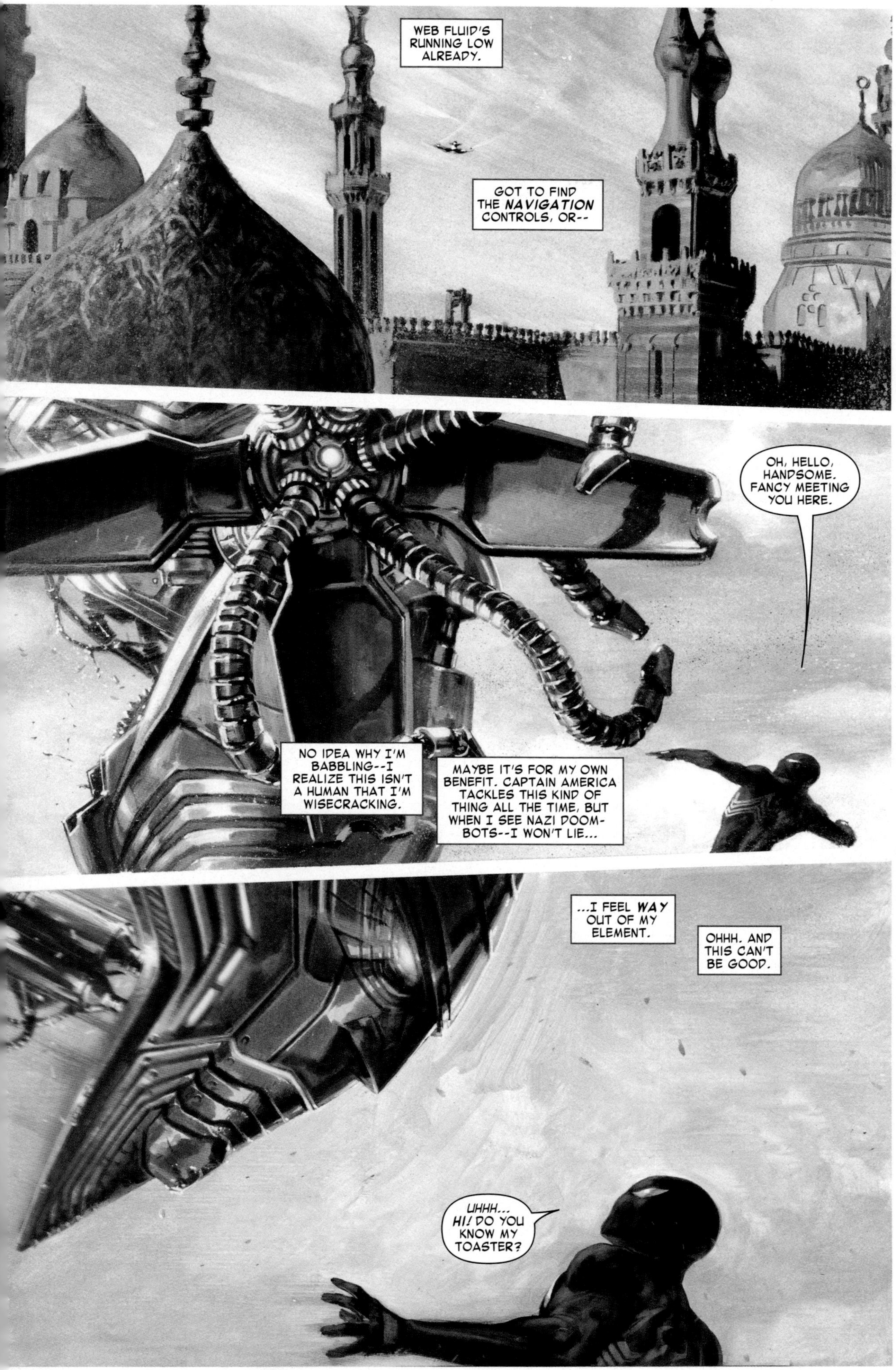
WEB FLUID'S RUNNING LOW ALREADY.
GOT TO FIND THE *NAVIGATION* CONTROLS, OR--
OH, HELLO, HANDSOME. FANCY MEETING YOU HERE.
NO IDEA WHY I'M BABBLING--I REALIZE THIS ISN'T A HUMAN THAT I'M WISECRACKING.
MAYBE IT'S FOR MY OWN BENEFIT. CAPTAIN AMERICA TACKLES THIS KIND OF THING ALL THE TIME, BUT WHEN I SEE NAZI DOOM-BOTS--I WON'T LIE...
...I FEEL *WAY* OUT OF MY ELEMENT.
OHHH. AND THIS CAN'T BE GOOD.
UHHH... HI! DO YOU KNOW MY TOASTER?

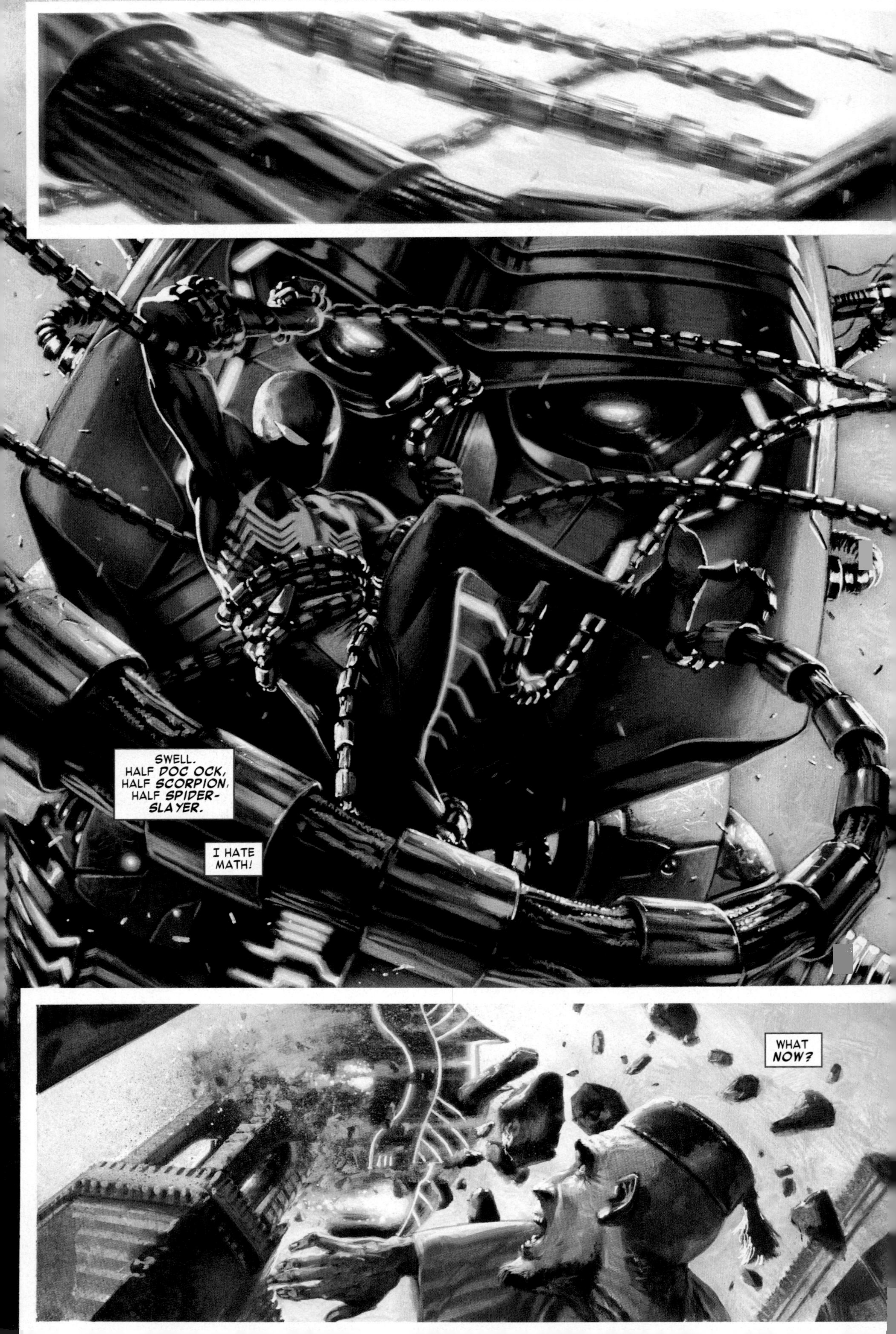
SWELL. HALF DOC OCK, HALF SCORPION, HALF SPIDER-SLAYER.
I HATE MATH!
WHAT NOW?

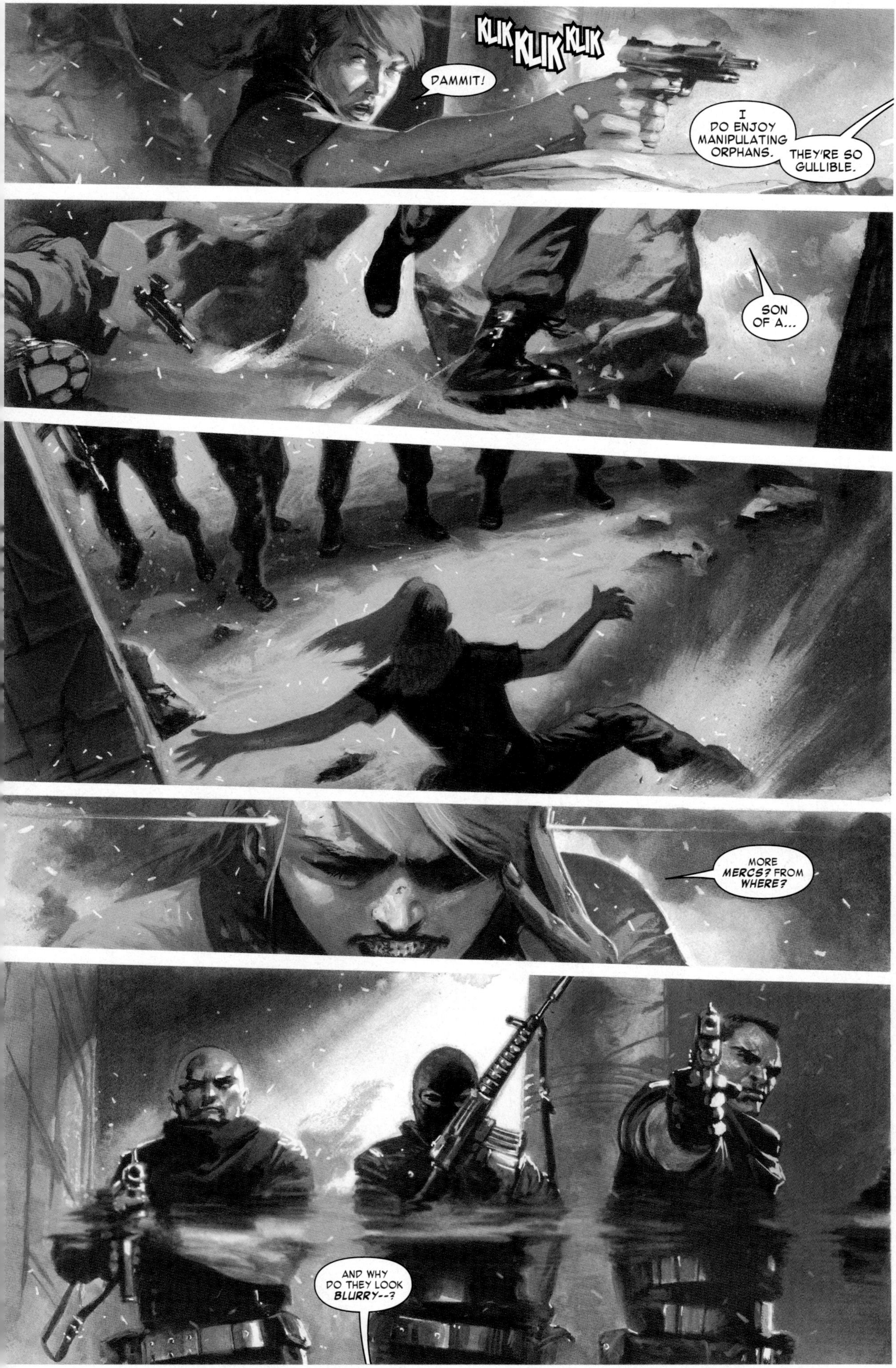
KLIK KLIK KLIK
DAMMIT!
I DO ENJOY MANIPULATING ORPHANS.
THEY'RE SO GULLIBLE.
SON OF A...
MORE MERCS? FROM WHERE?
AND WHY DO THEY LOOK BLURRY--?

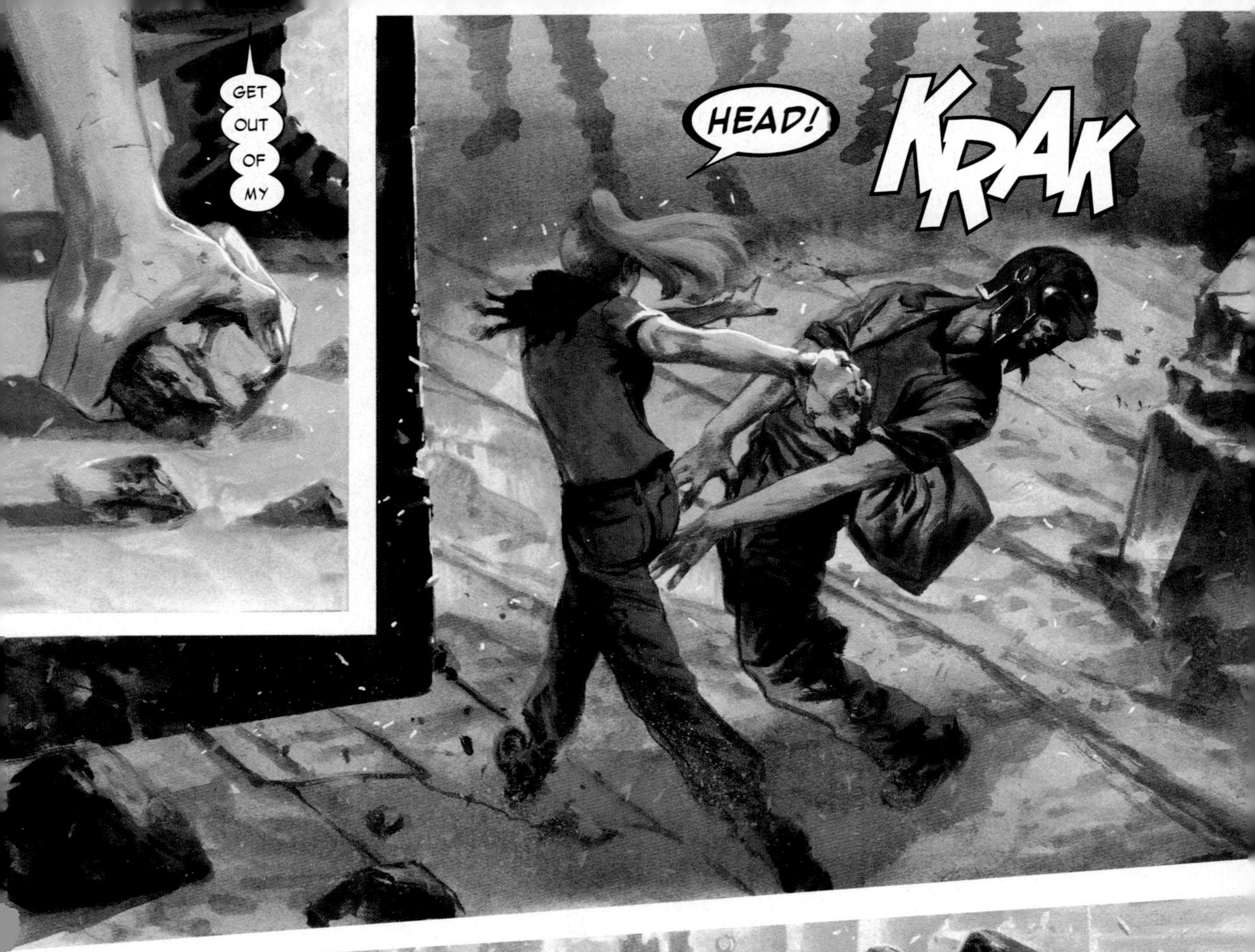
GET OUT OF MY
HEAD!
KRAK

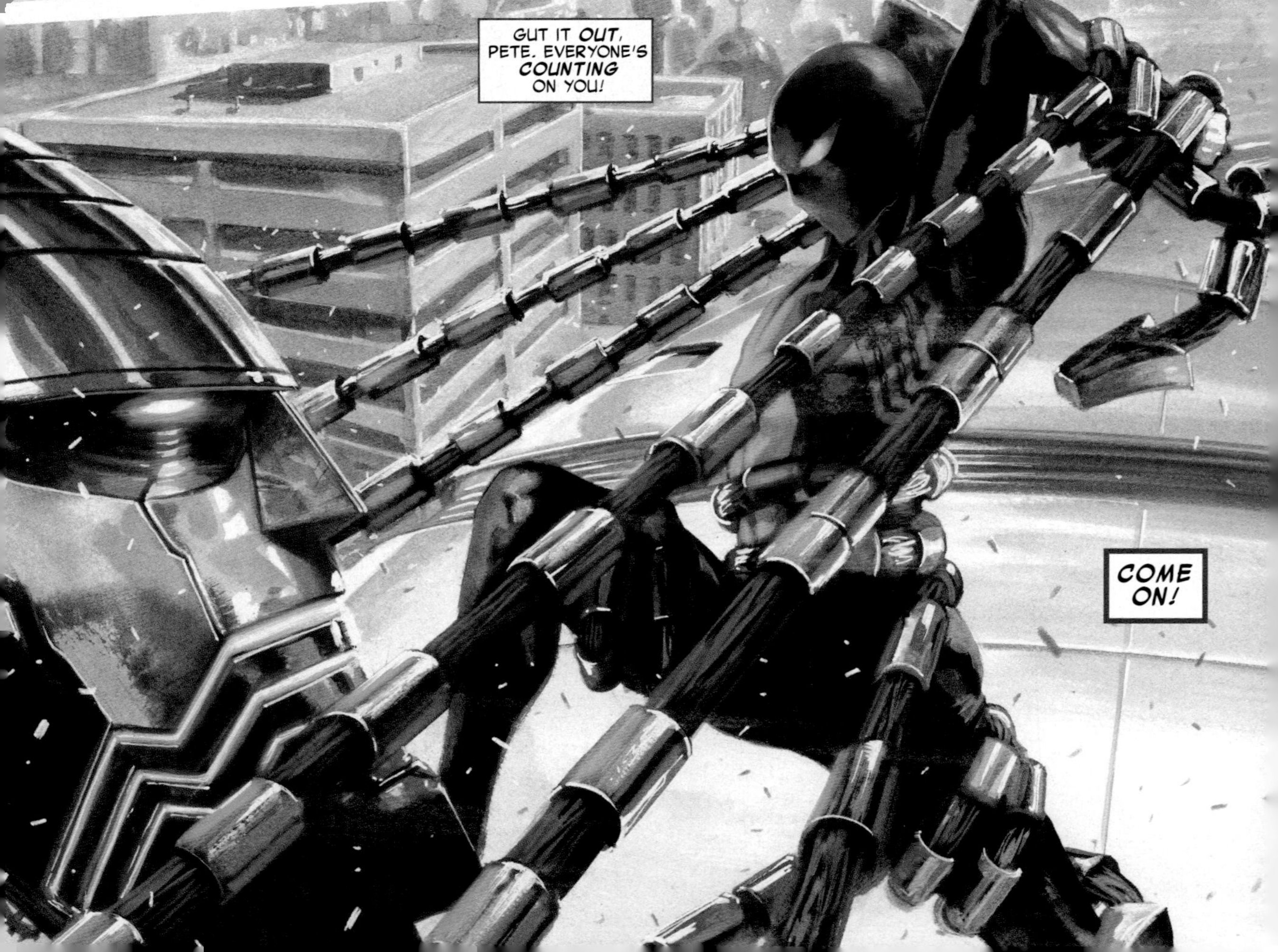
GUT IT OUT, PETE. EVERYONE'S COUNTING ON YOU!
COME ON!

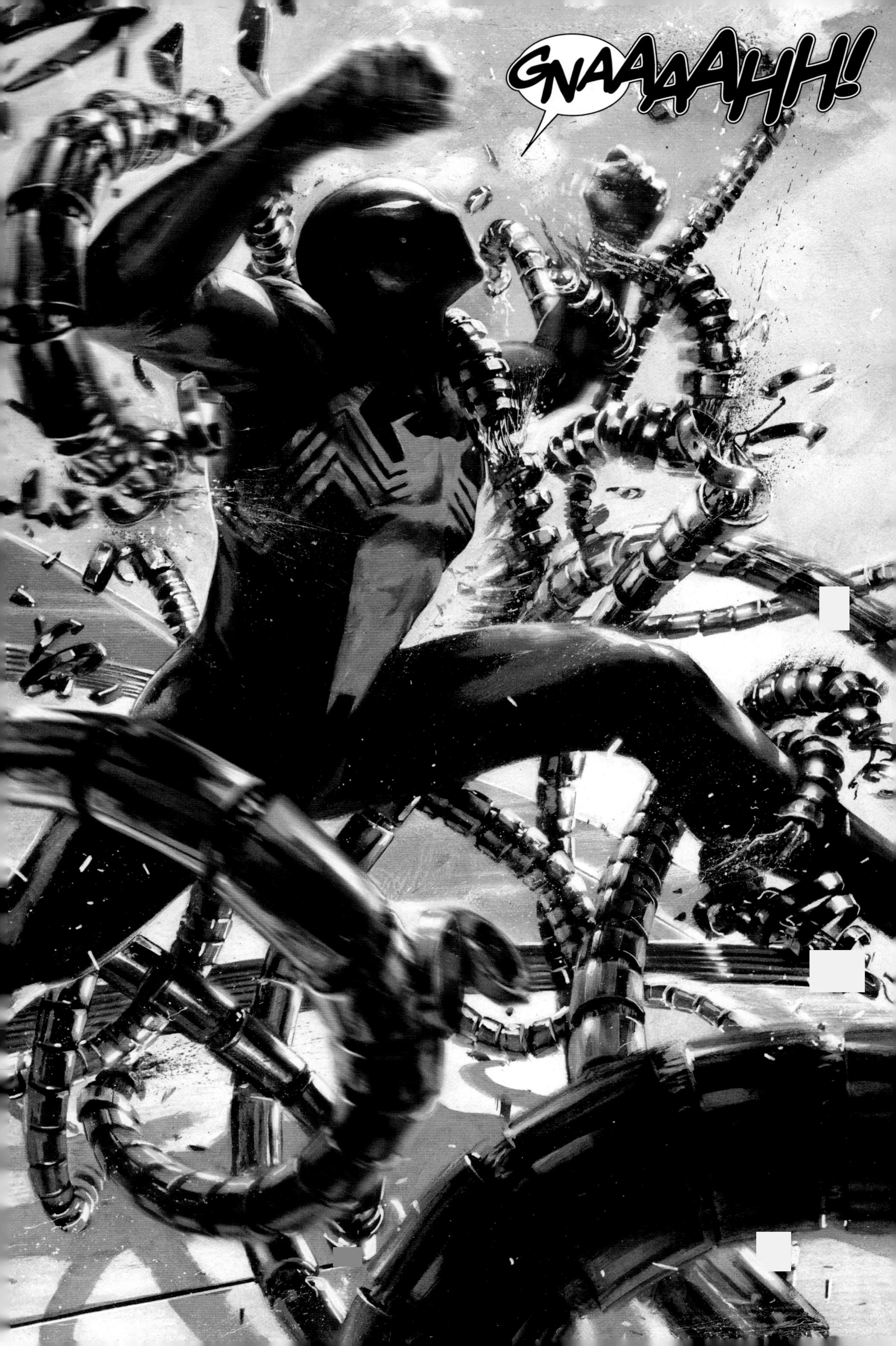
GNAAAAAHH!

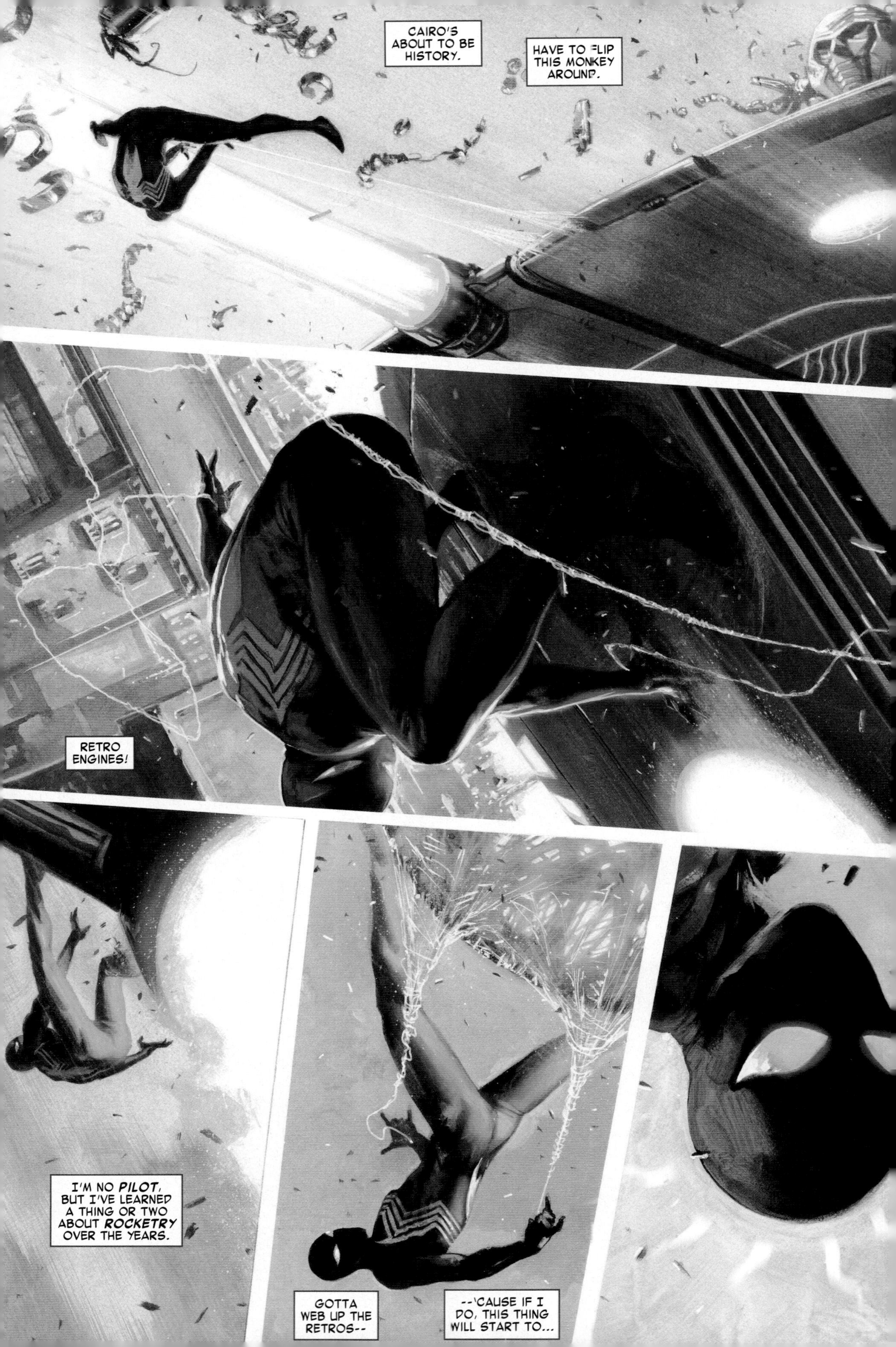
CAIRO'S ABOUT TO BE HISTORY.
HAVE TO FLIP THIS MONKEY AROUND.
RETRO ENGINES!
I'M NO *PILOT*, BUT I'VE LEARNED A THING OR TWO ABOUT *ROCKETRY* OVER THE YEARS.
GOTTA WEB UP THE RETROS--
--'CAUSE IF I DO, THIS THING WILL START TO...

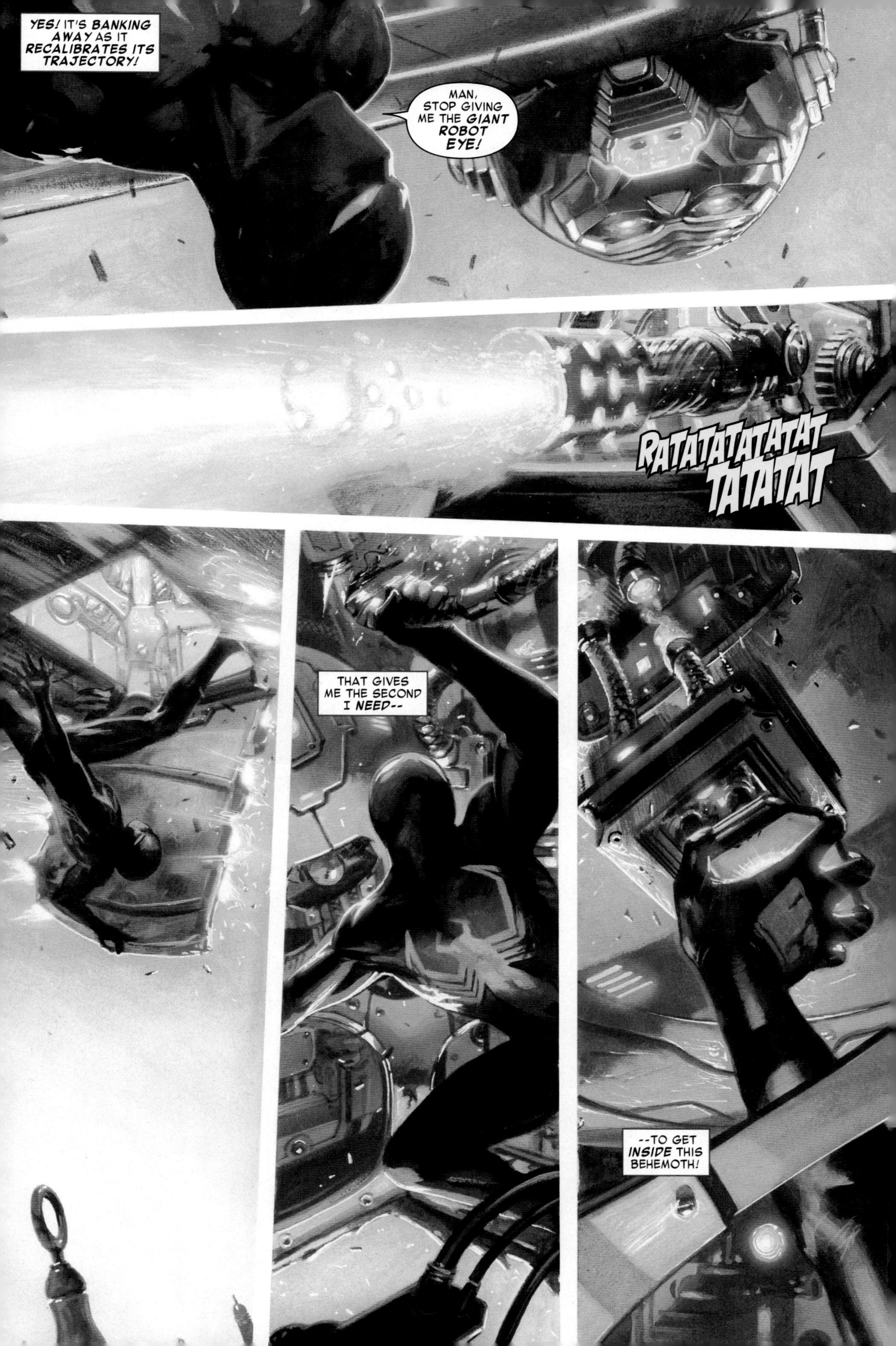
YES! IT'S BANKING AWAY AS IT RECALIBRATES ITS TRAJECTORY!
MAN, STOP GIVING ME THE GIANT ROBOT EYE!
RATATATATATAT TATATAT
THAT GIVES ME THE SECOND I NEED--
--TO GET INSIDE THIS BEHEMOTH!

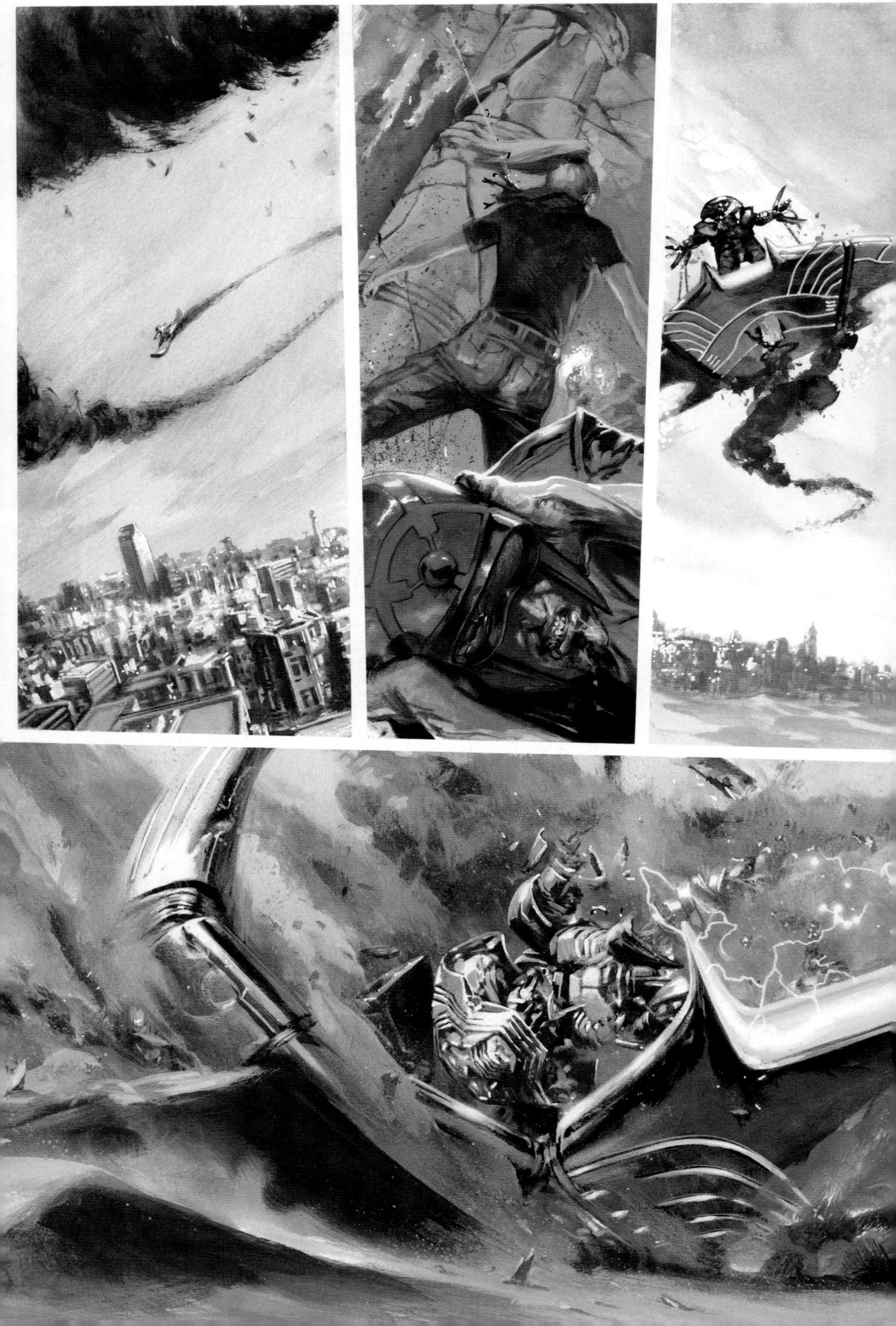

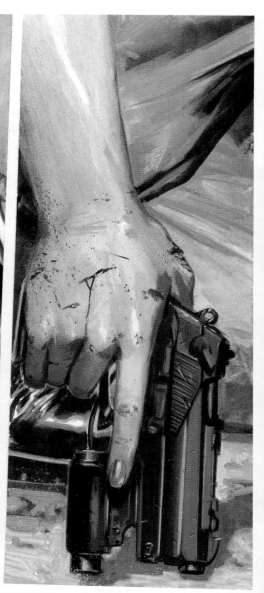

LOOKS LIKE CAIRO'S ANOTHER NEIGHBORHOOD SPIDER-MAN GETS TO BE FRIENDLY IN.

TERESA! YOU OKAY? TERESA!

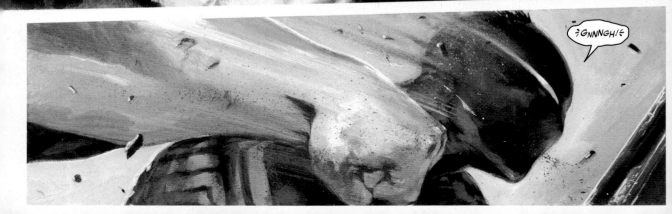

YOU VILE LITTLE INSECT!

YOU'VE BURIED THE GOLD EVEN *DEEPER!* YOU'VE RUINED *EVERY-THING--*

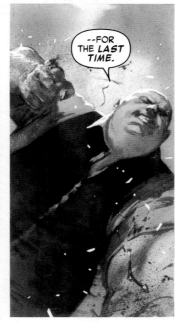

--FOR THE *LAST* TIME.

THAP

THWAM

YOU CAN'T IMAGINE HOW MUCH I WISH THAT WERE *TRUE...*

...YOU REPULSIVE WASTE OF *CARBON.*

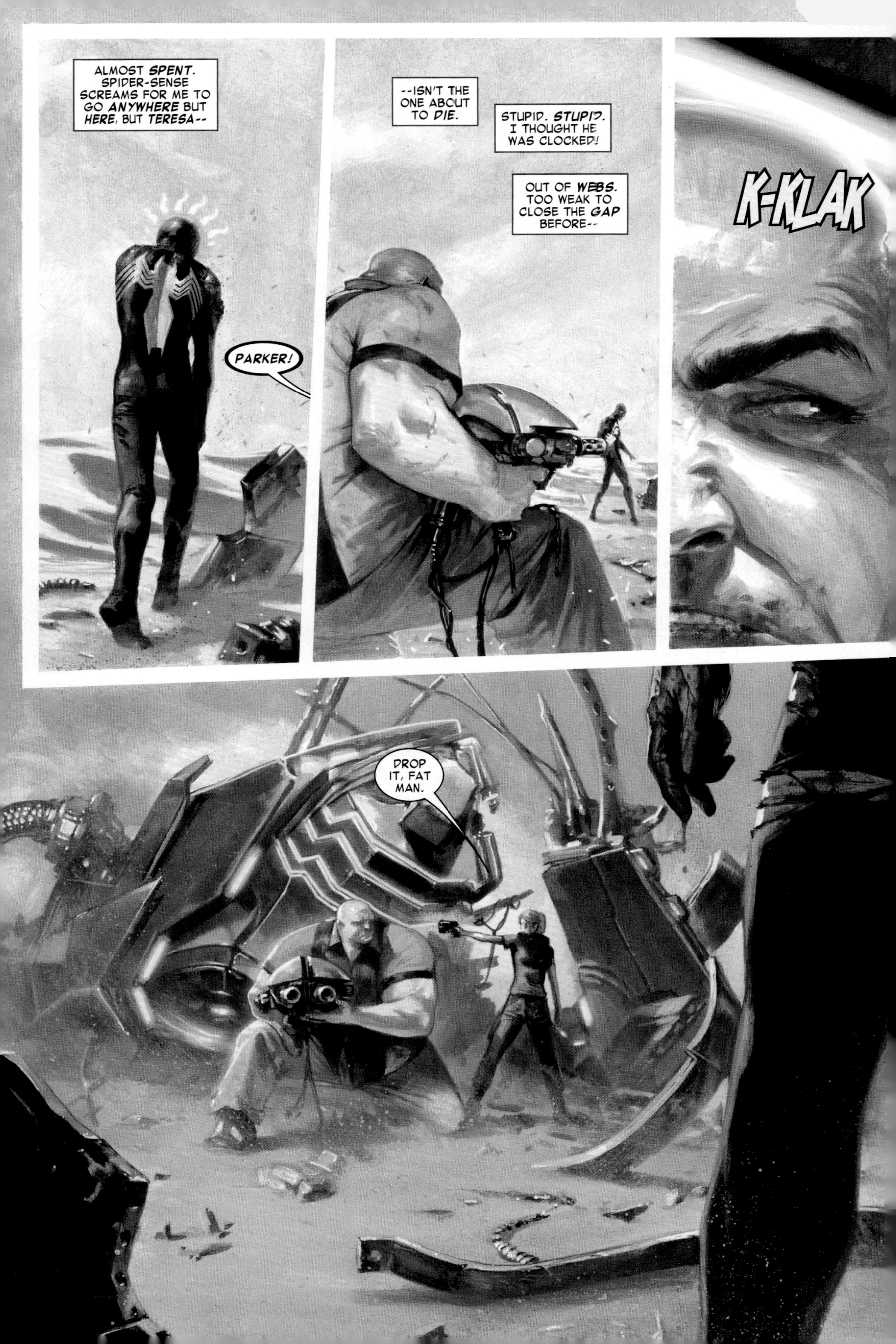

ALMOST SPENT. SPIDER-SENSE SCREAMS FOR ME TO GO ANYWHERE BUT HERE, BUT TERESA--
PARKER!
--ISN'T THE ONE ABOUT TO DIE.
STUPID. STUPID. I THOUGHT HE WAS CLOCKED!
OUT OF WEBS. TOO WEAK TO CLOSE THE GAP BEFORE--
K-KLAK
DROP IT, FAT MAN.

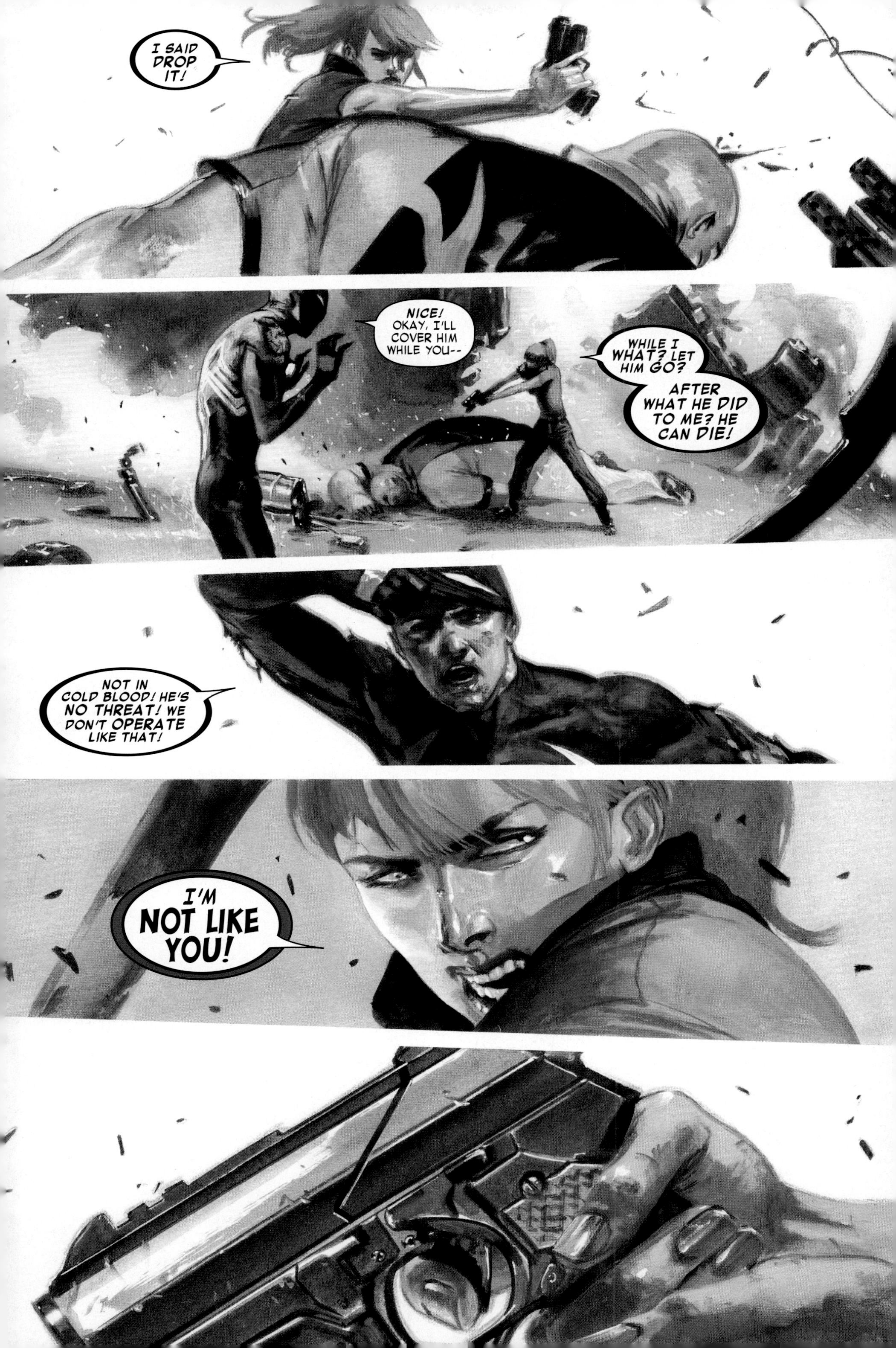
I SAID DROP IT!
NICE! OKAY, I'LL COVER HIM WHILE YOU--
WHILE I WHAT? LET HIM GO?
AFTER WHAT HE DID TO ME? HE CAN DIE!
NOT IN COLD BLOOD! HE'S NO THREAT! WE DON'T OPERATE LIKE THAT!
I'M NOT LIKE YOU!

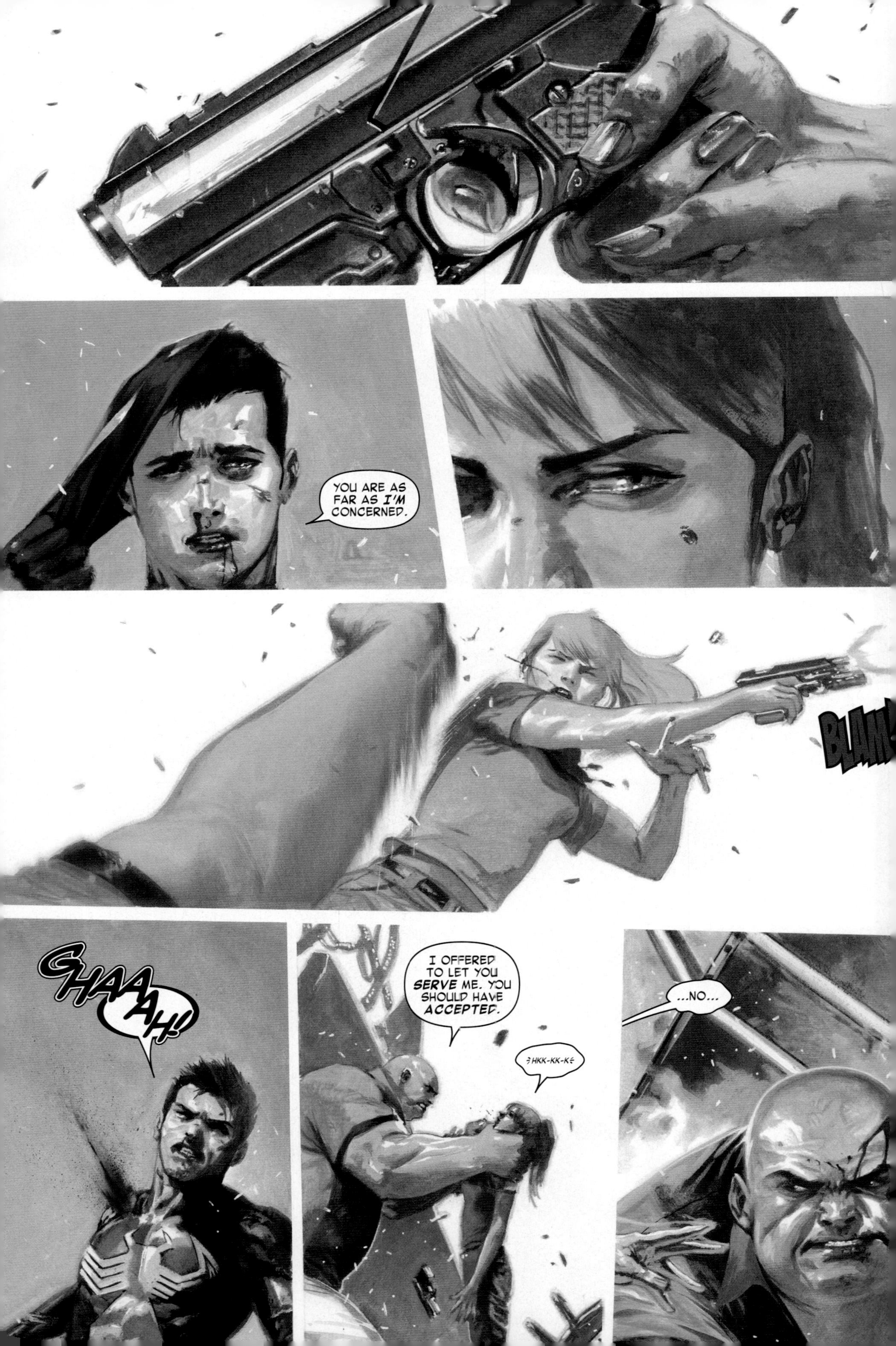
YOU ARE AS FAR AS I'M CONCERNED.
BLAM
GHAAAAH!
I OFFERED TO LET YOU SERVE ME. YOU SHOULD HAVE ACCEPTED.
HKK-KK-K
...NO...

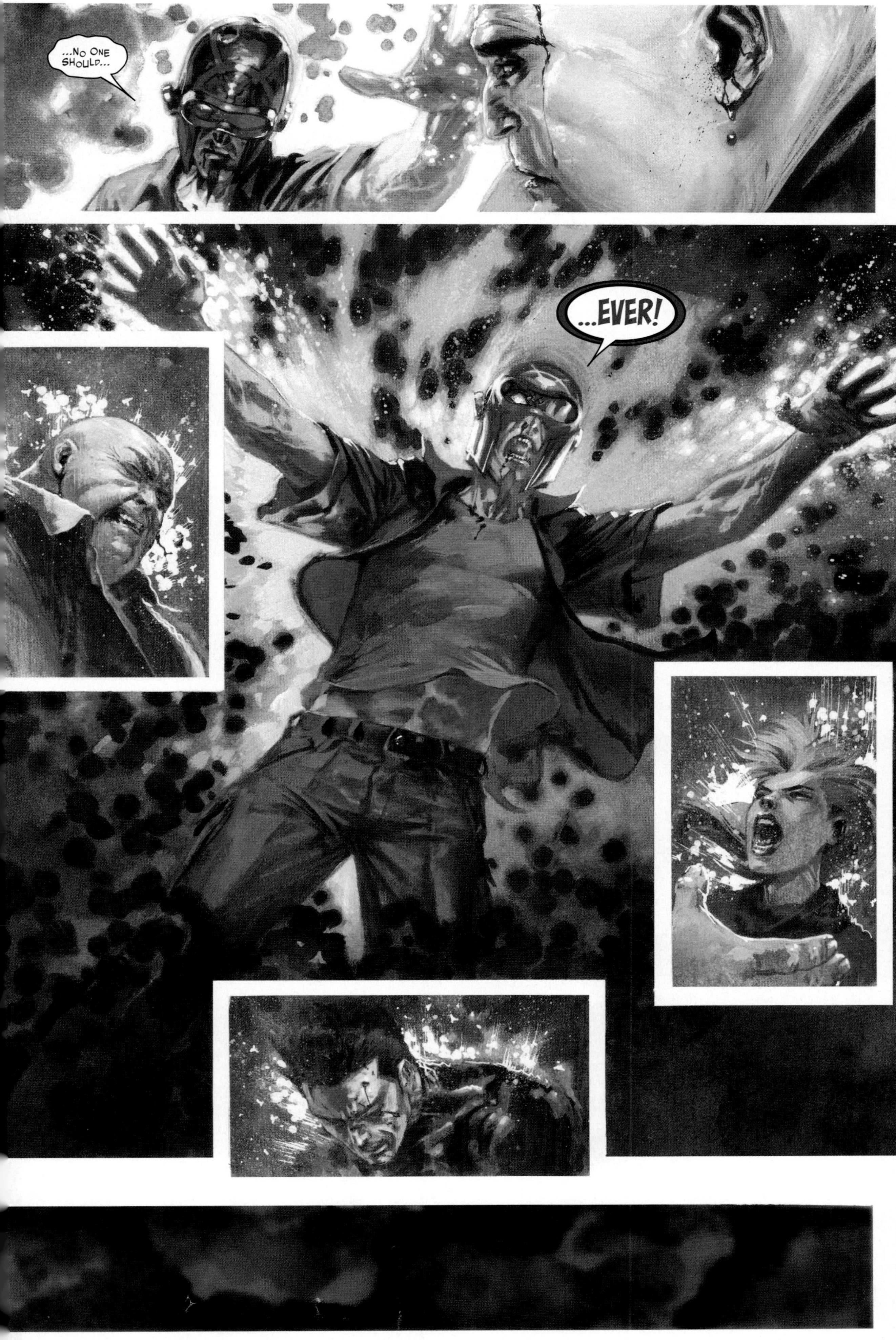
...NO ONE SHOULD...
...EVER!

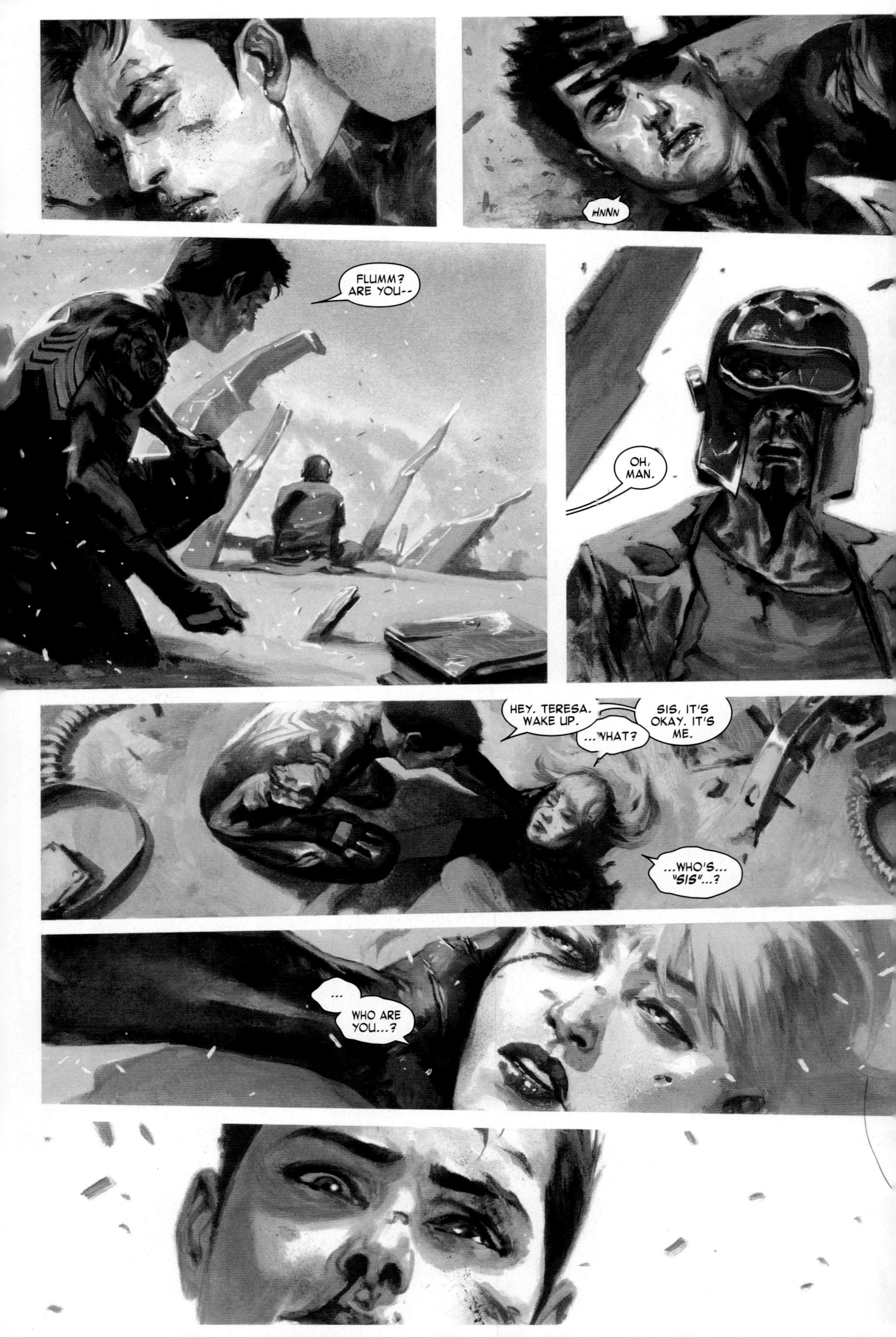
HNNN
FLUMM? ARE YOU--
OH, MAN.
HEY. TERESA. WAKE UP.
SIS, IT'S OKAY. IT'S ME.
...WHAT?
...WHO'S... "SIS"...?
... WHO ARE YOU...?

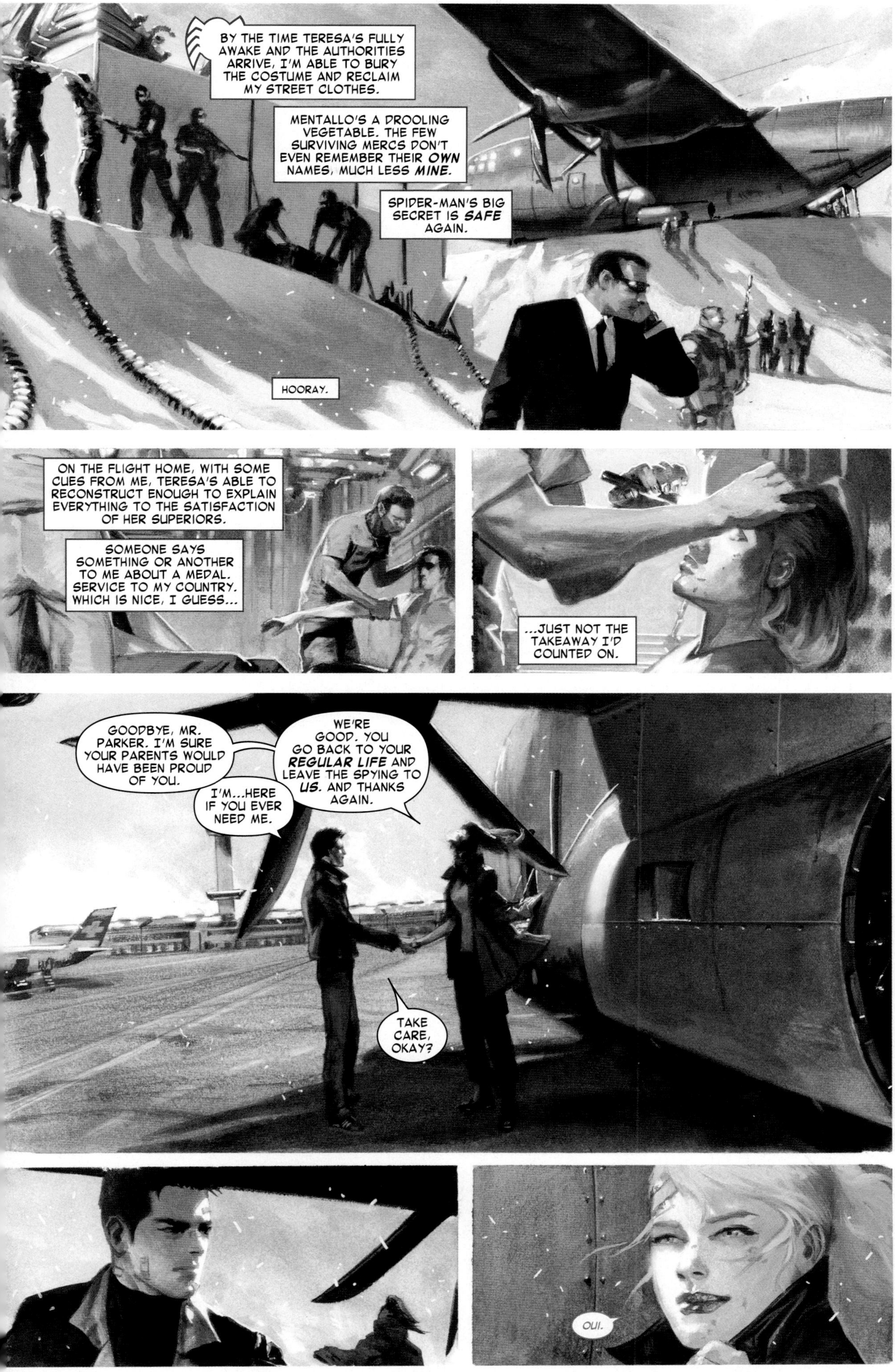
BY THE TIME TERESA'S FULLY AWAKE AND THE AUTHORITIES ARRIVE, I'M ABLE TO BURY THE COSTUME AND RECLAIM MY STREET CLOTHES.
MENTALLO'S A DROOLING VEGETABLE. THE FEW SURVIVING MERCS DON'T EVEN REMEMBER THEIR OWN NAMES, MUCH LESS MINE.
SPIDER-MAN'S BIG SECRET IS SAFE AGAIN.
HOORAY.
ON THE FLIGHT HOME, WITH SOME CUES FROM ME, TERESA'S ABLE TO RECONSTRUCT ENOUGH TO EXPLAIN EVERYTHING TO THE SATISFACTION OF HER SUPERIORS.
SOMEONE SAYS SOMETHING OR ANOTHER TO ME ABOUT A MEDAL. SERVICE TO MY COUNTRY. WHICH IS NICE, I GUESS...
...JUST NOT THE TAKEAWAY I'D COUNTED ON.
GOODBYE, MR. PARKER. I'M SURE YOUR PARENTS WOULD HAVE BEEN PROUD OF YOU.
I'M...HERE IF YOU EVER NEED ME.
WE'RE GOOD. YOU GO BACK TO YOUR REGULAR LIFE AND LEAVE THE SPYING TO US. AND THANKS AGAIN.
TAKE CARE, OKAY?
OUI.

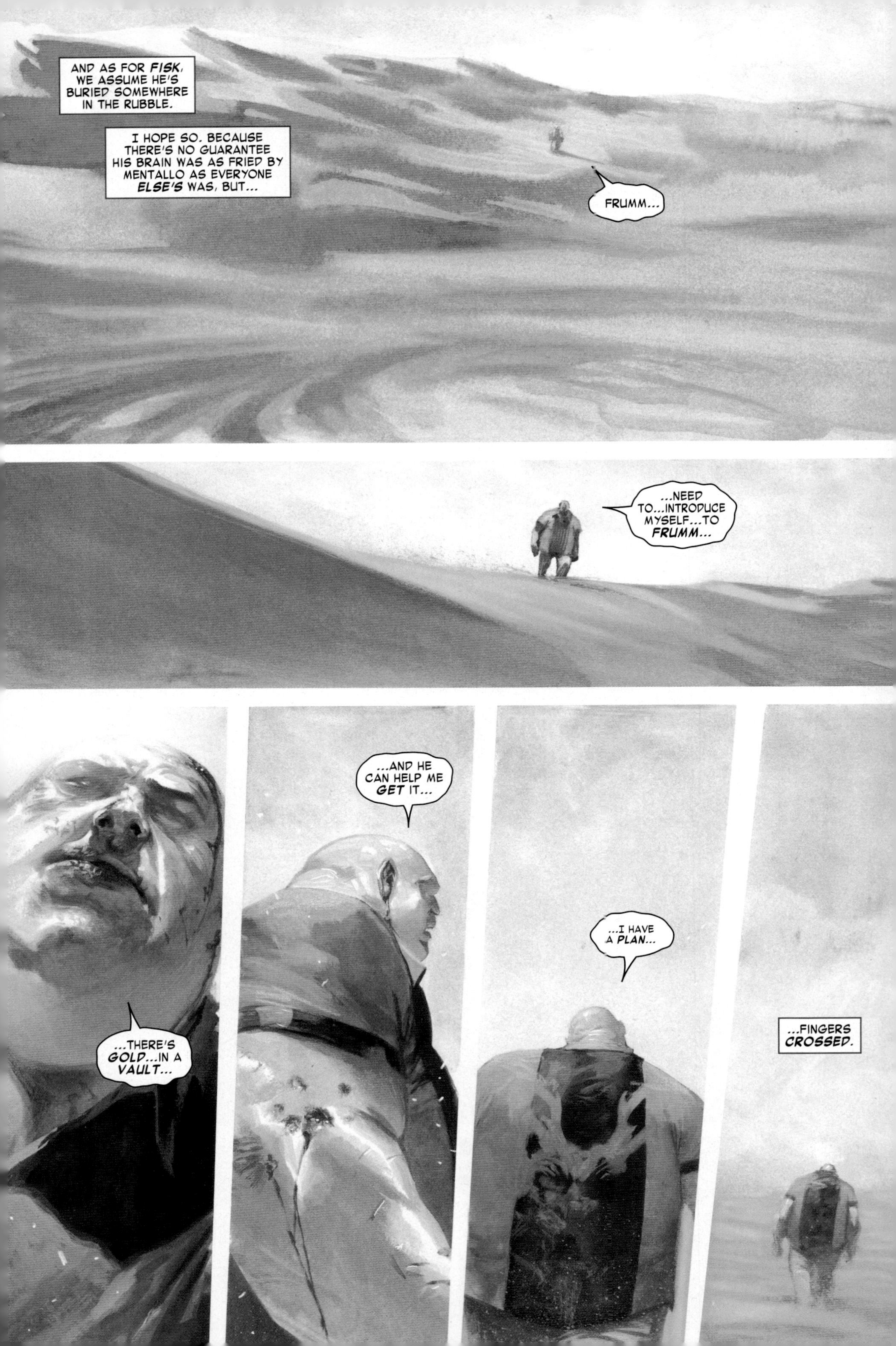
AND AS FOR FISK, WE ASSUME HE'S BURIED SOMEWHERE IN THE RUBBLE.
I HOPE SO. BECAUSE THERE'S NO GUARANTEE HIS BRAIN WAS AS FRIED BY MENTALLO AS EVERYONE ELSE'S WAS, BUT...
FRUMM...
...NEED TO...INTRODUCE MYSELF...TO FRUMM...
...THERE'S GOLD...IN A VAULT...
...AND HE CAN HELP ME GET IT...
...I HAVE A PLAN...
...FINGERS CROSSED.

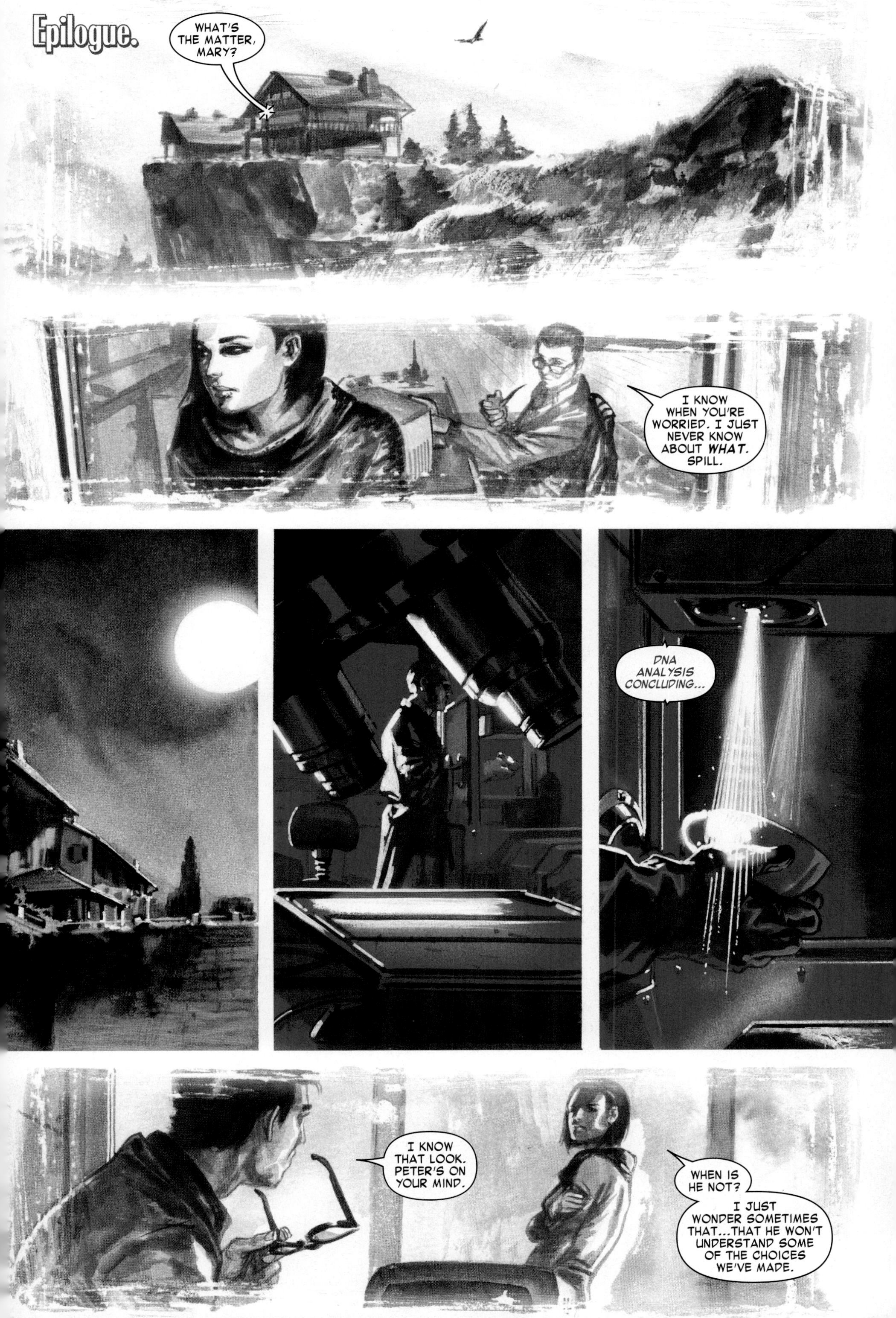
Epilogue.
WHAT'S THE MATTER, MARY?
I KNOW WHEN YOU'RE WORRIED. I JUST NEVER KNOW ABOUT WHAT. SPILL.
DNA ANALYSIS CONCLUDING...
I KNOW THAT LOOK. PETER'S ON YOUR MIND.
WHEN IS HE NOT?
I JUST WONDER SOMETIMES THAT...THAT HE WON'T UNDERSTAND SOME OF THE CHOICES WE'VE MADE.

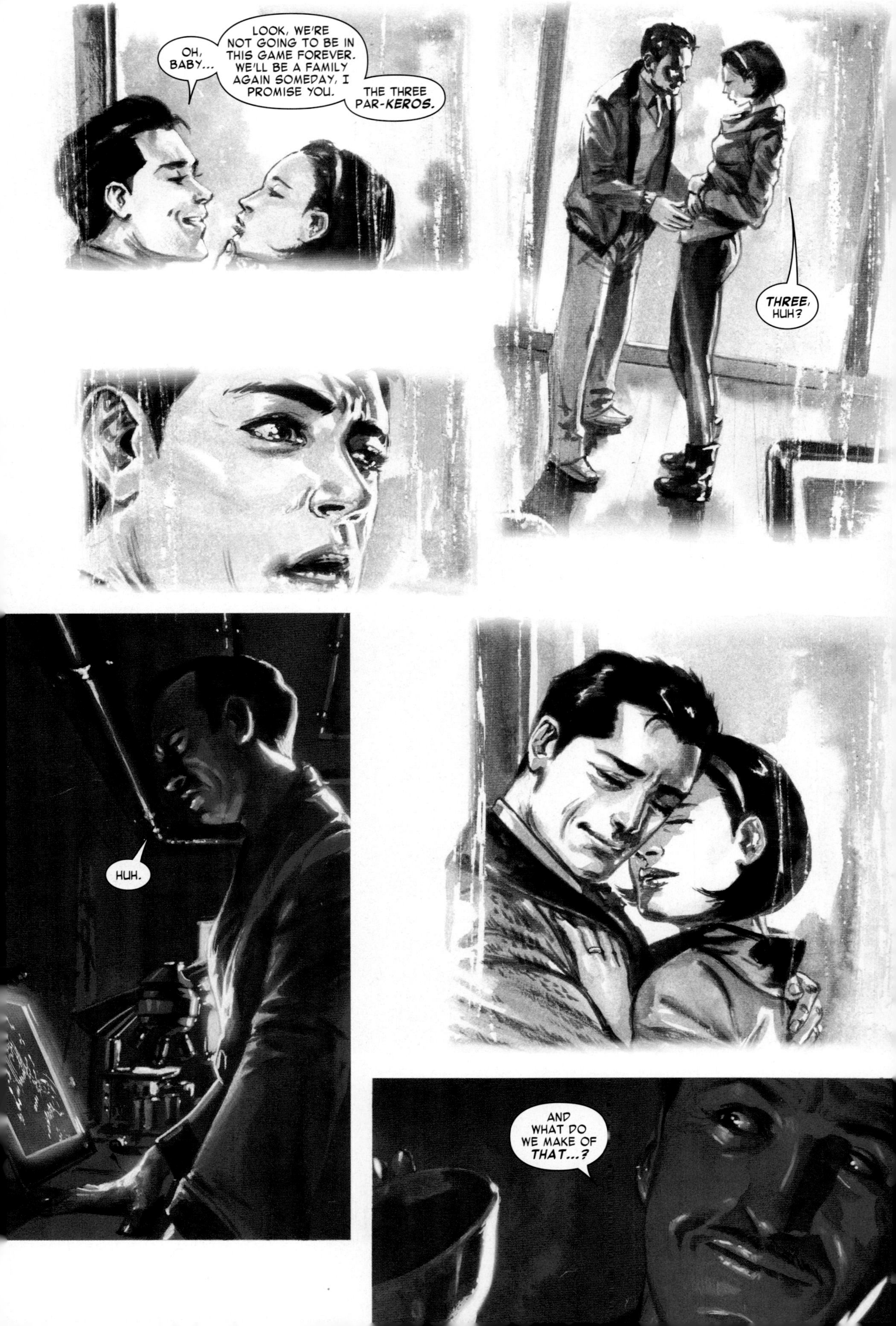
OH, BABY...
LOOK, WE'RE NOT GOING TO BE IN THIS GAME FOREVER. WE'LL BE A FAMILY AGAIN SOMEDAY, I PROMISE YOU.
THE THREE PAR-KEROS.
THREE, HUH?
HUH.
AND WHAT DO WE MAKE OF THAT...?

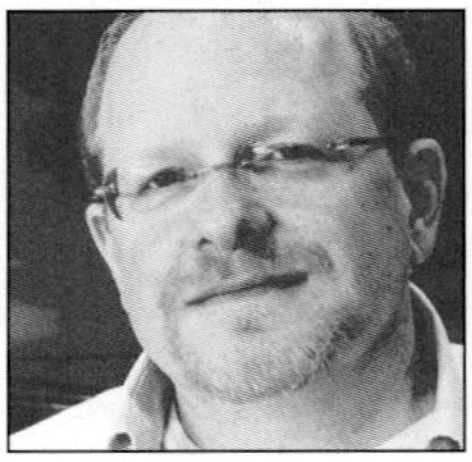

New York Times best-selling author **Mark Waid** has worked for every major company in the comics industry in a near three-decade career, writing thousands of issues including runs of *Amazing Spider-Man, X-Men, Ka-Zar* and *Fantastic Four.* His other works of note include his collaboration with painter Alex Ross, *Kingdom Come,* which earned an Eisner Award for Best Limited Series, and his long run on DC's *Flash.* He is enjoying great critical acclaim with the Eisner Award-winning *Daredevil.*

Biographies

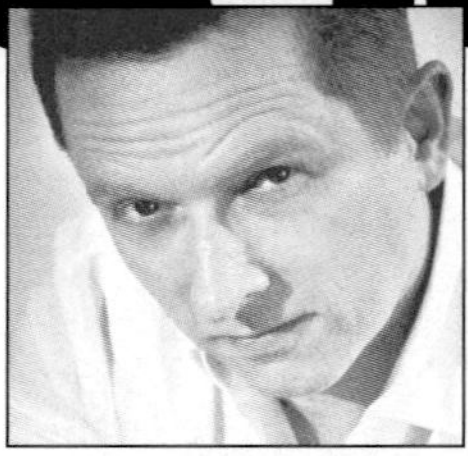

British writer **James Robinson** is acclaimed for his runs on DC's *Starman, Justice Society of America* and *Superman.* For Marvel, he has scripted *Generation X, Fantastic Four* and *All-New Invaders.* He has written several feature-film screenplays – including the adaptation of the comic book *The League of Extraordinary Gentleman* – and directed *Comic Book Villains*, which he also wrote.

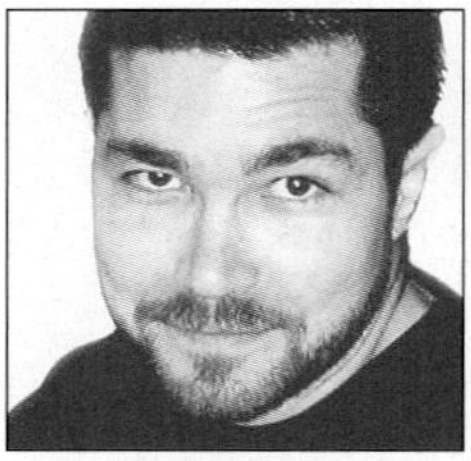

Hailed as "an instant legend" by writer Brian Michael Bendis, Italian artist **Gabriele Dell'Otto** established his reputation in the European comic-book industry with a series of painted covers for Panini. Dell'Otto's stunning work caught Marvel's attention, leading to a career-making assignment on the blockbuster *Secret War.* Propelled by Dell'Otto's stunning, fully painted work, the series became an instant sell-out and earned the artist *Wizard* magazine's prestigious "Breakout Talent of the Year" award in 2004.

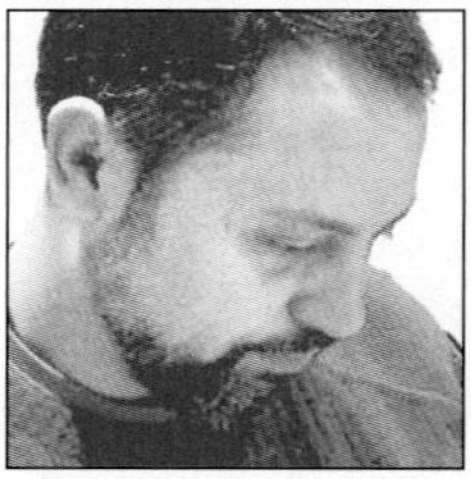

One of many Italian illustrators to find success in the United States in recent years, **Werther Dell'Edera** is quickly making his name as an artist capable of setting intense, simmering moods that can just as easily explode into unbelievable action. After drawing a run of the western comic *Loveless* at Vertigo, Dell'Edera came to Marvel, where he has worked with popular characters such as *Wolverine, Warpath* and *X-Force.*

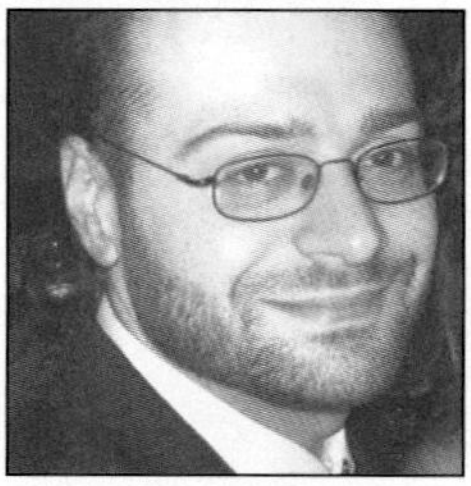

Joe Caramagna has been a regular writer and letterer for Marvel since 2007, most known for his work on *Iron Man and the Armor Wars, Marvel Universe: Ultimate Spider-Man, Amazing Spider-Man, Daredevil* and more. He has also written *Batman* and *Supergirl* shorts for DC Comics, and a series of *Amazing Spider-Man* novels for young readers.

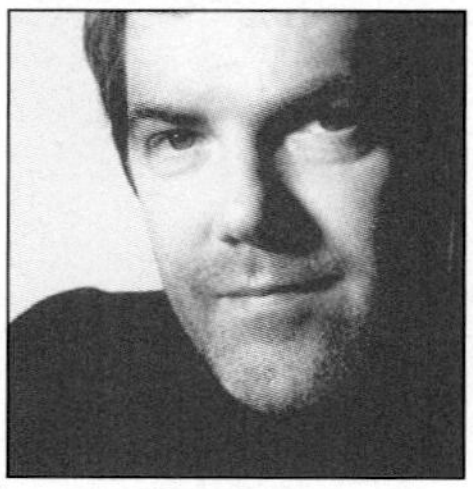

Designer and illustrator **Rian Hughes** began his career in the British music, advertising and fashion industries. His strips for *2000AD* and the short-lived *Revolver* with Grant Morrison and Mark Millar are collected in *Yesterday's Tomorrows* and *Tales from Beyond Science.* He has designed numerous logos, including *Batman and Robin, Batgirl* and *The Invisibles* for DC and *Iron Man, X-Men* and *Fantastic Four* for Marvel. Recent work includes writing and art for *Batman: Black and White.*

Behind the Scenes

Page 3

```
                          PAGE THREE

PANEL ONE: CLOSE-UP OF KINGPIN. SCOWLING MASTER OF MEN.

KINGPIN:        By not lolling about in SELF-PITY, Mr. Flumm.
                Once I was HERE, where I was UNDERESTIMATED,
                considered HELPLESS, I did what I ALWAYS do:

KINGPIN:        I observed those AROUND me. I exploited
                WEAKNESSES.

PANEL TWO/FLASHBACK: KINGPIN, CHAINED, SCOWLS AT AN OLDER,
WHITE-COATED NORTH AFRICAN DOCTOR ON HIS ROUNDS, POPPING PILLS.

CAPTION:        "I discovered the Chief Surgeon had a strong
                taste for a PRESCRIPTION NARCOTIC of reliable
                SUPPLY.

PANEL THREE/FLASHBACK: KINGPIN WRAPS HIS CHAINS AROUND THE
THROAT OF A GUARD AND STARES INTO HIS EYES, LIKE A PREDATORY
ANIMAL.

CAPTION:        "So with some...COERCED ASSISTANCE...

PANEL FOUR/FLASHBACK: NIGHT. THE SAME GUARD SETS FIRE TO A TRUCK
MARKED "ROXXON PHARMACEUTICALS."

CAPTION:        "...I made that supply UNreliable...creating a
                demand that only I could fill."
```

Script, layout, final art

100

Page 11

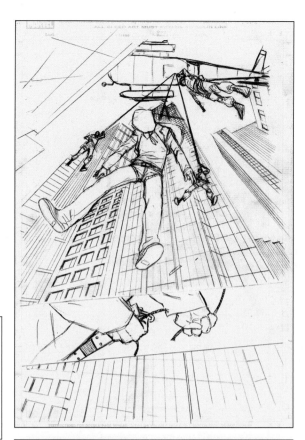

PAGE FOURTEEN

PANEL ONE/BIG: OUTSIDE. A SUPER-HIGH-TECH SILENT AIR TRANSPORT HOVERS IN THE AIR OUTSIDE PETE'S BUILDING, REELING PETE AND THE SOLDIERS TOWARDS IT!

PETER CAP: --maybe I should start taking this a little more SERIOUSLY.

PANEL TWO: TIGHT ON PETE'S HANDS BEHIND HIS BACK, SNAPPING THE ROPE.

SFX: whKSSH

Script, layout, final art

Page 17

PAGE SEVENTEEN

PANEL ONE: AS THE PURSUING AIRCRAFT OPENS FIRE ON THE FLEEING
CONVERTIBLE, PETE GAPES/GETS HIS FIRST GOOD LOOK AT THE DRIVER--
A BEAUTIFUL BROWN-HAIRED WOMAN ABOUT HIS AGE.

PETE: Not unless there's a JET ENGINE under the hood of
                this thing!

PETE: You KNOW me?

DRIVER: I've seen pictures.

PETER: Who ARE you?

DRIVER: My name is TERESA PARKER.

PANEL TWO, BIG: FOCUS ON THE DRIVER AS THE CAR ROARS DOWN THE
STREET TOWARDS US, THE PURSUING AIRCRAFT STRAFING THE STREET
WITH GUNFIRE! IF WE SEE PETE IN THIS SHOT, HE'S GAPING AT HER IN
SHOCK.

DRIVER: I'm your SISTER.

Script, layout, final art

102

PAGE THIRTY-ONE

PANEL ONE: WE LOOK AT THE SCENE FROM CYCLONE'S P.O.V.   WE SEE--

SPIDEY SWINGING IN, WITH A WEB ATTACHED TO THE CEILING.   HE IS
COMING STRAIGHT AT US, FEET ABOVE HEAD, YOU KNOW HE DOES HE IS
FIRING WEB TOWARDS US.

THE CROWD AROUND HIM (BELOW HIM, IF WE'RE LOOKING AT SPIDEY AND
HE'S IN THE AIR SWINGING AT US) ARE LOOKING UP AT HIM AGHAST.
SOME ARE RUNNING FROM THE SCENE, SOME ARE FROZEN ON THE SPOT.
MAYBE THE CROWD ARE CROPPED AT THE TORSO, BY OUR P.O.V. BEING
DIRECTLY ON SPIDEY HIGHER ABOVE THEM.

SOME OF THE CROWD ARE LOOKING STRAIGHT AT US WITH TERROR
(THEY'RE LOOKING AT CYCLONE AND NOT SPIDEY.)

LET'S GIVE THIS PANEL MORE THAN HALF THE PAGE.   MORE LIKE TWO
THIRDS OF THE PAGE, JUST TO SHOW SPIDEY AND THE CROWD AND THE
CASINO DÉCOR AROUND THEM BEFORE IT ALL GETS BLOWN AROUND.

PETER CAPTION: Forget the GUNMEN.

PETER CAPTION: Now someone's sending COSTUMES after the Parkers!

SPIDEY: Hey, Cyclone, where are your manners?

SPIDEY: Your folks never teach you not to break wind in a
               crowded room?

PANEL TWO: CYCLONE AIMS A TIGHT WIND-VORTEX RIGHT AT SPIDEY.

CYCLONE/small: No one mentioned SPIDER-MAN...

CYCLONE: Stay OUT of this, wall-crawler...for YOUR sake!

Script, layout, final art

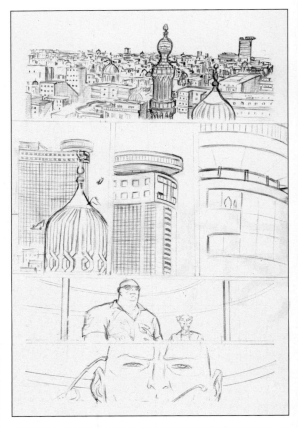

Page 45

PAGE FORTY-FIVE.
PANEL ONE.
THIS IS A WIDE CINEMATIC SHOT OF EGYPT.
WE SEE THE CITY AS A SWEEPING PANORAMA. HAVE SOME "OLD CAIRO" IN
IT TO MAKE IT VISUAL AND INTERNATIONAL BUT PUT IN A MODERN HOTEL
IN THE MIDST OF IT (EVEN IF IT DOESN'T EXIST IN REALITY -- AT
THE END OF THE DAY THIS IS A COMIC) SO THAT WE CAN TRACK IN PAST
THE ORNATE/OLD TOWARDS THE MODERN HOTEL PENTHOUSE/ROOF PANEL BY
PANEL.

CAPTION: Cairo.

MENTALLO: Can I go now?

PANEL TWO.
WE CLOSE IN ON THE HOTEL, BUT WE'RE STILL FAR ENOUGH OFF FROM
IT, THAT THE PENTHOUSE ROOF/BALCONY (AND WHO'S ON IT, ISN'T TOO
DISTINCT YET.)

MENTALLO: Mr. Fisk?

PANEL THREE.
WE NOW CLOSE IN TIGHTER ON THE HOTEL PENTHOUSE, SUCH THAT WE CAN
NOW SEE MENTALLO AND FISK ON THE PENTHOUSE BALCONY/ROOF (BIG
OPEN AREA -- LUXURIOUS), BUT THEY'RE STILL SMALL, SMALL IN SHOT
FOR NOW.

FROM WHAT WE CAN SEE MENTALLO IS FURTHER BACK AWAY FROM THE
BALCONY/ROOF RAILING WITH FISK CLOSE TO IT, LOOKING OUT AT THE
CITY WITH HIS BACK TO MENTALLO.

MENTALLO: Mr. Fisk, I've done all you asked of me, and my head
won't stop hurting, so I repeat...

PANEL FOUR.
WE'RE NOW IN THE AIR, FACING THE PENTHOUSE BALCONY/ROOF. FISK
IS STANDING THERE TO ONE SIDE OF PANEL, FACING US, LOOKING OUT
AT THE CITY.

MENTALLO IS TO THE OTHER SIDE OF PANEL, FURTHER FROM US, FACING
US TOO AS HE LOOKS AT THE BACK OF FISK'S HEAD.

MENTALLO: ...May I please go?

KINGPIN: I have always prided myself on never punishing
well-thought, honest question, Mr. Frumm.

PANEL FIVE.
SIDE-ON MED SHOT/PROFILE SHOT OF KINGPIN STILL LOOKING OFF PANEL
AT THE CITY, STILL TREATING MENTALLO AS A MINOR INCONVENIENCE.

KINGPIN: That is not one.

PANEL SIX.
TIGHTER CU OF KINGPIN, FACING HIM AS HE LOOKS OUT AT THE CITY.
HE'S BASICALLY LOOKING AT US IN THE FACE.

KINGPIN: Be thankful I still need your head attached to your
SPINE.

Script, layout, final art

PAGE FIFTY-SIX.
PANEL ONE.
EGYPT. A SMALL AIRPORT RUNWAY. TERESA'S JET IN MIDGROUND,
PYRAMIDS IN BACKGROUND. ON THE RUNWAY, OFF THE PLANE, TERESA AND
PETER TAKE POSSESSION OF A WAITING JEEP FROM A SALUTING SOLDIER.
WHATEVER PETER'S WEARING, IT HAS LONG SLEEVES AND LONG PANTS.

PETER CAP: So the flight to Egypt is anything but boring.
Teresa has a million questions.

PETER CAP: But also a change of clothes.

PANEL TWO
TERESA: Thank you for losing the costume.

PETER: What was LEFT of it smelled like a barbecue gone
horribly wrong. Not much point in hanging on, but that leaves
Spidey OUT of the rest of this mission.

PANEL THREE.
TERESA/off: Not necessarily.

PANEL FOUR
TERESA: I had my people whip up a little something. They didn't
ask why or for who, I didn't say.

TERESA: We had to make do with materials at hand, and I guessed
at the size, but...

PANEL SIX.
AS THEY RIDE INTO THE DESERT, PETE HOLDS UP HIS BLACK SPIDER-MAN
COSTUME.

TERESA: ...you're back in black.

PETER: Cool.

Script, layout, final art

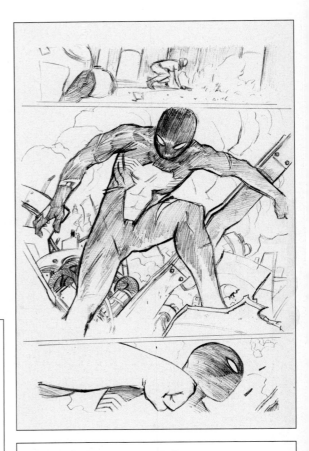

PAGE EIGHTY.
PANEL ONE.
KINGPIN, MERCS AND TERESA ARE ALL FELLED BY THE IMPACT OF THE NEARBY CRASH!

PANEL TWO.
GROANING, HIS COSTUME TORN IN PLACES, A LITTLE BLOODY, SPIDEY CRAWLS FROM THE WRECKAGE.

SPIDEY: =nnNNGGH--!=

PETER CAP: Looks like Cairo's another neighborhood SPIDER-MAN gets to be friendly in.

PETER CAP: Hope they put that on my TOMBSTONE, because I'm not sure I'm walking AWAY from this one.

SPIDEY/burst: TERESA! YOU OKAY? TERESA!

PANEL THREE.
BAM! SPIDEY'S SUCKER-PUNCHED FROM BEHIND BY KINGPIN!

SPIDEY/burst: =GNNNGH!=

Script, layout, final art

Page 81

PAGE EIGHTY-ONE
PANELS.
HOWEVER YOU FEEL LIKE CHOREOGRAPHING IT--KINGPIN BEATS ON
WEAKENED SPIDEY UNTIL SPIDEY MANAGES TO KICK HIM INTO THE GIANT
HOLE IN THE GROUND LEFT BY THE SLEEPER. KINGPIN FALLS.

[Banter to come]

Script, layout, final art

Cover design

AMAZING SPIDER-MAN
FAMILY BUSINESS
MARK WAID
JAMES ROBINSON
GABRIELLE DELL'OTTO
MARVEL

AMAZING SPIDER-MAN
FAMILY BUSINESS
MARK WAID JAMES ROBINSON GABRIELLE DELL'OTTO

AMAZING SPIDER-MAN
FAMILY BUSINESS

FAMILY BUSINESS

FAMILY BUSINESS

FAMILY BUSINESS

AMAZING SPIDER-MAN:
FAMILY BUSINESS

AMAZING SPIDER-MAN
FAMILY BUSINESS

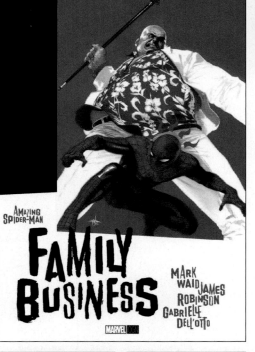

Some of Rian Hughes' alternative
cover design concepts

Also available

MARVEL
SECRET WAR
BRIAN MICHAEL BENDIS • GABRIELE DELL'OTTO

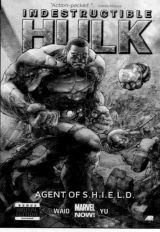

Secret War
Brian Michael Bendis and Gabriele Dell'Otto
978-0-7851-4228-7

"Action-packed."
INDESTRUCTIBLE
HULK
AGENT OF S.H.I.E.L.D.
WAID
MARVEL NOW!
YU

Indestructible Hulk Volume 1
Agent of S.H.I.E.L.D.
Mark Waid and Leinil Francis Yu
978-0-7851-6831-7

MARVEL NOW!
WAID • SIMONSON • SCALERA
INDESTRUCTIBLE
HULK
"Great dialogue, clever concepts and lovely art."
GODS AND MONSTER

Indestructible Hulk Volume 2
Gods and Monster
Mark Waid, Walter Simonson and Matteo Scalera
978-0-7851-6832-4

"An awesome spectacle."
INDESTRUCTIBLE
HULK
S.M.A.S.H. TIME
WAID
MARVEL NOW!
SCALERA
JACINTO

Indestructible Hulk Volume 3
S.M.A.S.H. Time
Mark Waid and Matteo Scalera
978-0-7851-8884-1

MARVEL
HERE COMES...
DAREDEVIL
WAID
RIVERA
MARTIN
RIOS
KANO
PHAM

Daredevil by Mark Waid Volume 1
Mark Waid, Paolo Rivera, Marcos Martin and Emma Rios
978-0-7851-6806-5

MARVEL
HERE COMES...
DAREDEVIL
THE MAN WITHOUT FEAR!
WAID
RUCKA
CHECCHETTO
SAMNEE
PHAM
ALLRED

Daredevil by Mark Waid Volume 2
Mark Waid, Greg Rucka, Marco Checchetto and Chris Samnee
978-0-7851-8479-9

An abomination, long thought buried, has resurfaced in a war-torn land. But now it wears an American flag. Faced with another nightmare reborn, Captain America will not stand for yet more death at the hands of a ghost from his past. Haunted by his greatest shame, Thor must renew the hunt for a familiar beast. At their side, an assemblage of allies united to end the threats no one of them could face alone. They are soldiers. Warriors. Comrades-in-arms. Mighty heroes led by a living legend, stronger together than apart. They are the Avengers.

Avengers: Endless Wartime

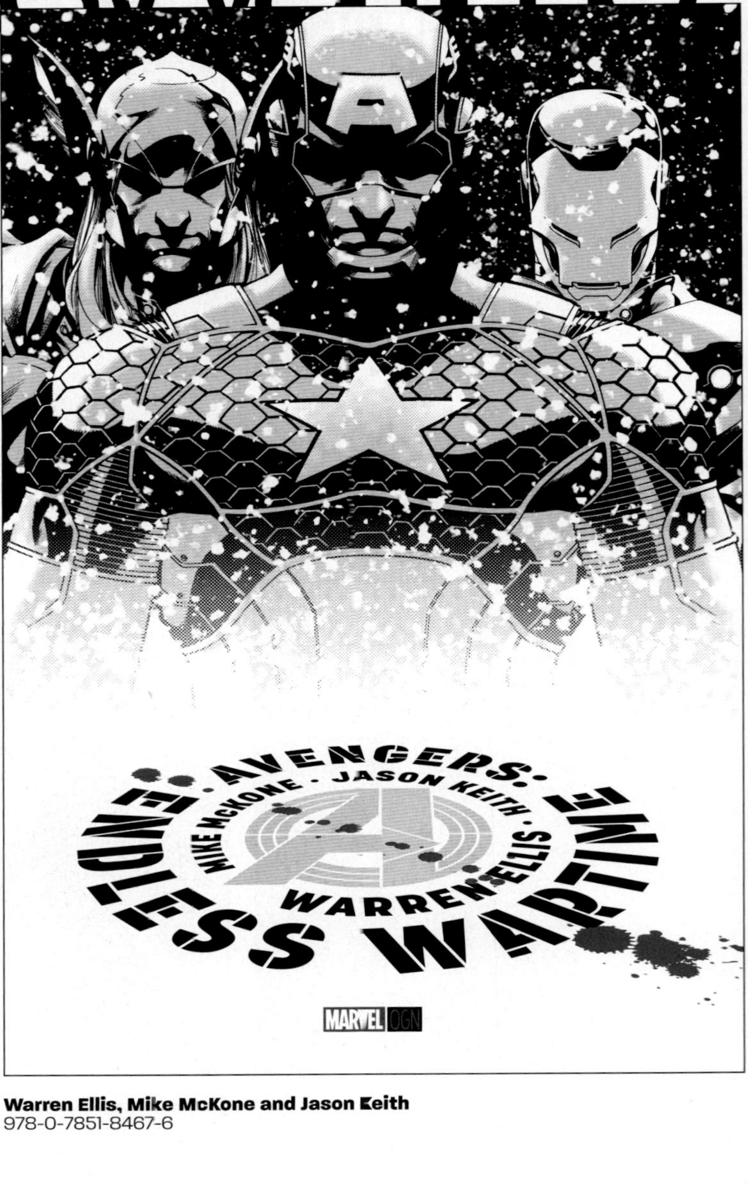
AVENGERS:
MIKE McKONE · JASON KEITH
WARREN ELLIS
ENDLESS WARTIME
MARVEL OGN

Warren Ellis, Mike McKone and Jason Keith
978-0-7851-8467-6

Following the shattering events of *Battle of the Atom*, the X-Men awaken to find all the world's humans gone. From normal everyday folks to the Avengers and Fantastic Four, all Homo sapiens have disappeared. It's up to the disparate sides of the X-Men to come together, get to the bottom of this mystery and find a way to get the humans back. But do all of the mutants want their human brethren to return? Available May 2014.

X-Men: No More Humans

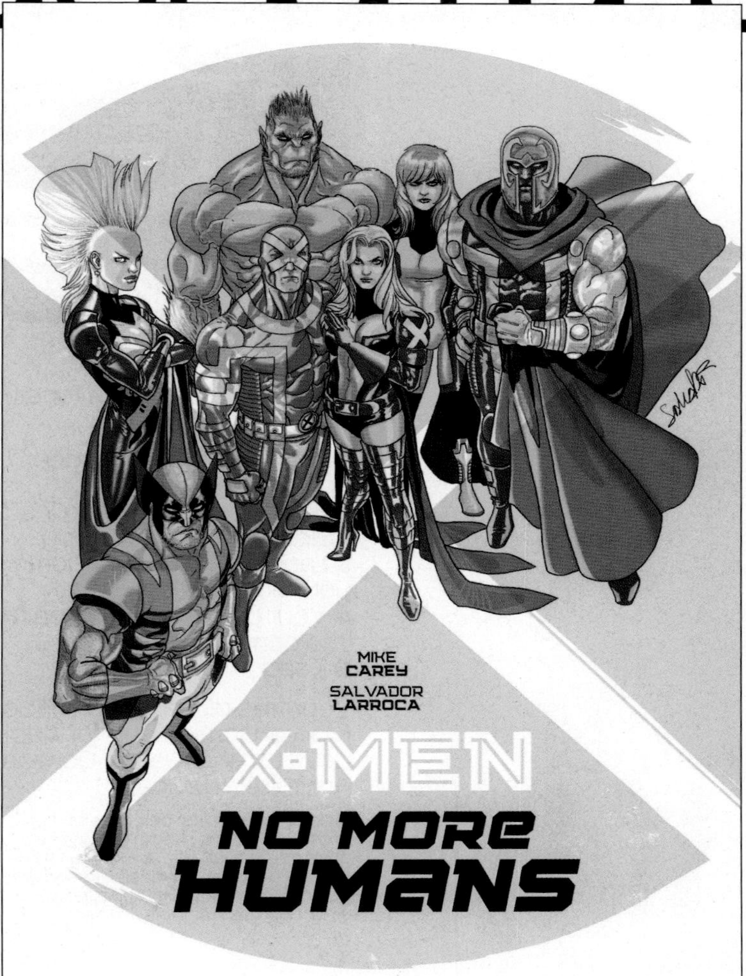
MIKE
CAREY
SALVADOR
LARROCA
X-MEN
NO MORE
HUMANS
MARVEL OGN

Mike Carey and **Salvador Larroca**
978-0-7851-5402-0

To access the free Marvel Augmented Reality app that enhances and changes the way you experience comics:

1 Download the app for free via marvel.com/ARapp.
2 Launch the app on your camera-enabled Apple iOS® or Android™ device.*
3 Hold your mobile device's camera over any cover or panel with the **AR** graphic.
4 Sit back and see the future of comics in action!

*Available on most camera-enabled Apple iOS® and Android ™ devices. Content subject to change and availability.

Augmented Reality

Free Digital copy

To redeem your code for a free digital copy:

1 Go to Marvel.com/redeem. Offer expires on 4/2/16.
2 Follow the on-screen instructions to redeem your digital copy.
3 Launch the Marvel Comics app to read your comic now.
4 Your digital copy will be found under the 'my comics' tab.
5 Read and enjoy.

Your free digital copy will be available on: Marvel Comics app for Apple iOS® devices and Marvel Comics app for Android™ devices.

Digital copy requires purchase of a print copy. Download code valid for one use only. Digital copy available on the date printcopy is available. Availability time of the digital copy may vary on the date of release. TM and © Marvel and Subs. Apple is a trademark of Apple Inc., registered in the U. S. and other countries. Android is a trademark of Google Inc.

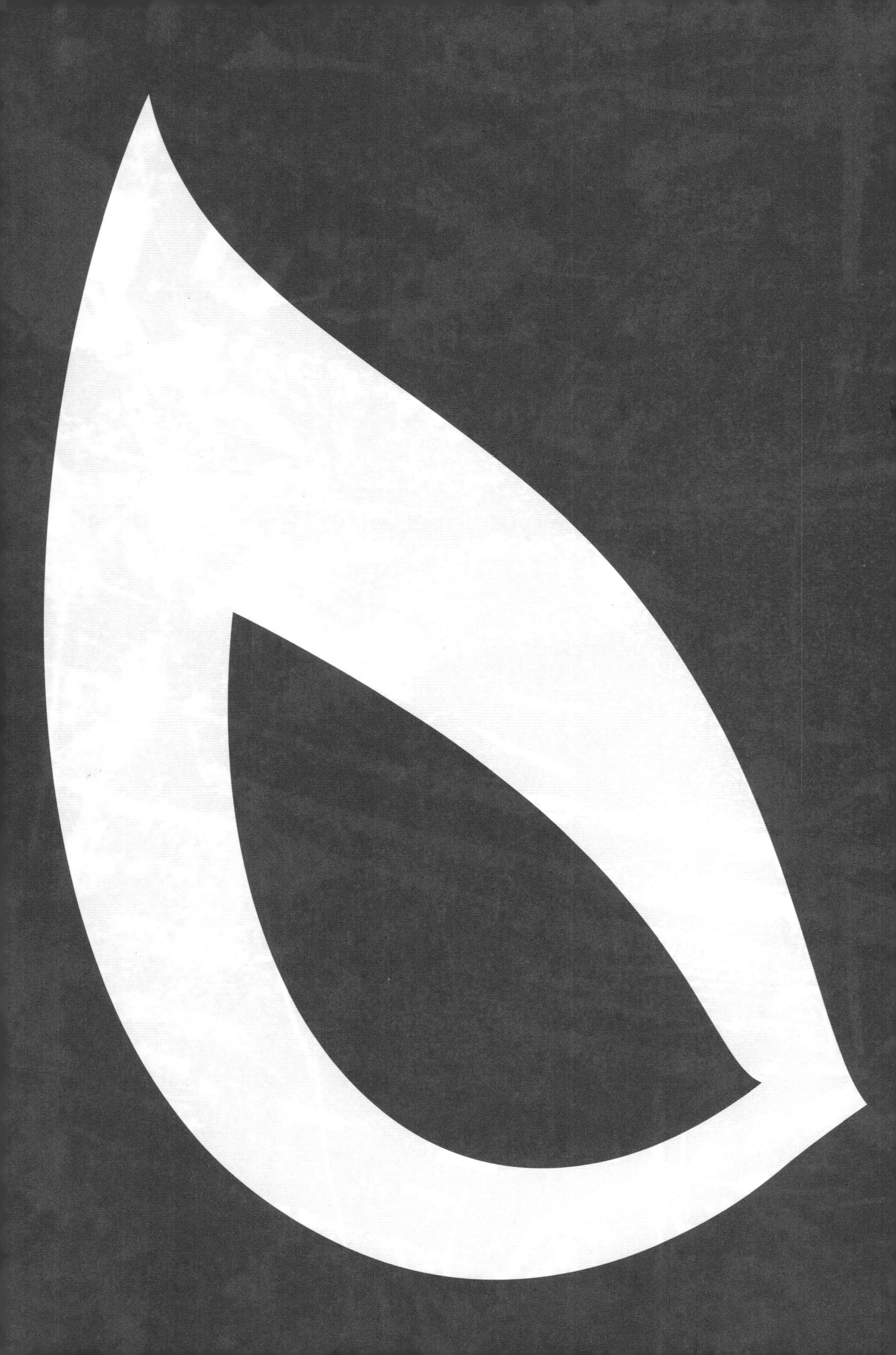